THE TASTEMAKERS

THE
TASTEMAKERS

A Celebrity Rice Farmer,
a Food Truck Lobbyist,
and Other Innovators Putting
Food Trends on Your Plate

DAVID SAX

PublicAffairs
New York

PublicAffairs books are available at special discounts for bulk purchases in the
U.S. by corporations, institutions, and other organizations. For more information, please contact the Special Markets Department at the Perseus Books Group,
2300 Chestnut Street, Suite 200, Philadelphia, PA 19103, call (800) 810-4145,
ext. 5000, or e-mail special.markets@perseusbooks.com.

Book Design by Jack Lenzo

The Library of Congress has cataloged the hardcover edition as follows:
Sax, David.
The tastemakers : why we're crazy for cupcakes but fed up with fondue (plus
baconomics, superfoods, and other secrets from the world of food trends) / David
Sax.—First edition.
pages cm
Includes bibliographical references and index.
ISBN 978-1-61039-315-7 (hardcover)—ISBN 978-1-61039-316-4 (e-book) 1.
Food habits—United States. 2. Food preferences—United States. 3. Food indus-
try and trade—United States. I. Title.
GT2853.U5S39 2014
394.1'2—dc23
2013045160

ISBN 978-1-61039-549-6 (paperback)

10 9 8 7 6 5 4 3 2 1

To Lauren,
my enduring trend,

and Noa,
the sweet cupcake
from your oven.

CONTENTS

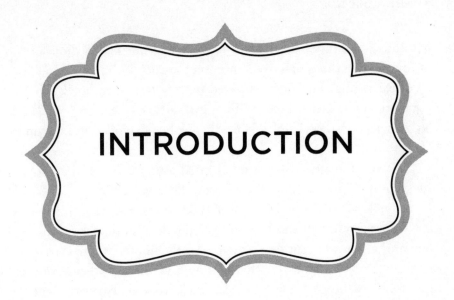

INTRODUCTION

The On Location Tours bus parked in the shadow of New York's Plaza hotel, idling in the damp January chill as its passengers trickled in from nearby sights. They ranged in age from their early twenties to late fifties, coming from as close as Long Island and as far away as Sweden. With the exception of two of their husbands and myself, the thirty-odd passengers were exclusively women. Some came with friends, others in large groups. All were here for the same reasons as everyone else on this bus: Carrie, Charlotte, Miranda, and Samantha, the four leads from the HBO television series *Sex and the City*, which aired from 1998 to 2004 along with two subsequent films. To the ladies seated around me, these were not only TV characters but also the hallowed names of prophets: icons of feminine identity, sexual liberators, and symbols of everything the Big Apple had to offer.

"All right, ladies!" said Staci Jacobs, practically singing into the microphone as the doors closed and the bus started to roll down Fifth Avenue. "Welcome to the Sex and the City Hotspots Tour!" Jacobs, who wouldn't divulge her age but is "old enough to have watched the show" (she was likely in her early thirties, like me), had been leading the tour twice a day, every day, since 2005. A stylish redhead in tight jeans and knee-high boots (think Charlotte with

Miranda's coloring), Jacobs had passed the same sights thousands of times, unleashing practiced anecdotes at each location.

"Remember Ed?" Jacobs asked outside the Plaza hotel, where Samantha once met her elderly fling for a drink in season two. "He had a saggy ass, am I right, ladies?" The bus exploded in knowing laughter.

"If you thought this was a PG-rated tour, you're on the wrong fucking bus!" Jacobs said. "Can I get a 'Fuck yeah'?"

"Fuck yeah!" the bus shouted back as Jacobs tossed her strawberry mane to the side with a devilish smile that's oh-so-Samantha. On we went downtown, past the library where Carrie—spoiler alert!—fled her lavish wedding and the church where the good-looking monk known as Friar Fuck worked. Two stops and a dozen video clips of the show later, the tour bus parked at the corner of Bleecker and West Eleventh Street, in the heart of the West Village, the picturesque, boutique-laden sun at the center of *Sex and the City*'s glittering solar system. The show had turned the leafy, bohemian neighborhood into a paradise of quaint cafés, high-end clothing shops, and giant handbags, drawing hundreds of thousands of fans a year to wander the narrow streets in awed disbelief, like medieval pilgrims in Jerusalem.

As we stepped off the bus, Jacobs instructed everyone that we had the better part of an hour to take in the neighborhood. "And when you come back to me I'll have cupcakes," Jacobs said, singing the last word with a cooing sort of siren call, her voice rising to a crescendo on "cakes." Oohs, ahhs, and giggles of anticipation greeted this news, but the show's seasoned fans already expected this.

"Are they Magnolia cupcakes?" one woman, from Alabama, asked hopefully, looking out her window at Magnolia Bakery, kitty corner from where the bus parked.

"No," Jacobs said, with a tense smile, "but they're just as good."

Alix Galey and Emily Pavlin, a pair of friends in their early twenties from Melbourne, Australia, exited the bus, and like most of the people on the tour, they made a beeline for Magnolia, where they purchased a pair of the bakery's signature red velvet cupcakes. "I'm obsessed with the show," said Pavlin between bites. "I've seen each episode five times." It was a gray, cold day, and the heat and moisture inside the bakery had fogged up all the windows so all you could see from the street were hazy round shapes, muted pastel colors, and the outlines of different magazine and newspaper articles taped to the glass.

Just by the door, barely visible through the condensation, was a small framed photograph of two women sitting on a bench in front of Magnolia. To the left sat Cynthia Nixon, the actress who played Miranda, and to the right was Sarah Jessica Parker, who starred as Carrie Bradshaw. Their legs were crossed, shopping bags at their feet, and they were looking directly at the camera. Each of them was holding a cupcake. At the bottom of the frame was a narrow piece of paper, which read, "Magnolia Bakery is featured on *Sex and the City* Season 3."

Thousands of years in the future, when archaeologists are combing through the artifacts of our age, what will happen when they excavate this photograph and the site around it? Will they have any idea what *Sex and the City* was or how it captivated the hopes and dreams of millions of women globally? Will they know that these two females in the photo were not just revered actresses but actually symbols of modern woman's sexual and social empowerment?

Will the archaeologists recognize cupcakes?

Will they know that in the first decade of the twenty-first century there were cakes baked in cups, cakes of every imaginable flavor and combination; that these cakes were covered in sweet frosting, in everything from simple vanilla creams to elaborate artistic 3-D creations; that for more than ten years these little cakes were a subject of great power and fascination all over the world; and that all of that, from the global tribes of devoted bakers to the chroniclers of the phenomenon to the multibillion-dollar cupcake economy, all began here, on this sacred corner of Manhattan, at this small bakery, with these two women and a twenty-second scene of a television show that, once upon a time, changed the way we ate dessert?

When I tell people I am writing a book about food trends, they usually just scratch their heads. Then I say the word *cupcakes*, and instantly their eyes open wide, their heads nod, and a torrent of passionate opinion pours forth from the depths of their soul. They love cupcakes. They hate cupcakes. They eat cupcakes every day. They avoid cupcakes like the plague. Cupcakes are everything they love about life. Cupcakes are everything wrong with the modern world.

Cupcakes, cupcakes, cupcakes. Glorious, cursed, beautiful, wretched, god-help-us, god-love-us . . . cupcakes!

As a child of North America, I am no stranger to the charm of cupcakes. In one of my earliest memories, right before my third birthday, I am standing in the kitchen with my mother, first tossing eggs on the floor and then hysterically crying at the results as she desperately tried to bake chocolate cupcakes for my party that afternoon. In later years my mother brought cupcakes to my school from Health Bread, a long-departed bakery near our house in Toronto. The whole class sat in hushed silence as they were carried from the doorway to our teacher's desk, twenty-five sets of little eyes locked like heat-seeking missiles on that pale blue box.

When our teacher untied the butcher's string and opened the box, it revealed the happiest sight on earth: row upon row of chocolate cupcakes nestled tightly in their accordion paper wrappers, frosted with a thin veneer of mocha-colored icing, and covered with a tasteful shower of rainbow sprinkles. We'd patiently wait in line, receive our ration, then head back to our desks, cradling the cupcake like a small bird in our hands. The girls would peel the paper off carefully, examining the best angle to approach the first bite, but not us boys. We'd tear into them with the senseless chomps of competitors in an apple-bobbing contest. Within seconds our faces and mouths would be painted in chocolate, our white shirts and sweat pants smeared with streaks of brown. What we didn't ingest, we figured, we'd simply absorb through the skin by osmosis. Within thirty seconds the classroom was a mess of crumbs, wrappers, and bubbling hyperactivity. Cupcakes were childhood at its peak.

But something happened to cupcakes over the past decade and a half. They became trendy. In fact, they became so trendy that the cupcake became the defining food trend of the age of food trends that we now find ourselves living in. When people talk about cupcakes today they don't talk about their sweetness, the colors and flavors they're made in, or any aspect that's inherent to how a cupcake tastes (you know how a cupcake tastes—it tastes like a small cake); instead, cupcakes are a lightning rod, drawing in the energy and emotion surrounding the complicated and rapidly expanding world of food trends, a world that has come to shape nearly everything we eat.

In truth, food trends are nothing new. They're a natural byproduct of civilization's evolution from hunter-gatherers, who ate whatever they could track down, to farmers, merchants, and traders, who had some choice in the matter. No one chased a woolly mammoth with a spear because the head of their tribe declared mammoth to be the hot protein in the Paleolithic era (back then the Paleo diet was the only option), but once we developed the economic means to select from a variety of foods, certain ones inevitably became more popular than others. Food became a fashion item, a status symbol, and a means of exerting power. It was a growing taste for exotic spices that drove explorers from Europe out into the unknown Atlantic, the prize of coriander, turmeric, and other edible Indian treasures as enticing as the gold and silk waiting across the void. Coffee spread from an obscure crop in Ethiopia to a global food trend that now anchors the morning of nearly half the planet and is grown wherever it can be cultivated.

In my three-plus decades on this earth I have witnessed the cyclical nature of food trends, including the chicken finger boom of my youth, the dismal Atkins diet years, and a bull market for fajitas during high school. I was born as sushi made its way to American shores as a rare delicacy alongside Japan's rising business culture, and I witnessed its transformation into a cheap takeout dinner for the masses, available at convenience stores and gas stations. I have read about trends that exist only in history books (the Roman royal habit of stuffing as many animals into each other for roasting as possible, like deboned matryoshka dolls or a turducken) and personally witnessed once-strong trends fade as they were usurped by competitors (those same fajitas and sushi platters giving way first to burritos and ramen soups and then to fish tacos and izakayas), while trends like espresso coffee have assumed a permanent role in my diet.

I've also seen heavily hyped trends vanish as suddenly as they have appeared, like thin snow hitting the ground. Watching Superbowl XXVII in 1993, I, like millions of others, was spellbound by the halftime commercial for Crystal Pepsi, with its new-age messages saying, "Right now, the future is ahead of you," set to the tune of Van Halen's "Right Now." Suddenly all the soda companies were rushing out with clear drinks of their own, eager to catch the transparent momentum. I remember going on a lunch break from high school with a group of friends to the nearest convenience store, literally lining up ten deep to buy our first bottle of Crystal Pepsi. We hustled to a nearby park, sat in a circle, and cracked open the bottle, passing it from one to another like hoboes around a campfire. Instead of ushering in a new era of transparent refreshment, however, my first eagerly awaited sip of Crystal Pepsi was a disappointing dram of uninspired sugar water.

Everywhere I look these days I see food trends, and what I see are trends springing up quicker and growing faster than they ever did before. Once the province of a few rich gourmands, they are now a mainstay of popular culture. Food trend news, reviews, and top-ten lists are splashed across the pages and screens of the media in an endless, incessant loop. We are living in a gold rush of food trends, mined with ladles and saucepans instead of pickaxes and dynamite. Each new trend I have witnessed in recent years left me to wonder how this whole ecosystem functioned. Why were certain items colonizing restaurant menus suddenly (fried chicken, pork belly, bourbon), while others, like paninis, seemingly disappeared after setting the trend just years before?

One day I craved a fish taco and could only find it in a single restaurant in Toronto. A year later my city was crawling with them, from a dozen dedicated fish taquerias that sprang up overnight to really bad fish tacos served in faux British pubs. How did this happen? I wondered why my father was suddenly eating pomegranate seeds with every meal and why my wife's best friend spent thirty dollars to attend a food truck event, lining up for an hour to get in, only to line up for another hour to buy a lobster roll, which sold out right before she finally reached it. Meanwhile the Sri Lankan samosa vendor twelve feet away sat and wondered why no one wanted what he was selling. Why was one food more popular than another? Both the lobster roll and samosa were delicious, and both cost around the same amount of money—so why the discrepancy in demand?

What made a diet healthy one week, then unhealthy the next? How did everyone crave hamburgers all of a sudden, simply because some blogger proclaimed it Burger Week? And do we really think, as eaters, that it is a good idea to infuse bacon into *everything*?

At its worst, when you've eaten your fifth mediocre fish taco in a week, you realize that this onslaught of food trends can be relentless, vapid, and exhausting. Why does food have to be trendy? Why can't it just taste good on its own merits? I often find myself just wanting to be given a grilled cheese and then left alone. Not "artisanal" aged cheese, mind you, or ancient grain bread. Just cheese. And bread.

Of course, I realize that my complaints are futile. Unless we all move to the woods and forage for our meals, it is inevitable that food trends will shape what we eat on a day-to-day basis (in fact, foraging is a big trend with chefs these days). Besides, I'm as guilty as any one of them. For all the times I may gripe about the invasion of ramen bars or the Greeks' colonization of the yogurt section, I am also the first to line up for a proper bowl of springy ramen noodles in a rich broth, and I haven't bought non-Hellenic yogurt since I first bought a tub of Fage in 2008. Not once.

If food trends are overtaking our thinking about the what, where, when, how, and even why of eating, then surely there must be something to them. I wanted to find out what drove these trends and made them such a potent force in our daily lives. First, how did they start, and who were the tastemakers behind them who took an idea, cultivated it, and changed the way we ate? (A tastemaker, in this book, is anyone with the economic or cultural power to create and influence food trends.) What did different types of trends have in common? How was a trend that a farmer started different from one credited with a chef or a diet guru, and where did they intersect? Second, who were the people and forces in the food business who took a food and grew it into a widespread trend? Who tracked and predicted trends? Who had the ability to market a food into a popular cultural moment? And where did a different set of tastemakers encounter these foods and bring them to a wider stage? Third, I wanted to understand just why food trends mattered. What impact did they have economically, culturally, politically, and socially? Were food trends a force for anything besides an excuse to eat more of one thing and not another? What happened to trends once they were no longer trendy? Did they leave a legacy or simply vanish into history, like the fondue set gathering dust in my parent's basement?

Finally, I wanted to come to terms with my own complex relationship with food trends. Were they indeed nothing more than a series of passing fads, a product of hype and bandwagon jumping that had corrupted our dinnertime? Or were they a force for good, opening minds and cultural opportunities, broadening our understanding of what we eat, cook, and grow?

Could I put aside my prejudices, tamp down my emotions, and once again stuff my face with cupcakes?

PART I

THE FOUR TYPES OF TRENDS

1

THE CULTURAL TREND

SEX APPEAL

The earliest cookbook references to cupcakes (or, rather, "cup cakes") reportedly date back to the late eighteenth century, though it's likely that miniature cakes, in some form or another, arose at the same time as, well, big cakes. On the Food Timeline, an online resource of food history, they are referred to as cupcakes, Vienna cakes, Queen cakes, fairy cakes, and Charlotte Russe, which was a simple sponge cake in cardboard, covered in whipped cream. The twentieth century saw cupcakes rise to their current form thanks to innovations in food processing technology, which allowed for packaged cake mixes and a rainbow of colored icing options. Months after World War I ended, Hostess launched its plastic-wrapped chocolate cupcake, with its iconic loopy spine of white decorative icing, and the corporate cupcake era officially began, bringing them to grocery stores across the country. Betty Crocker and Duncan Hines mixes followed, along with the Easy-Bake Oven, making the process so simple that cupcakes were often the first foods children made themselves.

For most of the latter half of the twentieth century cupcakes were a North American bakery fixture along with cookies, brownies, and other sweets occupying space in the display case. They came in vanilla and chocolate and were iced in the same two flavors, though the icing, which could be buttercream, ganache, or some processed variation, rarely amounted to more than 20 percent of the whole cake. Often they were topped with sprinkles, either chocolate or rainbow, or sometimes those silver-coated sugar ball bearings, called dragée, that rip through your molars like a diamond drill and are legally considered inedible by the Food and Drug Administration.

During the 1970s and 1980s muffins, not cupcakes, were the star of the bakery business, spurned by the high-fiber diet trend, which was believed to combat heart disease and other ailments. Bran muffins were a fixture atop diner counters and coffee shops everywhere, along with their cohorts, blueberry, banana, carrot, and chocolate chip. There were sugar-free muffins and frozen muffins, miniature muffins and giant muffins, muffin mixes and muffin franchises, including my personal favorite, mmmuffins, a Toronto bakery chain where the crisp top of the muffin was the size of a portobello mmmushroom. Every bakery worth their oven was into muffins, and Ann Warren, in New York City, was no exception.

"We actually opened up doing homemade-style donuts," recalled Warren, "but it was really part of the muffin thing when we opened in 1987. Muffins were very, very big. I mean literally. People were into very large muffins." She made these muffins to sell to other cafés and restaurants, but when a retail space opened up in their Chelsea neighborhood a year later, Warren and her husband figured that selling directly to the public might be an easier way to approach baking. They sold coffee and donuts, muffins, pies, and cakes, and because there was so much cake batter and an abundance of empty muffin pans in the afternoon, they made cupcakes as well. They called the bakery Cupcake Café.

"We weren't even trying to be a cupcake café," said Warren by phone, speaking between baking shifts at the Cupcake Café. "We just came up with the name, really, because we liked the association between cake and a cup of coffee," not, she insists, because they were bullish on cupcakes. As the realization emerged among customers that most muffins, even if they were made with bran and raisins, were in fact no healthier than the stick of butter they were made from, the muffin trend quickly faded. In response, Warren increasingly filled those vacant muffin tins with batter for cupcakes, which, she calculated, were less of a caloric indulgence than even a bagel and cream cheese.

Warren's cupcakes were comforting, pretty affairs—a moist cake base with a thin ganache frosting and a small buttercream flower on top—but they never kicked off any significant uptick in cupcake buying. Sure, she had a steady stream of clients, some of whom bought cupcakes, but people mostly came to the Cupcake Café for coffee and other baked goods. Cupcakes were popular there, but like most other bakeries, Cupcake Café largely sold them to children or for birthday parties. One customer who frequented Cupcake Café in the early nineties was the actress Sarah Jessica Parker, who was starring in a Broadway play nearby. "She used to come in, sit at the back table with my daughter, and have her coffee," recalls Warren, though she can't specifically remember Parker eating a cupcake. It's easy to imagine Parker, sipping her coffee and reading the newspaper as Warren walked by her with a freshly iced tray of cupcakes, neither of them realizing the significance of the moment as a future trend and its tastemaker passed unknown.

Like Cupcake Café, the Magnolia Bakery was not initially conceived as a business dedicated to cupcakes. In July 1996, when Jennifer Appel, a clinical psychologist, and her high school friend Alyssa Torey, who was working in her family's restaurant business, first opened up their seven hundred–square-foot retro-themed bakery in the West Village, less than two miles from the Cupcake Café, the only cakes they sold were Eastern European–style bundt cakes. "We were doing more bars, squares, sticky buns, muffins, and coffee cakes," recalls Appel. By September that year, neighborhood customers who liked Magnolia's products were requesting birthday cakes and other special occasion cakes from the two owners, even though they weren't on the menu. "People asked, 'Do you have birthday cakes?' and we realized, oh yeah, we kinda missed that," said Appel. Torey had a passion for southern food and baked goods, and she sought to re-create the fluffy, daintily iced, brightly colored layer cakes commonly found in the Deep South at church lunches, society teas, and country diners. However, the first two cakes someone ordered were different sizes—one in a nine-inch pan and one in a seven-inch pan—and Torey, like Warren, was left with excess batter.

She went to the deli next door, bought paper cupcake holders, and history was made. "We poured the batter into the leftover muffin tins from breakfast," recalled Torey. "We made a dozen extra cupcakes from the batter." Each time they baked cakes more cupcakes were the consequence. These cupcakes were in traditional flavors like chocolate, vanilla, and red velvet (basically chocolate with red dye), topped with a whirlpool swirl of buttercream icing in pink, lavender, and baby blue pastels that straddled the line between deliberate precision and homespun imperfection. They sold each for a dollar and a quarter. "People really liked them," Torey said. "So we started making cupcakes intentionally." By the end of the year word started to spread. Because the cupcakes were still a by-product of full-sized cakes and the tiny bakery had a limited staff and hours, their supply was small, so Magnolia's cupcakes frequently sold out before the end of the day. "Customers said, 'Where are the cupcakes?'" recalled Appel, "and it became obvious pretty quickly that cupcakes were becoming the number-one priority."

Magnolia's cupcakes steadily grew in popularity, first in the neighborhood and then around the rest of New York City. "It became a destination," said Appel. "You'd walk down from the Upper East Side to the West Village for a cupcake, like you'd do with your favorite slice of pizza." By 1997 Magnolia Bakery witnessed its first cupcake lineups forming outside the shop, and these soon snaked around the block. The shop instituted a hard limit of a dozen cupcakes per customer, which infuriated some but helped manage the incessant demand. These customers weren't exclusively children and their parents; in fact, they were largely adults—single and married, older and professional—who wouldn't come for a box of cupcakes but rather a singular, handheld indulgence that they had specifically traveled there to acquire. Each time the cupcakes ran out (eliciting groans from the people in the lineup, who watched them disappear from the window, one at a time), their currency rose in value. The harder they were to obtain, the more people wanted those cupcakes.

Magnolia Bakery was increasingly generating small local press clippings, though the first articles about the bakery didn't even mention the cupcakes. A few in-flight magazines flagged them as a destination for visitors to New York, but the first mention of their cupcakes in the *New York Times* only happened in early 1999, and it was very brief, just a few lines in a short story on the cupcake's potential revival, and also included mention of the Cupcake Café and several others. Still, the bakery was popular enough with the right people (cultural tastemakers in the media, fashion, and arts) that Torey and Appel were offered a book deal in 1998 with Simon and Schuster. By the time *The Magnolia Bakery Cookbook* was published in the fall of 1999, with a sun-drenched photograph of two full-sized cakes on the cover (one chocolate, the other coconut), much had changed at the bakery.

Appel and Torey's relationship had strained under the pressure of the business and the rapid success that the nascent cupcake mania brought with it. They jostled in the hot, cramped kitchen and argued over expansion plans with the passion that only old friends who go into business together can do. Finally, it reached a point at which Appel could take no more, and in 1999 she sold her share of Magnolia Bakery to Torey. Soon after, Appel opened the Buttercup Bake Shop uptown, specializing in the colorful, comforting baked goods that she sold at Magnolia, with a strong portfolio of cupcakes. Their rivalry only fueled New York's growing cupcake obsession, which was about to tip into a full-fledged national cultural food trend with a bite heard round the world.

∽

Sex and the City, Season III, Episode V "No Ifs, Ands, or Butts." Air Date: July 9, 2000.

Miranda and Carrie are sitting on a bench outside the Magnolia Bakery. Miranda wears flats, blue slacks, and an oversized red trench coat that matches her hair and lipstick. Carrie wears a dark blazer, gray linen dress, a silk scarf, and knee-high wool socks with chunky heels. Miranda holds a cup of coffee to her lips, while Carrie unpeels a vanilla cupcake with vibrant pink frosting.

Carrie: I have a crush.

Miranda: Yeah?

Carrie: Yup.

Miranda: Good. You haven't had a real crush in a while. Not since Big.

Carrie: Big wasn't a crush. He was a crash.

Camera cuts in tight on Carrie as she takes a large bite of the cupcake. Cut to a wide shot, where she licks crumbs and icing from sides of mouth.

Carrie: His name is Aiden, and I believe him to be very cute.

End Scene.

When I finally watched the infamous "cupcake scene" from *Sex and the City,* I was astounded by a few things. First, it is incredibly, unthinkably short, just twenty seconds, or about 1/90th the length of the episode. I can barely get the wrapper off a cupcake in that amount of time, let alone chew and swallow a bite without choking. Second, there is no mention of the cupcake Carrie eats. No "great cupcake," no "*mmmmm,*" no talk of anything except men. Third, aside from the first second of the scene, which shows the Magnolia sign, there is no mention of the bakery and no other sight of its name. Finally, it happens to be the only time in the show's history that anyone, let alone its lead protagonist, ate a cupcake. This is surprising, because the other trends that emerged from *Sex and the City*—cosmopolitan martinis, Manolo Blahnik high-heeled shoes, the Rabbit vibrator—were either constant fixtures over the life of the series or central to an episode's plot.

How, then, did this brief moment in television become the proverbial beat of a butterfly's wings that unleashed a hurricane of cupcakes onto the world? How did that one bite spawn the defining food trend of our age?

Georgette Blau believes she has the answer. In 1999 she started On Location Tours, which began offering its Sex and the City Hotspots Tour in 2001, a year after the cupcake scene aired. "We made *Sex and the City* synonymous with the cupcake," said Blau as we spoke in her Manhattan office, which was jammed, wall to wall, with framed articles from around the world mentioning the tour. Prior to the tour the cupcake scene was just a blip on the radar, accessible only to fans who saw that episode, lived in New York, and could recognize Magnolia in that first second of footage. "No one noticed. But then I did the tour, and cupcakes became synonymous with the show. The tour distilled the show down to key things," she said. "It's about fashion, eating, drinking, and sex." In other words, Manolos, cupcakes, cosmos, and Rabbit vibrators, all of which are incorporated into the tour in one way or another.

Appel, who has never even seen an episode of *Sex and the City*, noticed a change very quickly in Buttercup Bake Shop's business, which saw double-digit growth every year after the episode aired until the recession of 2008. It also shifted the demographics of cupcake eaters significantly. "Cupcakes changed from family-oriented customers to a tourist from Kansas saying, 'I need to go to Magnolia,'" she said, noting that her average customer became a size-four, twenty-seven-year-old female (though she still loves when big burly men come into her shop and say, "I'll have the pink one").

Initially the Sex and the City Hotspots Tour supplied their cupcakes from Magnolia, right across from their West Village midpoint stop, but after a few weeks that ended, as Magnolia's quantity limits were causing friction with the tour and the bus passengers were irritating customers in line. Blau switched to Buttercup Bake Shop for the tour's supply soon after, and the cupcakes rode in the bus until the West Village, where the bus still stopped by Magnolia, but its passengers were fed its competitor's cupcakes. More recently the tour's cupcakes, including the ones I ate, have been supplied by Billy's, a bakery run by another former Magnolia employee.

This was how the cupcake phenomenon initially spread: organically, from New York bakery to New York bakery, as bakers and cashiers and enterprising shopkeepers of Magnolia and its offshoots saw the success around them, looked at the lineups, the backlog of orders, the cash registers stuffed with thousands of dollars, and, like ambitious gangsters unhappy with their cut of the action, struck out on their own. Each new shop sought to be bigger, better, cuter, pinker, more elaborate, and more in tune with the strong single female image that the cupcake had risen to glory feeding. Each new cupcakery (a term that soon emerged) opening in New York tried to differentiate themselves in some unique way, whether it was minicupcakes, oversized cupcakes, stuffed cupcakes, frozen cupcakes, savory cupcakes, booze-filled cupcakes, or customizable vanity cupcakes with your face on the icing. Each new metamorphosis to the trend generated a sense of excitement and media attention, a cultural bonfire fueled by cupcakes.

Everyone, that is, except the Cupcake Café's Ann Warren, who watched the cupcake's wild success pass by her front window. "Magnolia and others took our idea and went crazy with it," said Warren. "They took our decor and went nuts with it. I mean, what can I say. We can't even pay our mortgage! I find the whole media coverage of it absolutely amazing and utterly ridiculous. A cupcake is a cupcake. Even a really nice cupcake is just a cupcake. I find it somewhat surreal. If I'd known when I was starting out, I might have gone in another direction. I don't understand it, and I know it's media driven, but I just find it, frankly, a little sick and tragic that something that's not really good for you is connected with being young and sexy and running around in high heels."

Why cupcakes?

That's the question that keeps Warren, muffin bakers, food writers, and flour suppliers up at night. Even well over a decade later the cupcake trend continues to baffle them. How did this child's cake, the simplest of treats that had been around for over a century, suddenly transform into a pink-frosted juggernaut in such a short period of time, and why did it happen when it did?

It's worth remembering that the cupcake trend's greatest period of growth happened in New York in the years following the September 11 attacks, which were not that far, geographically, from Magnolia and the epicenter of the cupcake craze. "September 11 unleashed this desire for a sense of security and pleasure and associations with a simpler, easier, sweeter time," said Christopher Noxon, a friend and journalist whose 2006 book, *Rejuvenile: Kickball, Cartoons, Cupcakes and the Reinvention of the American Grown-up*, examined the phenomenon in which childhood things, like Converse sneakers, cartoons, and, yes, cupcakes, became acceptable indulgences for North American adults. "Cupcake fanatics were part and parcel of the kitschy, hipster nostalgic boom of late nineties and late aughts," he said. "Nightclub parties with piñatas, pin the tail on the donkey, and cupcakes. Like a lot of things, it quickly became the norm. It went from a showy token of 'look how young and free spirited I am' to just part of the landscape. A cupcake is an instant passport to childlike pleasure, and it's simple. It's such a gateway drug. You can be a buttoned-up, uptight red-hot pig and order a green tea cupcake and seem instantly more whimsical." Practically, cupcakes also just make sense to eat. "It's just good. It's a personal cake! What could be wrong with that? You can peel back the layers of irony, but for a ten-year-old it's just cake."

It goes even deeper according to Dr. Jean Retzinger, a former baker who teaches media studies at the University of California at Berkeley and believes that cupcakes took off for a number of practical reasons as a cultural food trend. Cupcakes were a familiar food, easily recognizable to any American, unlike, say, French macarons (which required explanation and translation). They were accessible, so even if your city didn't have a cupcake bakery, you could find the ingredients to make them at any supermarket, and they were an individual luxury, which allowed a sort of guilt-free (or low-guilt) indulgence. More than anything, they were an easily adaptable symbol of whatever you wanted them to be. "Food represents so much more than calories consumed," said Retzinger. "I suspect the cupcake becomes an emblem of those characters on *Sex and the City*. If you identify with those characters and lifestyle, the cupcake is your road into it." One of the show's key messages, Retzinger believes, was that you could purchase your feminist independence and your power in the world as a woman. Cupcakes were a gendered treat. An edible, easily obtainable icon of modern womanhood that was also affordable, unlike a seven hundred–dollar pair of shoes.

Peter Naccarato, an English professor at Marymount Manhattan College in New York and author of the book *Culinary Capital*, agrees. "*Sex and the City* brought cupcakes to a whole new level," he said. What *Sex and the City* did for cupcakes was move them from a local culinary phenomenon, which mattered mostly to New York food fanatics, to a national media-driven trend, heavily invested in the popular culture, fashion, and status that the show was associated with. The show was the tastemaker, blessing the food with its social capital. It became cool to eat a cupcake, unlike, say, a chocolate chip cookie or a brownie, neither of which were nearly as sexy anymore. If you served cupcakes at your office party or wedding instead of sliced cake, it showed a certain sense of class and sophistication, like following the right band. "The cupcake is a brilliantly exploited opportunity to take a small, local phenomenon and blow it up into a national phenomenon," said Naccarato. "That's what the media can do."

Cupcakes were an intensely media-driven trend from the get-go primarily because they took off in New York City. The New York media world is an echo chamber, and the city is filled with thousands of journalists and media personalities from all over the world who tend to report the same cultural stories in their backyard, which is why trends tend to start there and not, say, in Wichita. The cupcake's coverage began in the local press, with small articles mentioning Magnolia's popularity. Other local writers and publications picked up on that and wrote their own versions of the story, and these were seen by editors and writers at national publications who, in turn, put their own spin on it, setting in motion an unstoppable spin cycle of publicity.

Stories about cupcakes were nothing new for the food media, but these were different. Fashion magazines became a particularly strong advocate of cupcakes, usually featuring them in short "what's hot" stories because many fashion editors and writers lived in the same neighborhoods as Magnolia and Buttercup and watched *Sex and the City*. "I remember the cupcake spreads from my mom's *McCall's* back in the 1970s," recalled James Oseland, editor-in-chief of *Saveur* magazine and a food journalist since the early 1990s. "When I was growing up in the sixties and seventies, every other food story in ladies' magazines or food spreads in the newspaper was a cupcake story." But as the trend grew in New York, Oseland began noticing all the other food publications coming up with their own versions of cupcake spreads because of what Oseland called their "collective narcolepsy." "It's an easy sell and an easy story to do," said Oseland. "It's an evergreen that can be dropped in wherever and whenever. It's not seasonally specific, and it's a crowd-pleaser among people who take in certain types of food media. You can make the cupcake story look very differently. You can do the Barbie fantasy palace version, or you can do your Luddite version of the cupcake, and you can tell the story visually and appeal to your readers. You can make these beautiful, gorgeous, appealing, very makeable-looking foods and splatter your pages with them, and you can resuscitate that often."

In the hands of the media cupcakes became the perfect chameleon: a shape-shifting combination of eggs, flour, sugar, and butter that could be grafted onto any storyline. What other food could run the gamut from cheap and cheerful to decadent and deluxe with a twist of the frosting or a sprinkle or two? What other baked good could be in a women's fashion magazine, symbolizing sexy single indulgence, right next to a parenting magazine in the newsstand, in which it was a smiling birthday party treat, without any sort of conflict?

No one understood the cupcake's versatility better than Karen Tack, a food stylist in Connecticut who had been elaborately decorating cupcakes for magazines like *Good Housekeeping, Women's Circle, Family Fun,* and other supermarket checkout titles since 1990. "I really think magazines drove the demand for cupcakes," she said, reflecting on the trend's increasing media presence in the late 1990s. "I mean, people were making cupcakes all the time, but it was just a realization that here's this thing we can do anything with. A blank slate, an untouched gem where people previously thought you could only do in vanilla and chocolate." In 1998 Tack and her photographer partner, Alan Richardson, styled and shot the photographs for the Magnolia bakery's first cookbook. The Magnolia cupcake was unlike any she'd seen before. It was topped with a confectioner's sugar–based icing, spread with a very specific swirling technique that left a sort of crater in the center that ended in a miniature peak. It was half cake and half frosting. "They had to close the shop for a couple of hours while shooting," recalled Tack. "You'd think we'd done something terribly wrong. People were throwing themselves on the sidewalk because they couldn't get their daily cupcake. 'Oh my god!' They'd scream, 'Are you kidding me?'"

As the cupcake trend picked up steam Tack and Richardson were increasingly busy with cupcake assignments from magazines, and each time they upped the ante, decorating the cakes as increasingly elaborate animals, cartoon characters, and figures. In 2008 they published *Hello Cupcake,* a cookbook filled with their decorations. They hoped it would sell two thousand copies. Instead, it went on to sell hundreds of thousands, spawning sequels, multiple appearances on the *Today* show and *Martha Stewart Living,* and innumerable copycat titles of a genre known affectionately as cupcake porn. Each article, TV segment, or book about cupcakes generated more of the same. The cupcake media trend fed on itself.

"The food media as a whole is generally lazy," remarked Joshua Ozersky, a food writer for *Esquire* and others and who is no fan of cupcakes. "There's very few people in the food media that really have their own tastes and trust their own tastes. Generally most of them are followers. That's why the food industry is dominated by trends. If you call something a trend, especially if you're an editor, then it artificially becomes that. . . . There's a group-think aspect. No one wants to be left out of the cupcake sweepstakes. It's a zeitgeist with frosting on top."

In terms of timing, cupcakes emerged onto the national scene just as the food media began its transformation from a cottage industry, largely aimed at women and an elite of gourmets, into a global, digital, omnivorous titan. Cupcake mania began just a few years after the *Food Network* first aired and North Americans began treating cooking as entertainment. The cable modem, which brought broadband Internet into homes across the world, was released onto the market in 1997, the year Magnolia's cupcake lines started forming. Its usage spiked in 2001, when the cupcake trend began picking up steam and coinciding with the rise of websites devoted to foods and a growing cadre of new blogs dedicated to cupcakes. Through these technologies and new media outlets, cupcakes became the most widely covered, rapidly disseminated, endlessly debated, and chronicled food trend of all time. One of the first and still most prominent cupcake bloggers is Rachel Kramer Bussel, a New York–based writer who is also well known as a writer of bondage erotica. I first met Bussel in 2006 at a sex-themed storytelling night in a former New York massage parlor that she helped organize. She passed around trays of cupcakes, and later in the evening guests were free to flog her with a leather riding crop. Bussel had launched her blog, Cupcake Takes the Cake in late 2004, chronicling the emerging field of cupcake shops around Manhattan and, later, the United States with her coblogger, Nichelle Stephens.

In 2012 I met Bussel again at Sweet Revenge, a cupcakery a few blocks from Magnolia that opened in 2008 and distinguished itself by pairing its extensive menu of freshly baked cupcakes with fine wines and other alcoholic drinks. Behind us four Dutch tourists sampled a quartet of cupcakes with a bottle of Prosecco at a wooden bistro table with worn chairs under a globe lamp as Edith Piaf played overhead. Here was just one slice of the cupcake craze among hundreds: its boozy Parisian Belle Époque evocation, scented not with talk of radical politics and tobacco but of browning butter and caramelizing sugar. Bussel ordered the day's special, the Very Strawberry cupcake, a Mexican vanilla bean cake stuffed with macerated strawberries and topped with strawberry cream cheese frosting. She removed a camera flash from her overstuffed handbag and lit up the cupcake, taking photos at various angles with her phone to upload to her blog.

The cupcake blogs lifted the cupcake out of New York and allowed them to proliferate anywhere there was an Internet connection. Cupcake fanatics would read Cupcake Takes the Cake and send Bussel their own photos and stories, either of cupcakes they made at home or of cupcakeries that were opening in their respective cities. In turn, the blog and all the accompanying press inspired numerous cupcake entrepreneurs to enter the business. "People saw the stories we wrote, and they thought, 'Hey, I can do that,'" said Bussel, who consumed her cupcake as though performing its autopsy: she laid it on its side, mashed it down with her fork, and ate the icing and cake separately, allowing her to taste their distinctive components. (To me it tasted like a denser version of strawberry shortcake, with a tart edge to it.)

Bussel believed the cupcake's unique advantage was that it started to really take off nationally around 2006 to 2008, shortly after the launch of Facebook and Twitter, both of which helped elevate the cupcake as the world's first viral food trend. "Suddenly," says Bussel, "bakers could reach customers directly. They could experiment with the persona of the business and test what they were selling in terms of its image." She also pointed out that one of the first popular videos on YouTube was a *Saturday Night Live* music video called, "Lazy Sunday," in which a rapping Chris Parnell and Andy Samberg "hit up Magnolia and mack on some cupcakes."

Then, in the fall of 2008, the Great Recession hit America, and cupcakes reached a fever pitch. Suddenly you had a tremendous sense of insecurity, which was perfect for a renewed interest in American comfort food (similar to the one that had lifted Magnolia after 9/11). You also had thousands of young professionals who either lost their corporate jobs or became disenchanted with them. Sitting up late at night, fine tuning their résumés, more than a few flipped back and forth to cupcake blogs and articles on cupcakes, read about the financial success of some of these bakeries, and thought, *Hey, I could do that.* As a result, cupcakes became big business. They were cheap to make, the profit margins were very high, and customers tended to be loyal and buy multiples. Adam Sternbergh, writing in *New York* magazine at the time, likened them to the bakery equivalent of crack cocaine: They were addictive, and the high demand caused turf wars to spring up between cupcake dealers. As former investment bankers and lawyers around North America entered the business and began to set up local chains and franchises with an eye on global domination, the lawsuits started to fly. Buttercup launched a lawsuit against Little Cupcake, founded by former employees, for apparently pilfering the feel of Appel's bakery. Sprinkles, a Beverly Hills–based cupcake chain founded in 2005 by Candace and Charles Nelson (the first cupcakery to bake cupcakes exclusively), ruthlessly pursued any other cupcake bakery they felt impinged on their brand, using multiple lawsuits and cease-and-desist letters to prevent other shops from using the word "sprinkles," their store's pink color, or their trademarked use of a fondant dot within a dot atop their cupcake's icing.

The largest chain to come out of the cupcake wars was Crumbs Bake Shop, which first opened in New York City's Upper West Side in 2003 by Jason Bauer and his wife, Mia. Crumbs expanded quickly, first in the New York area and then to other cities such as Boston, Chicago, Los Angeles, and Washington, DC, totaling more than sixty stores in 2013. The company sells over fifty different varieties of cupcakes, including miniature cupcakes and gigantic cupcakes (basically a tall regular cake), in flavors like cannoli (topped with a cannoli), brewski (topped with a beer stein cookie), and the pigskin (topped with a candy football on green-icing turf). Crumbs cupcakes are baked and iced in four large central kitchens (each employing around five bakers and twenty decorators) around the clock, and they are delivered each day to stores in that region. In 2011 Crumbs set a precedent by taking the company public on the NASDAQ exchange with a $58.9 million market valuation based on monthly sales of over $1.5 million, with cupcakes selling at $3.75 apiece. Cupcake speculators didn't even have to get their hands dirty with flour and butter anymore; they could call up their broker and buy as many shares of the cupcake trend as they could afford.

The economic impact of the cupcake trend is difficult to quantify because cupcakes aren't tracked like a commodity such as oil or corn, and aside from Crumbs, all other cupcake businesses are privately held. According to articles in the industry trade journal *Modern Baking*, which tracks the bakery industry nationally, cupcake sales grew 56 percent from 2008 to 2012, a period when they continually gained market share against regular cakes. "We've seen an explosion of a new market segment called cupcakeries, popping up around the country," said Heather Sisson, director of sales and marketing at Lucks Food Decorating Company, one of the largest and oldest bakery supply companies in America. The wholesale market for cupcake-specific decorations more than doubled in the past decade, drawing in a whole new group of suppliers (of everything from branded cupcake tins to transport trays) and making cupcakes Lucks's number-one product category. Where the previous cupcake market was focused on mom-and-pop bakeries and packaged supermarket cupcakes that cost a dollar per dozen, the rise of the cupcakeries changed the cake business fundamentally.

"More [cupcakeries] began popping up in every state," said Sisson, "and that of course caused the independent bakeries to change cupcake programs, and then in-store bakeries jumped on the bandwagon. We then jumped all over the cupcake craze." Cupcakes are now at the point of the trend's economic evolution at which they are moving into the mass market. "We meet with Walmart and talk to them about cupcakes being an important part of their bakery program," Sisson said, estimating that there are already around eight to nine thousand independent cupcake bakeries in America alone. They are in big cities and small towns, red states and blue states, from I Love Cupcakes in Key Largo, Florida, to Kastle's Kreations, a cupcake truck in Eagle River, Alaska, and everywhere in between. Even if each bakery doesn't pull in the millions that a Sprinkles or Magnolia does, it's safe to say that the annual cupcake GDP in America is in the multibillion-dollar range.

The cupcake trend has also spawned a cottage industry of accessories and affiliated products that has generated untold millions more. Johnny's Cupcakes sells hip clothes with a cupcake-and-crossbones pirate logo out of stores designed around a bakery look. On the weekend you can enjoy your red velvet cupcakes with a chilled bottle of Riesling from California's Cupcake Vineyards (one review calls it "overpoweringly sweet, creamy, with a touch of acidity on the finish") or a cocktail with the company's brand of vodka, which comes in flavors such as Chiffon, Frosting, and Devil's Food. Houseware companies, from Sunbeam to Babycakes, sell electric cupcake-baking machines and decorating stations, including one shaped like Hello Kitty (presumably for the enthusiastic Asian market). There are cupcake-themed novels and children's toys, cupcake jewelry sold online, plastic cupcakes used to sell women's shoes (not to mention high heel–shaped cupcakes), and even a Sprinkles cupcake ATM machine in Los Angeles that takes cash or credit cards and in return dispenses cupcakes twenty-four hours a day.

The most significant cultural offshoot of the trend is television, which not only rakes in big money from advertising and syndication but also fuels cupcake growth even further by inspiring a wider audience to bake, buy, and sell cupcakes. The summer of 2010 saw the launch of the Food Network's *Cupcake Wars,* a fast-paced baking competition show that pitted teams of cupcake chefs against each other. Similar to Bravo's *Top Chef* or pretty much any other reality cooking show, *Cupcake Wars* features lots of running around, highly edited moments of "tension," and catty judging from the likes of Sprinkles's Candace Nelson. A month after *Cupcake Wars* had its debut TLC premiered *DC Cupcake,* a show focused on the daily life of Washington's famed cupcakery Georgetown Cupcake, owned by sisters Sophie LaMontagne and Katherine Kallinis, who constantly struggle in each episode to get orders out the door just in time. The series premier of *DC Cupcake* drew over a million viewers, and many more watch each week as well as in reruns. The two times I visited Georgetown Cupcake the lineup (mostly tourists, though some locals) snaked up the block, even on a scorching summer day. Every person who walked in made sure to photograph their order, the surroundings, the cupcake they bought, and the act of eating that cupcake, photos that they instantly uploaded to social media, doing their part to keep spreading the trend around the world.

 ❧

In November 2011 I was walking on a crowded street in Buenos Aires, Argentina, as a man in front of me was talking on his cell phone:

"Yeah yeah, it was a fun party . . . yeah good wine, pretty girls, too. . . .

The food? They had a big sushi bar, lots of sushi, and then all sorts of cupcakes. . . .

Yes, cupcakes. . . .

It's like a small cake. Like a sweet muffin. It's like a sweet muffin cake or some bullshit, I don't know. People were going crazy for them. . . .

Yeah . . . CUP CAKE . . . like a cake in a cup. Who knows . . . it must be an American thing."

I had lived in Buenos Aires from 2003 to 2005, and never once during that time had I heard about or set eyes on a cupcake, even for the birthdays of my expat American friends. Argentines love their sweets, especially anything filled or smeared with dulce de leche, and they tend to be pretty inflexible in their food choices. But in the years that I'd been gone not only had the cupcake arrived in Argentina; it had begun its spread around the party scene, pairing with sushi (a trend that was in full bloom when I lived there) to attain the same iconic status with upper-class tastemakers as it had in New York more than a decade before. At least half a dozen cupcakeries have since opened in Buenos Aires, each with its own highly stylized décor, website, and interior. Local and international media coverage on them inevitably makes reference to *Sex and the City* and Magnolia. Muma's Cupcakes, one of the most popular shops, with four locations (including one in Uruguay), has the song "Seasons of Love" from the *Rent* soundtrack playing on their website in an infinite loop, driving the bohemian spirit of the West Village into your brain like a frilly pink hammer.

Not even two decades into its rise, the humble cupcake has become a power instrument of globalization, spreading good old-fashioned American culture throughout the world. Spin a globe, put your finger down, and it's pretty much certain that cupcakes have begun appearing in whatever country you are pointing at. In Dhaka, Bangladesh, Cherry Blossom Cupcakes splits the market with Silver Lining Cupcakes, and in Dar es Salaam, Tanzania, owner Kelsey Malaika McKinney claims her Dots Cupcakery is the "sassiest cupcake shop in all of East Africa," something that Nairobi, Kenya's Just Cupcakes might dispute. The world's most expensive cupcake is, naturally, found in Dubai, going on sale in 2012 under the moniker the Golden Phoenix. For around $1,000 the discerning (or at least very wealthy) cupcake eater gets a cupcake with imported organic flour and butter, premium Italian cocoa, Ugandan vanilla beans, and the obligatory edible gold 23-karat sheet, all presented on a gold stand with a golden spoon, and strawberries dipped in edible gold. Home Made Cake sells cupcakes (as well as cakes) in Baghdad, Iraq, and although there isn't a dedicated cupcakery yet in Kabul,

Afghanistan, Christian American missionaries have reportedly been working there in recent years, teaching Afghan women to bake cupcakes so they can cater to Western aid workers and embassies.

The main American military base in Afghanistan, ISAF HQ, was nicknamed Camp Cupcake because it was so plush, and cupcakes are regularly sent to troops on the front line. On the Fourth of July, 2011, the American embassy in Kabul served soldiers, Afghan dignitaries, diplomats, and assorted friendly warlords a giant American flag made of cupcakes. A month before, Britain's MI6 intelligence service had hacked an al-Qaeda online magazine, which features calls for holy war and bomb-making instructions. The British intelligence service then systematically replaced all the jihadist material with step-by-step baking and decorating instructions that they had lifted from an Ohio cupcake shop. They dubbed it *Operation Cupcake*. Cupcakes can also help international development. Bloom Cakes in Phnom Penh, Cambodia, is a not-for-profit organization that teaches Cambodian women the art of baking, employing many in their popular cupcake shop and café that is operated by an Australian mother who moved to Cambodia in 2009 to spread the buttercream gospel.

I was shocked to find out that Asunción, Paraguay, had not one but two dedicated cupcakeries in addition to a number of individuals who baked cupcakes for events. I have been to Asunción, and it is the last place on earth I expected to find cupcakes. It is a small city ringed by slums—a shantytown actually leans against the walls of the presidential palace—and yet it proved the perfect place for local resident, Giselle Taborda, to open up Dolcito Cupcakes in 2010. "I saw all these little cakes with different colors and decorations on the Internet, and I fell in love with them," recalled Taborda over e-mail. Initially Dolcito began out of Taborda's own kitchen, and her first cupcakes were simple, homey creations, more like sugar-dusted muffins and the types of small cupcakes I recall my mother making when I was a kid. As the business evolved, however, Taborda obsessively studied photos of cupcakes online, and today her retail bakery (which opened in 2012) makes some of the most elaborate cupcakes I've seen, with everything from three-dimensional Angry

Birds characters to an entire sushi menu, with maki rolls and toro belly tuna rendered in intricate layers of icing and fondant.

As in North America, most of the international cupcake entrepreneurs were younger women who came from business backgrounds, often with no professional baking experience. Basma Azfar, a banker with an MBA in Karachi, Pakistan, began Cupcakes by Cookie in 2008 after making a batch of applesauce-infused *Sesame Street* cupcakes for her son's second birthday. "It has blossomed today into something far beyond my expectations," Azfar told me in an e-mail. "I thought cupcakes to be a fad that shall soon fade, but the trend seems to be now a staple dessert here." Though Cupcakes by Cookie remained a special order–only business, numerous other retail cupcake bakeries have since opened around Pakistan, such as Sugar and Crumbs in Islamabad and Redolence Bake Studio in Lahore.

As it did in America, the media played a role in fanning the flames of cupcake fever in every single one of these countries, making the trend as much about culture as taste. "Cupcakes can be found in all the major magazines here in Germany," said Betsy Eves, the American owner of JavaCupcake, a blog and cupcake recipe site based in Bavaria. "From lifestyle magazines to high-end fashion magazines and food magazines, cupcakes are everywhere." Her friend Iris Wagner, who owns Mir Wachen Cupcakes in Munich, credits a significant amount of her business to the articles she's been featured in. The appeal is the cupcake's novelty. "It's new," says Eves. "It's Western. It's definitely caught the eye of the twenty-somethings." In Paris, where the cupcake craze began in 2008 (there's around a dozen stores now), Cat Bernier, an American who runs Sugar Daze in the 9th Arrondisement, said that initially it was still powered by *Sex and the City* associations in the press, drawing "young, single French girls who had either seen cupcakes on TV or were reading about 'la folie de Cupcakes' in the fashion magazines." Over time it branched out into a greater French mainstream audience, though one television appearance Bernier did ended with the presenters denouncing this invasion of inferior American desserts, crying, "Vive le patisserie Française!!" on air.

American cupcake companies are eyeing this global demand as the American market becomes increasingly competitive and, in many cities, oversaturated. At the forefront of this is Magnolia Bakery, which is now headquartered in an office building just off Columbus Circle, across the street from Central Park. The office is built around an open kitchen where new cupcake recipes are being tested, and teams of eager new hires at Magnolia locations around New York (there were five in 2013) are instructed in the art of the perfect frosting swirl, which remains Magnolia's distinguishing feature along with its pedigree as the trend's originator. Amazingly, thanks to reruns, two movies, and widespread international syndication, Magnolia's *Sex and the City* association still has legs more than a decade after the show went off the air. The company appears in anywhere from one thousand to twelve hundred global media stories annually, and this is only a fraction compared to the volume of requests they receive and turn down.

Since 2006 Magnolia has been owned and operated by Steve Abrams, a tall, fit, silver-haired former waiter from the Catskills with a passion for fast cars, and his wife, Tyra. A veteran of the restaurant business, Abrams purchased Magnolia from Torey (who moved to the country to raise dairy cows) for $1 million. When I met Abrams in 2012 the company had seven American locations and four in the Middle East. "We get three to five international franchise requests daily," said Abrams, who opened the Dubai store in 2009 as a lark. "That ratcheted us up just by being in that part of the world." He saw potential everywhere, from Turkey and Japan, to Rwanda and, yes, even Paraguay. "When I go to Spain I might have sixty stores. Brazil could support twelve to twenty stores. We're probably looking at three hundred international stores in five years. . . . As much as America is disliked in many countries, our popular culture is overwhelming, and that's the culture that most of the world follows. Especially their middle class."

Even though the cupcake trend began in rarefied, elite enclaves like the West Village and Beverly Hills, those were just the entry point to the mass market. "Cupcakes are becoming more mainstream," said an executive at Crumbs who didn't want to be named, who explained that the company's expansion plan was to target malls in the heart of America. "Those malls have more fluid shoppers. It definitely caters to a different type. Yes, it could be high end, but it also could be potential for people who want to buy an affordable cupcake who are not affluent, and that's a huge opportunity. You wouldn't compromise the quality of the product. We'd maybe change the pricing of it and expect a higher volume."

The elephant in the room is that at some point the mania for cupcakes will subside and the market won't be able to support an increasing number of dedicated cupcakeries. The public's interest in the trend will move on to donuts, some say, or maybe a pie revival, and many cupcake shops will either close or branch out to serve more products. "I, too, wonder how sustainable it is," said the Crumbs executive. "Is it a short-lived trend and something you can sustain and build a business out of this? We grapple with that as well. It's the million-dollar question." Or, in Crumb's case, a multi-million-dollar one.

The media had been calling the end of cupcake fever since the trend began. Joel Stein, writing in *Time,* called them a "sickness" in 2006, and *Vanity Fair,* in a 2009 essay on the epidemic of cute in America, likened eating cupcakes to sitting on your couch in a Snuggie while gazing at photos of kittens online (though cupcakes are still served at the *Vanity Fair* Oscar party). Business writers predicted the cupcake trend would implode as it grew, like Krispy Kreme donuts had a decade earlier. "In America, bubbles form because any good business idea gets funded a dozen times over," wrote Daniel Gross in *Slate* back in 2009. "That's the American way. Cupcakes are now showing every sign of going through the bubble cycle. The first-movers get buzz and revenues, gain critical mass, and start to expand rapidly. This inspires less-well-capitalized second- and third-movers, who believe there's room enough for them, and encourages established firms in a related industry to jump in." The recession would right this, Gross predicted, as people traded down for more affordable options. Others searched for the "next cupcake," holding up whoopie pies, macarons, and cake pops as the rightful dessert salvation. Instead, the opposite happened. Cupcakes only grew further. The recession swelled the ranks of cupcake bakeries (led by newly unemployed professionals) and eaters. Cake pops and whoopie pies flashed in the pan. Each time someone predicted that cupcakes had jumped the shark, they were forced to eat their words as cupcakes rose to new heights.

I'm not immune to cupcake fatigue. Where I was once excited about a cupcake shop opening in my neighborhood, I now shake my head and sigh when yet another pops up nearby. Two years ago I moved into a new house, and a few weeks before, the nearest business to us, a hair salon, had transformed into a cupcake bakery called Le Dolci. On our first night in the house a friend brought us a box of their cupcakes in flavors like s'mores and key lime. The icing took up half the weight of the cupcake, and the designs were overly elaborate—one had chocolate cake, embedded chocolate icing, another layer of icing frosting the cake, itself covered in chocolate sauce swirls, topped off with a chunk of brownie as though it was created for some chocolate industry–sponsored bake sale. It wasn't a cupcake, that delicious, sinful treat of my youth, but rather a Cupcake, the very evocation of this global trend that had turned baked goods into an arms race of cuteness, sacrificing the subtlety of taste for an onslaught of gimmickry and sugar, the boy band of desserts. When I heard a few months later that a cupcake martini bar was opening in Toronto, with sweet alcoholic drinks garnished with your choice of minicupcakes, I prayed for the rapture to arrive and drown this wretched trend in a cleansing lake of fire.

Perhaps it will come to pass. On April 17, 2013, as I sat in Georgetown Cupcake eating a cherry blossom specimen (vanilla with real cherries, and a glob of cream cheese–cherry icing), having just come from the nearby Sprinkles, where I tried a selection of minis and nearly broke my tooth on their trademarked fondant dots, my brother e-mailed me an article that the *Wall Street Journal* had just posted, titled, "Forget Gold, the Gourmet Cupcake Market Is Crashing." Crumbs had posted significant earnings downgrades for fiscal year 2012, and their stock plunged 34 percent in one day, down to $1.70 from a high of $13 a share in 2011. The chain would scale back its aggressive expansion plans, and other cupcake bakeries were quoted as saying that sales were declining. That night in DC I went to my friend Gail's house for dinner, and her son Zachary, who had just turned six that day, asked to be excused from the table to go play with his new Lego set. "Okay, Zachary, you can still have a cupcake for dessert," my friend offered, and Zachary, to our collective shock, said he didn't want one. A six-year-old was tired of cupcakes. Surely this was the cupcake's death knell.

Not so, said the cupcakers, including Alison Robicelli, owner of an eponymous bakery known for its cupcakes. In a swift and damning blog post responding to the Crumbs news, she carefully dissected and refuted the cupcake Cassandras's arguments with in-depth economic and social commentary. "Know why cupcakes aren't going anywhere?" Robicelli wrote. "Because you need something to be 'the next cupcake' just like you need something to be 'the new black.' It's not a bubble; it's a genre—individually portioned dessert. You can talk about feminism, and *Sex and the City*, and nostalgia all you want; it comes down to the fact that just about everyone on earth likes cake. Not rocket science."

Steve Abrams at Magnolia echoed those sentiments when I'd asked him about the trend's limits. "You have a food media that's all fucking pissed off that they haven't killed the cupcake," he said. "By the time I bought this business it was no longer a craze in my mind," said Abrams, noting that Magnolia's business is evenly split between cupcakes and their other baked goods. "In a hundred years from now there'll still be a brownie troop that needs a fund-raiser, and they won't be baking macarons . . . or fondue."

Eventually cupcake fever will break. Some cupcakeries and overextended chains will close or shrink, but their legacy will continue on in commerce and culture. Cupcakes arguably created what has been called the "single-focus premium-indulgence" retail market, a mouthful of industry jargon that basically means small treats people will pay more money for. They have paved the way for every artisanal donut shop, grilled cheese pop-up, and slider miniburger that has come along since the mid-1990s. Starbucks didn't create the cappuccino and latte, and the chain reached its pinnacle in 2008, before the recession forced them to close thousands of stores. But the trend Starbucks fostered with coffee-drinking behavior, in the way Magnolia did with the cupcake, fundamentally changed the coffee market around the world, creating demand for high-end coffee products in places where low-budget instant coffee once was king. Now you find small independent "third wave" latte art shops around the corner from your home and push-button espresso machines in every single restaurant. Joel Stein, he of the snide cupcake remarks in *Time,* told me the cupcake has now become the "default American dessert" like pie was a century ago.

As for the cupcake itself, I believe it will slowly revert to the kid-friendly birthday treat I recall from my youth, which is its logical end. "Cupcakes are cheaper to buy and cheaper to bake," said my cousin Caroline Davis, whose Toronto bakery, Two Moms, has practically cornered the city's kosher cupcake market, especially at schools. (Okay, disclosure time: she also made cupcakes for my wedding, and I was delighted to have them.) The cupcake's advantage remains central to its form: it costs less than regular cake, requires no cutlery to serve or eat, can be customized for groups (a dozen vanilla, a dozen red velvet, two nut-free, two dairy-free, etc.), and they look great. "I like cupcakes," said Davis, who had recently visited Georgetown Cupcake with her kids on a trip to DC, "but I just don't understand this craze. I mean, I wouldn't want to wait in line for one." The cupcake trend, for all its fireworks and sex appeal, was merely the symptom of the cupcake's inherent perfection and familiarity, something I knew from the first time I ate one, and this is why it was able to grow so wide and large. But transforming something as familiar and fun as a cupcake into a trend was one thing. What I wanted to find out was how someone could cultivate a food trend from the ground up, starting with an idea, a patch of dirt, and a seed for a food that almost no one had ever tasted.

2

AGRICULTURE

THE SLOW BOAT TO CHINA BLACK

Parking is not an easy feat in Charleston's historic downtown, and no one knows that better than Glenn Roberts, who has a story to tell about each spot he passes. One is in front of a building that belonged to his old friend, now dead, and another spot is in front of one of his first houses here, back when this upscale area was a mixture of eccentric bohemians, conservative members of South Carolina's grand families, and the African American workers whose culture they all drew from. "Oh hell, let's just park here and hope the guard is asleep in the booth," Roberts said, pulling into a private lot. "We aren't going to be more than an hour anyway." Roberts peeled his long body out of the car and went around to the trunk.

Though Roberts is in his mid-sixties, his Dennis the Menace–worthy flop of silver hair, faded jeans, and heavy work boots makes him look like a much younger man. He speaks in a booming voice that quickly fills any space he occupies with a mixture of personal tales ("I once drove mangoes cross-country in a big rig through here!"), arcane local history, and a passionate diatribe for what he loves, which is the traditional food of the Deep South and America. Roberts is a first-rate adventurer and wanderer, the type of all-American man they once sent to space, not because he was a physicist but because he'd jump on a missile and ride that bastard just for the hell of it. He is a Californian with feet in New York and his heart firmly in the South, and in the world of American food he is a legend both for his outsized personality and the fruits of his carefully wrought labor, which I came down to Charleston to experience firsthand.

Digging around the trunk, Roberts eventually found what he was looking for: a large Ziploc bag filled with four pounds of ink-black rice. In fact, the rice in Roberts's hand was IAC600, also known as China Black, a variety he had worked for close to a decade to bring to the culinary market in the United States and was on the brink of releasing for the first time to a select few tastemakers. Ten pounds of this year's test crop had been set aside to give to the chefs in Robert's orbit, regular customers of his heritage grains company, Anson Mills. The four pounds in his hand, two-fifths of his entire available yield, were destined to enter the hands of Sean Brock, one of America's hottest chefs and a leader of South Carolina's modern low-country cuisine. The China Black rice was so scarce that Roberts valued its worth at $500 a pound, almost half the price of France's coveted black Périgord truffles, the so-called black diamond of the food world.

"Okay," Roberts said, slamming the trunk with a big grin. "Let's go bribe a chef."

We walked around the corner and down a cobblestone alleyway to the entrance of McCrady's, the city's most renowned restaurant. Originally a tavern where George Washington used to drink (and steal across the alley to an adjacent bordello, according to Roberts), the stately dining room, nestled under brick arches, had become the center of a southern food revival ever since Sean Brock took over the kitchen in 2006. A native of rural Virginia, Brock was raised growing and cooking almost all of his family's food. He built his kitchens around a dedicated commitment to farm-to-table cuisine, with an emphasis on traditional southern ingredients (many of which he raises on his nearby farm, including grains, vegetables, and pigs) and a mixture of time-honored cooking techniques (at McCrady's, he has cooked by a wood-fired hearth, and he pickles, cans, and preserves extensively) as well as modern (he'll employ molecular tools like emulsifying agents and dehydrators). In 2010 Brock won a James Beard Award as the best chef in the Southeast, the same year he opened Husk, a more casual, increasingly southern-focused restaurant in Charleston that many publications, including *Food & Wine*, have since named the best restaurant in America.

When we came in Brock was standing behind the bar, talking to a couple of Swedish journalists. He was dressed in a Black Sabbath T-shirt and "Virginia is for Lovers" trucker's hat and had an impressive full-color arm tattoo depicting a multitude of southern vegetables.

"Hey Glenn," the soft-spoken Brock said, sticking out his hand. "What have you brought me today?"

"This is China Black," Roberts said, ceremoniously holding up the baggie, like a drug dealer would, before dropping it onto the counter in front of Brock. "In China there are tons of entries about how it used to be a tribute rice for emperors. White rice was something anyone could eat, but black rice was so coveted that it was used to pay tax."

"Man, it's gorgeous," Brock said, dipping his fingers in and pulling out a few dozen grains, which he examined in his open palm. "I can't wait to cook it."

"Me, too," Roberts said, "but this is almost half of all that exists in the world right now, and it's worth a lot of money." He paused a second, for dramatic effect. "Tell you what. I'm going to give this to you, but only if you promise to cook some of it for David and me tonight." Roberts smiled knowingly, and Brock just smiled back.

"I don't think that will be a problem," Brock said, grabbing the rice. The two had played this game before.

Roberts and Brock had been collaborating for a number of years, working to bring back, grow, and cook antebellum southern grains that were on the verge of extinction. Those ingredients formed the core of Brock's cooking, and much of what he did with them unfolded in the restaurant's immaculate kitchen laboratory, stacked to the ceiling with shelves of precisely labeled food containers and where he worked with Josh Fratoni, his "fermentation guru." On a large chalkboard was a list of sixty-odd vinegars,

misos, and fermentation experiments currently going on with local grains, most of them supplied by Anson Mills. Brock handed
around several plastic vials of liquid fermented from Sea Island
red beans, which we dropped onto our tongues and unleashed its
unique flavor, something like a sweeter, milder soy sauce. Next, the
chef grabbed plastic spoons and scooped red pea and faro shoyu
paste from a tub. It was tangy and sweet but also tasted like por-
ridge, thanks to the natural sugars brought out through a yearlong
lactic fermentation, which Brock still wasn't sure was long enough.
He took out another tub and passed around spoons with its contents. "Tell me what you think this is," Brock said as I took a taste.
Buttery and salty but somewhat sweet, it was incredibly familiar,
like a richer version of something I'd eaten all my life. "It's popcorn," Brock said, with the slightest hint of the magician's smile. "A
miso made from whole popcorn and popcorn stock. Actually, from
Glenn's own Appalachian heirloom sweet flint corn."

Miso paste is typically made by fermenting rice or soybeans.
When mixed with stock it becomes the soup often served at Japanese
restaurants. Brock had not only created a stock with popcorn but
also found a way to ferment popcorn kernels. I shut my eyes and took
another lick, transported instantly to a movie theater's sticky seats.

We tasted more misos, including one made from benne seeds
("It's like peanut butter on sex," said Roberts), and one that was
actually a fermented peanut butter ("like peanut butter with MSG
on top" countered Brock, with great pride). "I've got an idea," Roberts said, turning to Brock quickly with a flick of his hair. "Because
with that rice, when you cook it, the dregs taste like black cherries.
I mean, think about that," he said, motioning to the popcorn miso,
then, looking at the bag of rice on the counter, "and wow!"

∾

In the world of *Sex and the City*–themed cupcake tours, it is
tempting to think of food trends as 10 percent creativity, 90 percent fashion fad, with the herd flocking toward the latest taste of
the week. Even though the great cupcake boom took years to reach

its maddening apex, it was fundamentally a relatively simple thing. Someone decided to bake a cupcake in New York, those cupcakes became popular, and that popularity spread around the world, inspiring others to bake their own cupcakes. Yes, it took tears, long hours, and enough butter to fill the Grand Canyon to make the cupcake into a trend, but no one had to paddle a canoe into alligator- and snake-infested waters at the crack of dawn to hand-harvest cupcakes with a scythe in hand, as Glenn Roberts has regularly done with certain types of rice. Never had there been a year when cupcakes simply weren't available because a hurricane, flood, or insects decimated tray after tray of cupcakes in one fell swoop before they could even be iced. No one ever lost the original DNA for a cupcake, setting the entire industry back years before another cupcake could be eaten. For Glenn Roberts, these regular catastrophes are the acceptable, everyday risks he weathers in order to bring his grains into the world.

To start a food trend from agriculture is one of the riskiest, most ballsy things an entrepreneur can do. Yet every day there are countless farmers, scientists, and gardening dreamers with a trowel in their hand, digging in the dirt and planting the seed that they hope will one day change the way we eat. Agriculture's tastemakers are arguably the most potent trendsetters in the food world and have been for all of human civilization. Ten millennia ago someone in the plains of the Fertile Crescent had the thought to take the seeds from the strands of wild emmer and Einkorn wheat growing in the fields (grains that Roberts has lately revived) and plant them in a controlled area, which they could water, protect, and harvest on their own. At the same time, in China, farmers in wet lowlands were using the heartiest varieties of wild rice they collected, known as Oryza sativa, and planting them in paddies that they shaped to retain water (Roberts uses similar techniques). These innovations, which are some of the earliest forms of agriculture, not only led to better food supplies for these enterprising farmers, they also completely shifted humanity's way of life from mobile hunter-gathering tribes to geographically rooted agricultural societies. We built our towns and cities not because we liked an area but because it was where our wheat and rice were growing, and we had to stay nearby to guard and tend to it. With a predictable source of grain, humans were able to domesticate animals by feeding them, leading to a tremendous increase in protein, which allowed more of us to survive and procreate, and a form of labor, which allowed us to farm larger areas of land more efficiently and to travel greater distances.

The excess food from these crops formed the backbone of what would become the financial system, as farmers in one village exchanged grains and surplus foods with others. A new crop or a better variety of a staple crop provided a substantial advantage for trading with others and led the tribes and groups who developed them to sources of power. In his best-selling book *Guns, Germs, and Steel*, author Jared Diamond argued that the rise in Eurasian civilization and its continued dominance over civilizations in the southern hemisphere can all be traced back to what essentially were the food trends that came out of the early days of agriculture. Those who developed better grains for cultivation grew bigger and stronger; were able to devote more free time to specialized tasks, such as developing education, technology, and political alliances; and could use domesticated animals to acquire power through trade and warfare. Each subsequent agricultural innovation, from the ability to make oil and ferment dairy for cheeses and yogurt to the invention of preservation techniques, which facilitated travel, fundamentally altered the world. Each new agricultural trend, whether it was a new spice or variety of vegetable or a better breed of animal, pushed our interconnectivity and civilization along.

As it evolved, the business of agriculture focused increasingly on efficiency. Agricultural faculties at universities allowed the greater study of plant and animal breeds, and the emerging fields of agricultural science focused the study of breeding and selection to find newer, more profitable plant and animal breeds. Chemistry opened up our understanding of plant physiology and made possible the introduction of pesticides and fertilizers. The Agricultural Revolution in England, led by these advances, opened the door for the Industrial Revolution, which in turn provided the machines that made modern high-yield farming possible. Though this trend has had dramatic social and political consequences, ranging from a decline in global famines to the shrinking of rural communities and environmental degradation, industrial agriculture has allowed many in the industry to focus their energy on innovation around new products, ranging from new conventional breeds of fruits, vegetables, and animals to genetically modified strands of rice with bits of fish DNA in them in order to make them more drought and pest resistant. By the twentieth century, concerns over soil erosion and pesticide use led to the development of organic farming, a trend started by the British couple Albert and Gabrielle Howard, who based their ideas on the traditional farming practices they had observed in India. Though it remained a niche trend for many decades, organic farming grew rapidly from the 1990s onward and today represents one of the fastest-growing segments of the agriculture industry, driven largely by consumer food trends that have embraced organic products as healthier and their agricultural practices more environmentally sustainable.

Today's agricultural food trends range greatly in their scope. They can be industry-altering shifts, such as the introduction of genetically modified seeds by agrobusiness giants such as Monsanto, or the development of animal breeds that grow fatter, quicker, and with less propensity for disease than their predecessors. They can involve specific farming practices with political undertones, like the emergence in the 1970s and onward of more natural and "humane" methods of raising meat and dairy animals, from free-range farming for cattle and chickens to codes of conduct for aquaculture and fishing that ensures the sustainability of ocean life. Agricultural trends are also focused on bringing more variety and flavor to our plates. Each trip to the produce section of the grocery store brings us into contact with the latest innovation in plant breeding. One season there is one type of kale, and the next thing you know there's kale in five different sizes and three colors. Each new fall brings in whole new varieties of apples from growers around the world, many created by university agriculture labs and farmers, such as Wisconsin's Honeycrisp or the Red Prince (which you'll meet in a later chapter). This type of work takes years, often decades, to bear fruit (so to speak). Breeding plants or animals is a grueling process of trial and error, requiring thousands of experiments, with results taking shape over many seasons until an edible prototype is available. That's why agricultural tastemakers tend to be exceedingly driven, often obsessive individuals whose devotion to the trend they're working to establish borders on the maniacal and cannot be dismissed as flights of fancy. They are a mixture of alchemist and entrepreneur, with a warrior's passion. Basically, the opposite of a cupcake baker.

Glenn Roberts fits precisely into this category, and his influence as an agricultural tastemaker falls somewhere between the political and culinary. The company he founded, Anson Mills, has emerged over the past decade as the preeminent cultivator and supplier of gourmet grains in the United States, if not globally, selling hundreds of varieties of heritage wheat, rice, corn, and other grains to customers and restaurant chefs around the world. He is one of the leaders in organic and sustainable grain production in America, using traditional, environmentally friendly methods of planting, harvesting, and milling at every step of the process. Roberts has done more to revive lost or neglected species of American grains than any single individual in the country and has been a key player in the resurgence of the South's historical food culture, centered around the low-country cuisine of South Carolina's coastal plains, known as the Carolina Rice Kitchen.

"The oldest intact cuisine in the United States was based on Carolina rice," said Roberts, who has worked with historians over the years to discover everything he could about food and agriculture in the area. We were back in his car, driving out of the city's historic center, along its inner harbor. Charleston had been a major trading port since the British founded it in 1670, and a great variety of cultural influences shaped its food culture over the centuries. As we drove to the outskirts of the city, past barbecue joints owned by Klansmen and high-end bike shops that also sold guns, Roberts painted an enthusiastic picture of a global mixing pot of flavors and cuisines unlike any that had existed before. Venetians originally brought rice to the area in the 1670s, planting half a dozen varieties at the edges of bays where the tides would irrigate them, and designing the coastal rice canals the industry grew around.

The British colonists brought their influence with other staple crops along with the flavors of outposts in India, Jamaica, and other far-away places. Sephardic Jews (the city's Jewish population was once greater than New York's) introduced Mediterranean rice dishes, including rice breads, and French settlers made casserole cooking the core of Charleston's kitchen culture. The Irish, German, Scottish, and Spanish populations who settled in the city lent it their flavor, too, along with those of nearby Native American Cherokee and Creek tribes, who worked in the rice fields.

Charleston was also the principal destination for the human cargo of the African slave trade, and their influence in the development of the Carolina Rice Kitchen cannot be understated. African slaves who had worked on rice plantations in other British colonies were put to work establishing Carolina's plantations with their knowledge and forced labor. Every kitchen in the city's grand houses, hotels, and restaurants was staffed by black cooks, first as slaves and later as freed servants. They were the ones who pulled together the disparate influences from the city's global population, creating the cuisine of the Carolina Rice Kitchen. "It was a full wrap cuisine," Roberts said with longing, existing today only as scattered recipes and fading memories. At the high point, prior to the Civil War, there were over a hundred varieties of rice grown in the region, ranging from commodity varieties, which were exported to Europe (the region was once a main source of the global rice supply); multiple varieties of bay rice, which used the Italian methods of planting along the edges of bays; and so-called secret rice, grown by black farmers in hidden plots and used as sacramental offerings for traditional African religious practices.

The Civil War, however, put an end to all that diversity, said Roberts. "Sherman blew up the seed houses, skilled farmers died on the war's battlefields, and emancipation killed off the labor model," which relied on slavery. A series of storms and floods ruined many fields in the early twentieth century, and with each farm that closed, local rice mills, which knew how to process each grain in ways that preserved its best flavor and texture, also shut their doors. Cotton plantations replaced rice fields because the cash crop could bring in more money, but cotton plants depleted the soil until it was barren. Monoculture replaced seed diversity in the fields that remained, and the hundred-plus rice varieties, grown in various different ways, were replaced by a handful of common commercial seeds that were heartier and could store better but lacked any of the aromatic flavor and cultural significance of those original Carolina rice varieties. By the 1980s the last small-plot rice farmers were dwindling, and the rural families, largely African American, who toiled in the fields and kept the traditional recipes alive were moving to the cities without passing on their knowledge to the next generation. Countless recipes were lost to history and only exist today in scattered memories and the research files of a few dogged academics. "The term *Carolina Rice* meant something before the war," Roberts said wistfully as we pulled into the Clemson Coastal Research and Education Center, just outside the city limits. "We lost a sense of place, our identity, and a market."

The introduction of China Black was just one step in Roberts's mission to rebuild the diverse world of Carolina rice, and he was here to see how it was taking shape. Clemson University, with help from the US Department of Agriculture, operated the farm. Roberts drove past a few small buildings and greenhouses and out onto a field bordered by a tall forest of eucalyptus on one side and a large pond with blooming magnolias on its shore. The trees were pregnant with dozens of squawking white egrets that two large alligators watched hungrily from below. Roberts saw me looking nervously at the alligators and told me not to worry; the alligators would run away from us, he said, unless, of course, they didn't. Then it would be us doing the running. "This land is just like Africa," Roberts said with excitement as he stepped out of his rented Camry and greeted Hal Harvey, the farm manager, who had a great white mustache and wore a faded camouflage hat. The two men stood by a plot of earth that was about the size of two parking spaces and was surrounded by small mounds of mud and flattened reeds. In the next few weeks they would plant five strains of rice in this small plot, including China Black, which would take up roughly 1/240th of an acre, a tiny test planting about the size of a bathtub, because the idea was simply to see whether it could take root here. Larger trial plots of China Black would also be planted two hours south, near the Georgia border, and in Arkansas and Texas to see how the crop would fare in different conditions and climates.

Though there are several varieties of black Chinese rice dating back thousands of years, the rice labeled as IAC600—Roberts's rice—is a relatively recent creation. In 1994 a Brazilian crop breeder named Candido Bastos imported several strands of black rice from China and began selecting from their breeds for varieties that grew well in São Paulo state. Though dozens of other black rices existed on the market, almost all cultivated in China, the strain that Bastos isolated had surprisingly aromatic flavor properties when grown in Brazil: a nutty, fragrant bouquet and taste, making it desirable and unique for cooks. Bastos eventually contacted Dr. Anna McClung, research leader at the Dale Bumpers Rice Research Institute in Arkansas and one of America's foremost rice breeding authorities, to see whether this black rice might be something that the American market would respond to. McClung grew out a test patch and checked for problems. She contacted several commercial rice farmers, but none were ultimately interested in growing it because of the color, which created a quality-control nightmare in a production facility. "Because it's black, it looks like a weed seed if you mix it in with regular rice," said Dr. McClung over the phone. "It'll contaminate your white rice in processing, and vice versa. People said forget it. Unless you are only farming black rice, it's a pain to work with." McClung turned to Anson Mills and Roberts, who she had worked with previously on other rice varieties the company sells. "You need someone like Glenn who can say, 'I know there's a market for this, and I'm going to bite the bullet and do what it takes to bring it out.'"

In the second year of the seed's development McClung split the breeding crop, which contains plants that act like parents for producing seeds, into two, growing one in Arkansas and the other in Puerto Rico in order to expose it to different climates at different times of the year. The seeds flew down to the Caribbean, first-class freight, and returned in the spring, as first-class bushels, to be planted again in Arkansas. In the fourth year the testing continued, and McClung and Roberts, who has funded most of these experiments out of his pocket, sent IAC600 to a food science laboratory in Louisiana to test its nutritional, milling, starch, and other characteristics, all of which were very good and, in some cases, such as antioxidant levels, excellent. "When you're going that far, that's when you realize whether you want to let others grow it," says Roberts. "Then you have to find growers who are willing to take it."

By the fifth year enough rice was available to do a few taste tests, so Roberts took some of the precious grains into his kitchen and cooked up a pot. "I said, 'Wow, that's tribute rice, and it's beautiful!' It had a great inkiness, and the rice wine I made was amazing." The crop was stabilized, and slow-scale production began on a sixty-six-day yield cycle, from spring planting to fall harvest. In 2009, with a steady supply just a season away, Roberts began talking up China Black to the chefs in his vast network, initially approaching some of the most trusted and powerful tastemakers in his circle and, indeed, America—California's Thomas Keller, New York's David Chang, Chicago's Charlie Trotter, New Orleans' John Besh, Sean Brock, and others—with the promise that his next delivery was going to contain a fantastically aromatic black rice that would be a perfect fit for where their cooking was going. There was a ton of interest from the chefs, who couldn't wait to get their hands on China Black.

"Then," Roberts recalled, with a shake of his head and a chuckle, "the seeds crashed." The seed stock was already limited, and for some reason the facility storing the seeds accidentally sent Roberts the breeding seeds (the parents), basically the foundational DNA of the crop, that were irreplaceable. Without knowing what had happened, Roberts planted them, only later realizing he'd basically put China Black's entire family tree into the ground, with no chance of recovery and no ability to replicate easily. "It was like slaughtering my prized breeding bull and selling it to me as steak," Roberts said, still smarting at the monumental screwup. Everything had to start back at square one, and only now, in the spring of 2013, had Roberts gotten back to the point at which China Black could be grown as a trial on a decent enough scale to provide samples to a few chefs. Not only that, but in the past year the trials at Clemson with China Black had not gone well. "It's probably the worst of the six varieties out here," said Harvey, as an alligator slowly crawled into position nearby, under the oblivious herons. "The field conditions weren't the best last year, and the plot wasn't level." Most of the crop hadn't survived. The fate of China Black was resting in this little plot plus the others around the country, all of which amounted to no more than a handful of acres.

"If we get a hurricane," Roberts said, "Hal and I will be sitting here saying, 'Well, that was fun, let's do it again!'"

We left the farm and drove back toward Charleston, stopping for lunch at the Glass Onion, a sustainable soul food restaurant that served some of Anson Mills's products. Over a buttermilk-battered fried chicken po' boy, beers, and a platter of shrimp and grits, Roberts told me how he'd become the nationally recognized tastemaker of American grains.

Glenn Roberts was born in Delaware, though his mother was originally from South Carolina, and her family included preachers and mule farmers. He mostly grew up in La Jolla, California, near San Diego. His father was both a professional singer and aerospace worker, and his mother owned restaurants in La Jolla and, later, Marin county, near San Francisco. Though Roberts grew up in the kitchens of these restaurants, with their French-speaking kitchen staff and Continental menus, he never really picked up the hang of cooking (he says he can make one dish really well, but not a meal). His mother, however, taught him what she knew about the Carolina Rice Kitchen, making traditional dishes at almost every family meal. Over the years Roberts, who is a restless and adventurous soul, has dabbled in a number of things. He flew jets in the Air Force, sailed around the world on yachts, rode horses, drove long-haul trucks, crewed on shrimp boats out of Charleston, and even tried his hand at growing corn, working at a cotton mill, and making moonshine (which he still has a soft spot for every so often). Eventually Roberts settled into restaurant consulting, working with chefs and owners on everything from concepts and menus to architecture and construction, a discipline that demanded that his pulse rest firmly on the latest food trends. He opened, closed, and revived restaurants in California, DC, and the South, getting to know the country's emerging top chefs, such as Thomas Keller, before they were household names. By the 1990s he had settled down in Charleston.

Anson Mills came about thanks to a stroke of bad luck. In 1998 the Smithsonian Institution was conducting a series of historical dinners focusing on the railroad cuisine of the post–Civil War era, and they asked Roberts to help put one on in Charleston. He began working with a historian to learn about the cuisine from that time period, leading him to the Carolina Rice Kitchen, which had been named by historian Karen Hess. Roberts wanted to serve the rice that was central to many of those recipes, a strain called Carolina Gold, and he ended up at the Turnbridge Plantation just north of Savannah, which is one of the few places where that rice was still growing. Arriving late in the day, he looked out over the flooded fields of Carolina Gold rice, their stalks lit by the glow of the setting sun pouring across the water like spilled paint. "Man, it was gorgeous," he said, the image still in his eyes. Glenn Roberts fell in love with growing rice right then and there. The first thing he did after leaving was send his mother a bag of that same rice for her approval. "She flipped out. She hadn't seen anything like it since the Depression."

Unfortunately, the Smithsonian dinner turned into a disaster. The church group that was cosponsoring the event had no idea how to properly store the rice, and when Roberts opened the bags in the kitchen, an hour before service began, the precious grains were full of corn weevils, a common agricultural insect. He freaked out, then calmed down, told the kitchen to switch the order of the meal around, grabbed a few busboys, and got down to the dirty work of salvaging the rice. "Imagine sitting in a pair of Gucci loafers and an expensive suit, picking dead bugs out of rice for three hours," he said. "It fucking sucked." At the end of the night what stuck in people's minds was the food, and the reaction they'd had to the rice more than made up for the agony of its execution. "I decided a lot of chefs would like that rice," Roberts said. "It was the real thing." Anson Mills began the next day.

Roberts started growing corn right away because he had done it before and it was easy to cultivate quickly, and he used the proceeds to finance his first crop of Carolina Gold, which was more labor intensive. Using historical records and seeking out seed experts and backwoods farmers, he began pulling together a breadbasket of heritage southern grains, most of which were no longer commercially available. Anson Mills brought back native blue corn, heirloom yellow hominy corn, yellow flint popcorn, traditional couscous, Sea Island red peas, Carolina Graham wheat, Sonora white wheat, Einkorn wheat, Italian grains like several varieties of polenta, farro, buckwheat Taranga, and a whole slew of Carolina Gold products. Everything was grown using traditional, organic, sustainable methods, including hand harvesting, to retain flavor, preserve soil integrity, and keep a historical continuity with the grains. Multiple crops shared the same soil in rotation because they complemented each other's flavors and doing so improved soil health. Rather than use large commercial rollers to mill corn, hull rice, and grind wheat, Anson Mills operated with antiquated equipment, like granite mill stones, so the product retained a traditionally coarse texture, which affected taste tremendously because it left many aspects of the grain, such as the germ, intact. Anson Mills products, which require very specific storage and cooking instructions (they are not shelf stable), are packaged simply and sold directly to the chefs Roberts knew from his past life in the restaurant business. He asked them to spread the word, and their enthusiasm for his products soon grew within the upper echelons of America's culinary tastemakers.

The first product that Anson Mills put on the map was grits. Grits are technically a very simple product, with origins in Native American culture, and are made of coarsely ground cornmeal. Over time the varieties of corn used to make them had grown so efficient that grits were practically devoid of all taste. The large industrial mills that ground down kernels to cornmeal did so with pulverizing force, resulting in a grit that was much too small and uniform, with the plant's germ, where much of the flavor is stored, largely destroyed. However, grown at organic farms in three states, the heirloom corn for Anson Mills's grits, in varieties such as Carolina Gourdseed White, John Haulk Yellow, Burris White, and Boone County White, is naturally soft, hand harvested, and stone ground, resulting in an uneven appearance and large grits that are hearty in texture and ready to soak up flavor. David Chang, the chef and owner of the Momofuku group of restaurants, first encountered Anson Mills's grits in 1999 when he was cooking at Craft, a restaurant run by chef Tom Colicchio. "No one was using the grit cut at that time," Chang recalled, noting how chefs like Colicchio and Mario Batali first used it to make Italian-style polenta. "It shows you where American dining has gone. No one was going to put grits on a fine-dining menu. Then [fine dining] became a little more rustic and slowly evolved from there and grew." Chang's own shrimp and grits dish, made with Anson Mills grains and laced with ramen stock and soy sauce, was a nod to his own Korean American–southern roots and was one of his first standout hits at Momofuku Noodle Bar, his flagship New York restaurant. As word of Anson Mills's grits spread from kitchens like Chang's, the demand among chefs soared, and grits became a must-have item on menus around the country, prompting others to grow and sell their own stone-ground grits in imitation of Roberts.

"Glenn Roberts's reputation began spreading like wildfire years ago when he first reintroduced us to the proper grit and to Carolina Gold rice," the New Orleans chef John Besh recounted. "Word spread through the upper-echelon kitchen ranks by word of mouth." Besh, whose grandfather had ground his own grits, hadn't seen a proper grit in decades. "Then came Anson Mills, who in turn inspired others to begin milling again. I credit Glenn with this renaissance of not only the mill but of southern food and culture as well." Charleston soon became a food destination at the center of this movement, on par with San Francisco as a magnet for culinary tourism, as hush puppies, shrimp and grits, and fried chicken dishes began populating menus all over the country, from fine-dining spots such as Charlie Trotter's in Chicago to small neighborhood bistros and even national chains such as the Cheesecake Factory.

During our lunch at the Glass Onion I tasted the shrimp and grits Roberts had ordered, piled in a wide bowl with pan-fried fat prawns and thick slices of spicy Andouille sausage. These were Anson Mills hominy grits made from John Haulk corn grown nearby, cooked in the Charleston style by quickly boiling them in milk. Their color was a deep, custardy yellow, but there were flecks of brown and caramel in there as well. I didn't really expect much; having tried grits many times before, I'd always felt their taste was somewhere between baby's cereal and unsweetened oatmeal, but these were something entirely transcendent. Buttery, sweet, and chewy, they had the consistency and heft of perfectly scrambled eggs, and I found myself actually pushing aside the shrimp and sausage to get every last bite of grits that I could.

Today Roberts runs Anson Mills with his wife, Kay Rentschler, a cookbook writer and journalist who met Roberts when she came to write about him and his grits for the *New York Times* in 2004, and she fell in love after he sent her home with his only bag of yellow nixtamal grits, which, she said, "blew me away." She works out of New York and Martha's Vineyard, testing recipes to accompany the two hundred–plus grains the company now sells—a daunting task, considering the need for historical accuracy as well as precision in cooking what are very temperamental foods. Though Anson Mills grains are freely available for purchase online, according to Roberts, direct-to-consumer sales only make up 4 percent of the company's $3 million annual revenue, with roughly four thousand restaurant clients, ranging as far afield as Italy and Japan, being the main driver of the business. Each year it's been in business the company has grown between 20 to 25 percent, almost all of it driven by more chefs and restaurants coming to Anson Mills for their grains. Aside from his work in the field, Roberts works closely with chefs who buy his products, sometimes talking on the phone with them, often as they're in their kitchens, to explain not only the cooking process but also the cultural legacy behind what they are serving that night. That hand-holding and his attention to personal relationships has really paid off. "We know what chefs want, we know how to deliver it the way they want it, because we've all been in the restaurant business.

We've all worked with some of the best in America. I'm a rotten cook and a terrible chef, but if I work with chefs, I become better," said Roberts, ordering a second beer. "The idea behind what we do is only dealing with concepts we can make relevant to the American public. We stumble across things that can become relevant. We were never restricted by trends. We set our own trends."

Each year Roberts picks one new food he will push out to his clients, and this year, if everything works out in the fields, he is hoping it will be China Black. The combination of its flavor, the stark black sheen of its color, and the story of its history make it a grain he believes could eventually generate revenues of $1 million annually. Though other rice producers, such as Lotus Foods, sell varieties of imported black tribute rice (grown largely in China), these mostly lack the deep aromatic flavor of the organic, American-grown China Black that Anson Mills is bringing to market. Even before it was available, the company's website listed several products it hoped to sell, from straightforward China Black rice to black rice grits, black rice flour, black rice polenta, crème de riz, and a toasted black rice powder. With its high antioxidant levels, Roberts imagined being able to sell some of the by-product for health supplements and saw the potential market of pastry chefs as a particular springboard into a food trend. "This must be begging for some sort of out-of-the-way crazy congee rice dish," he said enthusiastically.

Roberts was also driven by a desire to redeem China Black's fortunes after the crop's failure in 2009. "When the seed went away, the beatings I took from the chefs were brutal. I'd promised it, and when chefs want stuff, they want it now. They don't want to wait." For the sake of Roberts's reputation and that of Anson Mills, China Black had to succeed and become a trend. "I promised the chefs I'd do it. I failed, and now I'm coming back and tripling down on it." When I asked Roberts how he planned to create a demand for China Black, he told me the marketing plan was already done. His strategy was simple: choose grains that will be relevant to chefs, put those grains in their hands, and use the chef's own star power and network to kick-start the trend. In short, let the clients do the work for you. "I just gave two thousand dollars of rice to Sean," he said, with an all-knowing grin. "I guarantee you within two weeks from now Anthony Bourdain and David Chang will be sitting somewhere together, eating this very rice I gave Sean today."

໑

We sat down for dinner at McCrady's a few hours later as the restaurant slowly filled with well-dressed Charleston families, led by men who wore seersucker suits and bowties and opened car doors for their wives and daughters with a gentlemanly grace. Roberts was still in his dusty jeans and boots, but the restaurant's staff greeted him with a hero's welcome. After all, his name graced the menu under the section devoted to the local farmers whose products Brock used, crediting Roberts and Anson Mills for *Grains, Knowledge, Inspiration.*

"Well, one of the three, anyway," Roberts said with a chuckle.

The meal unfolded over many boozy hours, with Brock pulling out all the stops to showcase his cooking, his heirloom products (ham from African guinea hogs he'd raised, ember-roasted carrots he'd grown), and what he could do with Anson Mills grains. There were bright, briny roe from sunburst trout sprinkled on a smoked trout pate atop crisp, earthy crackers baked from Anson Mills red fife wheat; Anson Mills airy popcorn served with a startlingly buttery popcorn miso and pea stew; a buttered slice of chewy, dense, flavorful bread made from Anson Mills grits, oats, and benne; chocolate chess pie with toasted benne seeds and benne butter; and finished with Robert E. Lee cake baked with Sea Island red pea flour. Each dish was presented with a minimal rustic elegance. In one, Brock plated what looked like two small, thin rice crackers on an earthenware plate and topped them with some sort of cream. The waiter would explain with great ceremony that these were actually crispy fried beef tendons, topped with a truffle cream. I bit in, and the deep flavor of beef stock quickly emerged from that lithe airy crisp, with the rich, woodsy funk of the truffles tying it back to the earth. It was one of the most amazing, epic, and yet somehow humble meals I'd eaten in years.

As the cocktails and wine flowed (and flow they did—we'd already had three different drinks before the first course even arrived), Roberts got to talking about what drove him to keep pushing out new tastes and trying to forge new trends, like China Black. Seed research these days was becoming digitized. Agronomists could sit at a computer, sequence a grain's DNA, and concoct new varieties without ever having to step foot in a field. A connection to the land was being lost and, with it, the sense of place and culture that came along with agriculture and with eating something grown on a farm. Yes, Anson Mills was a company that existed to sell grains to high-end customers (their products are much more expensive than their competitors'), but at its core Roberts saw his mission as part of a "Robin Hood syndrome." In 2003, when the company began taking off, he founded the Carolina Gold Rice Foundation, a nonprofit that funds research into heirloom grains from the Carolina Rice Kitchen and distributes those grains for free to interested farmers around the United States as well as cofunding research projects with the USDA, such as the China Black trials. "My mission is to recover something from extinction and make sure the avenues to scale it up are open." Already, he had distributed up to seventy tons of seed entirely free, including donations of Einkorn wheat to the radiation-ravaged farms around Japan's damaged Fukushima reactor, and aided the southwest's Hopi Native Americans in recovering their nearly extinct blue corn crop. To Roberts, Anson Mills was just the means to fund and publicize the work he was doing at his foundation.

"The public doesn't respond to the system [behind the growing] at all. They just think the product is wonderful," he said, summing up the divide between the two sides of his business. "The public responds to taste if they have a good palate, which is why this goes back to the elite—getting the one percent interested." It was a trickle-down approach to social change via food trends. Anson Mills grains composes a tiny percentage of the grain produced in South Carolina, let alone America. But because he had targeted the most respected, visible chefs in the world and had his company's name on all their menus, Roberts had harnessed their visibility and influence as tastemakers, turning those grains into a trend and using the trends' success (and profits) to further his mission of restoring the Carolina Rice Kitchen as well as the greater cause of saving American grains. The culinary trend he'd created was itself a kind of Trojan horse—for the social, environmental, and historical trends he truly cared about implementing.

"I started this when I'm old," Roberts said, "and that's a good thing, because if I was young, I would have to prove a point. I just want to get enough seed out there that there's a tipping point—that anyone can get China Black rice if they want to grow it and want to sell it. I think about my age, and I probably need to make money at some point. I'm on a decade-and-a-half startup."

Just then Brock came out of the kitchen, carrying two dark, handmade ceramic bowls and pewter spoons. A sweet, nutty aroma steamed out of them, and as he set them in front of us, we saw that each contained a mound of China Black rice, about half a cup's worth, glistening and perfect. "We just cooked them simply in water, in a low oven, and added a little butter at the end," Brock said, clearly pleased with the product. "Everyone in the kitchen was freaking out. It doesn't need anything else. You understand the work that goes into it. It's the best food in the world."

I had never eaten rice like this: straight and pure, in which I noticed the firm, al dente texture of each grain, its subtle fragrance of toasted earth, and the slick, buttery coating from the starch coaxed out of it. I could see how Chinese emperors would have demanded this rice in tribute, hoarding it for themselves, like gold and rubies. It was rice that tasted like candy. It was a grain as art.

"It's nuts," our waiter said, looking over us as we savored it. "Chef Brock gave us each a little spoonful, just a few grains, and it reminds me of ice cream. The density has that pop to it. Oh man, it's incredible."

"Sean, I haven't eaten this in three years," Roberts said, his nose hovering over the bowl with an ear-to-ear grin. Suddenly, the years of work, the high hopes and crushing disappointments, were evaporating for him like the steam coming off the rice.

When our dinner ended at eleven that night, five hours and far too many drinks after it had begun, Roberts ordered a cup of strong black coffee, which he downed in several gulps. I could barely stay awake at the table, but he was going to drive two hours to his mill in the town of Columbia, sleep there for two hours, and start milling seeds at three in the morning to prepare orders for shipment the next morning, when he would meet me at another rice plantation, then drive another four hours to Charlotte, where he would catch a flight back home to New York that night. Here was a man who was hitting the stride of a twenty-year-old at an age when most men were thinking about retirement, and in his mind, Roberts's trendsetting had only just begun. He was a farmer and advocate and dreamer who had tapped into the fantastic trendsetting power of chefs and leveraged that to change the way the culinary world ate its grains. As he drove off into the night with the Camry's seatbelt warning bell clanging away (he never wears them), I thought of something Dr. Anna McClung said about Roberts when I asked whether he was a trendsetter or just plain nuts.

"Well," she replied without a pause, "I guess most trends start with eccentric lunatics."

3

CHEFS

A CEVICHE IN EVERY POT

"You definitely have to try the quinoa locro," said the waiter on my first visit to Picca, a popular restaurant in Hollywood run by the Peruvian-born chef Ricardo Zarate. Hollywood servers are remarkable creatures. They're the alphas of the waiting world: the top tier of aspiring actors who are both better looking and vastly more dramatic than servers in any other city. After his initial five-minute introduction, in which he explained Picca's concept (basically, an upscale Peruvian cantina), its signature spirit (pisco, a grape brandy), and ingredient (aji amarillo, a bright, spicy yellow pepper), our server let us in on a little secret. "You know, it's good you came on a Monday night, because that's industry night," he told me and my three friends, locking eyes with each of us to seal in the enthusiasm. "It's when all the chefs and food bloggers come here." At that moment, as though he were acting on the waiter's cue, in walked Danny Bowien, the chef of San Francisco's hotspot Mission Chinese Food, with a crew of beautiful friends, all dressed liked they owned an upscale vintage clothing boutique, and they sat at the table behind ours. The waiter beamed, then pushed us toward the quinoa locro once more. "Trust me," he said, "it's big on all the food blogs."

We obligingly ordered it, along with nearly a dozen other small dishes that expressed Zarate's signature elevation of Peruvian flavors, all in an atmosphere that's similarly loud, boisterous, and Latin but with crisp Japanese design elements like a robata-style open grill set behind a wooden bar. I started off drinking an Apricot With Your Pants Down, a cocktail of Italian pisco, apricot brandy, lemon and cane juice, Aperol, seltzer, and a spritz of "juniper air," which gave the first sip a forested whiff. My friend Marko ordered a perfect pisco sour, the Peruvian national cocktail: pisco, lime and lemon, and a beaten egg white, a drink that the menu claimed was "shaken like a Polaroid picture." There was a whimsical, cutesy element to much of the menu's descriptions, all of which would have been annoying had the food not been so damn good.

The chicharrones de pollo was the first dish to hit the table: a pile of golden fried chicken skins, like schmaltzy chips, which we dunked in a spicy rocoto pepper aioli. There was a salad of sweet baked pumpkin chunks in a tangy miso sauce; a tiradito of firm sashimi-grade tuna, brushed with miso and seared to a caramelized crust on the outside, then dressed with a soy ceviche dressing; and a trio of mashed potato causas topped with smoked salmon and aji amarillo yogurt. The pumpkin stew with fried egg, raspberry-sized kernels of Peruvian corn, parmesan cheese, and fried crispy tomato strips was definitely worth its hype. In all we had around ten small dishes, all great, but the waiter was right in his enthusiasm for the quinoa locro (a bright, brothy squash, pumpkin, and quinoa stew). A deep, satisfying dish of comforting ingredients whose bright flavors shone through, the quinoa locro exemplified Zarate's cooking style, with the humble food of his roots remade as something unexpected and even daring.

"I've never eaten anything like this," my friend Kyle said, and we all chimed in, mumbling praise while strategically eyeing the last bites of quinoa lying unguarded in the bowl.

❧

In the battle to establish the next food trend, chefs are the equivalent of Marines. Many aspire to join the top ranks of their field, but few are chosen. Most cannot survive the grueling hours, the physical and psychological hardship, and the shockingly low pay it takes to get to the elite ranks. Their dreams of becoming the next *Top Chef* champion evaporate during that initial service rush, as orders pile up, proteins overcook, sweat pours from their bodies, and their bosses hurl verbal abuse. For the few who do endure, there's still no guarantee of success. Everyone wants to be the face of the next big dining trend, but that success is as much a product of serendipity as it is of raw talent and hard-earned experience. Significant new trends often come from unknown chefs cooking out of restaurants scraped together through sweat, tears, and a few maxed-out credit cards as the multimillion-dollar temples of dining created for big-name chefs often fizzle upon opening, their only legacy being a for-lease sign in a picture window.

Chefs are the creative class of the food world. Sure, the majority of chefs cooking in restaurants aren't culinary Picassos and Beethovens. Most execute the same recipes day in and day out because the dining public expects a high level of consistency in restaurants, and for good reason. No one wants their roast chicken and potatoes reinvented each time it's ordered, but even in the most tightly controlled kitchen there's a degree of inventiveness, whether it's the chef's ability to look into the fridge and concoct a nightly special from an abundance of turnips that someone ordered or her idea to use sesame oil instead of olive oil in a salad. Occasionally that slight change, brought on by a combination of experience and imagination, of circumstance and dumb-assed luck, leads to a dining trend that can raise the fortunes of that chef and their restaurant. If it is big enough, a chef-created food trend even has the power to fundamentally alter the way we all eat.

Today, chef-driven trends are more powerful and visible than ever before. The media attention chefs have embraced over the past two decades, brought on by the rise of the Food Network, competition shows such as *Top Chef* (which releases twenty-one freshly minted "celebrity chefs" into the restaurant world each season), and a ravenous online ecosystem of food blogs, review sites, and social media opportunities, has not only cemented the idea of the chef as artist and celebrity but has also given chefs everywhere a vastly greater audience, well beyond those who actually come into their restaurants and eat their food. The popularization of chef culture is a change to the industry as powerful as the invention of recorded music for musicians. Before the phonograph, bands and singers could only build their audience and influence on the stage, one show at a time. Once they could sell records, however, their impact was limited only by where those recordings could sell. Today's chefs are no different. No longer constrained to their physical kitchens, they can create and shape food trends quicker, more widely, and with a greater impact than any generation that preceded them. Their ideas trickle down from a single kitchen to a city's restaurant scene, spreading out across nations and oceans, until one day you find yourself asking the butcher in your supermarket whether he carries beef cheeks, without even knowing how you developed a taste for them.

Chef-driven trends can take several forms. The most significant and longest lasting is an introduction of a comprehensive style of cooking and eating, and this trend is almost more philosophical than technical. It affects not just restaurants and their menus but also the way food is cultivated, sold, and cooked at home. One of the best examples is the trend started by cook and personality Alice Waters at her restaurant Chez Panisse, which opened in 1971 in Berkeley, California. "Chez Panisse is the ultimate manifestation of the baby boomers' contribution to the American food revolution," wrote David Kamp in his history of American dining, *The United States of Arugula*. "These are folk who revel in the fact that they changed the landscape, man." Waters's high-minded cooking, which focused on the provenance of ingredients more than specific recipes and flavors, set the mold for the farm-to-table ethos of fresh/local/seasonal/organic dining that trickled down from a few select hippie spots serving "California" cuisine to large national chains such as Chipotle, which now boasts about the ethics of their meat and produce sourcing, and the existence of supermarket products like Heinz Organic Ketchup.

Trends started by chefs can also take the form of entirely new business models for the food service sector. In 1989 Nancy Silverton, a Los Angeles–based pastry chef, opened La Brea Bakery, which focused exclusively on artisan breads. In the wake of La Brea's highly publicized success, in which Silverton was credited as the queen of sourdough, specialized artisan bread bakeries and accompanying bakery cafés popped up all over the world, creating two new categories of businesses that barely existed before. Then, in 1998, Silverton and her partners opened a new plant where they made partially baked versions of their loaves that could be instantly frozen and shipped nationally and then finished off in the ovens of stores and restaurants so that the bread tasted as though it had been freshly baked. La Brea Bakery soon became the largest specialty bread supplier in the country, and the success of their product again revolutionized the bread industry, putting high-quality, fresh-baked bread within the reach of anyone with a freezer and an oven. "It turned the American people into a far more sophisticated bread-eating customer," said Silverton. "The consumption of that style of bread is here to stay."

A chef can initiate a trend around specific flavor profiles, popularizing a mixture of ingredients and seasoning that gets incorporated into everything from other restaurant dishes to the new flavor of potato chips in your local supermarket. In the 1980s New Orleans chef Paul Prudhomme made Cajun cooking a nationally recognized phenomenon. Although Cajun cuisine had a rich cultural history in Louisiana, melding French, Indian, and African American cooking methods and flavors, Prudhomme's largest impact seemed to be around his so called blackened spice rub, which involved dipping fish or other proteins in butter, then dredging it in spices that include thyme, oregano, chili pepper, peppercorns, salt, garlic powder, and onion powder, and searing the protein in a hot skillet. Although Cajun budin noir blood pudding and crawfish bakes never became household staples in places like Minneapolis or Vancouver, nearly every seafood restaurant still offers blackened fish, and the mere mention of a dish as "Cajun" triggers a familiar association with something that's spicy, fragrant, and darkly crusted.

Finally, a chef's trend can take the shape of a single, iconic dish. In 1991 the molten chocolate volcano cake burst forth onto the world's dessert menus like the buttery peak of Vesuvius. Though

French chefs in New York claim to have been the originators (most vocally Jacques Torres and Jean-Georges Vongerichten), others credited new-wave chefs in France, such as Michel Bras and Alain Ducasse, with the individual warm chocolate soufflés and their gooey centers. They are so simple to make, so economical and consistently delicious (who could resist a warm, liquid bite of chocolate sugary butter?), that they are still a mainstay on menus over two decades later. Like cupcakes, they became a universe unto themselves, with innumerable variations (spiced Mexican chocolate, white chocolate, raspberry chocolate) and a trickle-down economy of volcano cakes that had them appearing on menus in places like Applebee's and as premade hockey pucks in Costco's freezer section, ready to heat and serve.

∽

Ricardo Zarate believes he is a chef with the potential and desire to start a trend like these. Since 2009 the forty-year-old has opened three high-profile restaurants in Los Angeles, each presenting a different variation on his modern, Japanese-inflected interpretation of Peruvian cuisine. His cooking has garnered favorable reviews from local critics, attracted the praise of other chefs, and made Zarate a known name in the Los Angeles culinary landscape. Increasingly, that reputation is going national. He is an aspiring tastemaker, but he is also a good example of how difficult it is for a chef to actually start a food trend.

Zarate was born in Lima and is broad shouldered with a full head of shiny black hair. He has a wide Cheshire cat's grin and the plump cheeks of a newborn baby, which are often bearded or covered in stubble. The eleventh child of a housewife and a taxi driver, Zarate grew up in a crowded, modest house where every one of his dozen siblings pitched in. At twelve years old each child was expected to enter the kitchen and assume the position as the family cook, occupy it for six months, then hand it off to the next in line. "There was no choice. It was your duty, but I liked to cook before that," recalled Zarate over a coffee one day at his restaurant

Mo-Chica in downtown Los Angeles. "I was always trying to sneak myself into that position."

Once Zarate entered the family kitchen he was hooked and quickly grew addicted to the praise he would receive from the family after cooking a good meal. He fed this ego boost by constantly trying to outdo his last meal, vowing to put something new on the table each night. Zarate picked up tips and techniques from his friends' mothers and saved up to take cooking courses advertised in the newspaper. At sixteen he was working as a security guard at a large corporation, where many of the executives were Japanese (Lima has a large Japanese population). Zarate overheard one of his bosses talking about the annual employee's Christmas barbecue, given for all eight hundred of the company's workers, and Zarate immediately offered to cater it, despite lacking any experience beyond his family's house. As Christmas approached, he learned some recipes from a friend's mother who worked as a maid for a Japanese family, and he built the feast around a dish of octopus with soy sauce, wasabi, sesame, and aji limon (a hot, citrus-flavored pepper central to Peruvian cooking).

That meal would come to define Zarate's cooking. He quit the security job and enrolled in culinary school for the next three years. At this time Peru's government was in the midst of a brutal conflict with the Shining Path, a Marxist guerilla group, and life for most Peruvians was pretty miserable. "I was angry," said Zarate. "The country was at war. There were bombs everywhere. It was destroyed." In 1994, with great reluctance, he fled to London on a student visa and landed in a city that was incredibly foreign. Zarate found work in a Japanese restaurant during the height of the sushi trend and worked his way up the ranks in a number of Japanese kitchens until he moved to Los Angeles in 2004, when he assumed the role of head chef in another sushi restaurant.

By 2009 Zarate was getting antsy. He had comfortable work, but he was already thirty-six years old, and though he knew sushi inside and out, he really wanted to cook the food close to his heart. Zarate believed he could advance Peruvian cuisine beyond a cheap ethnic staple of rotisserie takeout chicken, which was how most Americans saw it. There had been a buzz building around Peruvian cuisine internationally, spearheaded by the success of Lima-based chef Gastón Acurio, who operated a series of popular ceviche restaurants around Latin America and abroad. Acurio's success had many, even in nonculinary publications such as the *Economist*, heralding the imminent global upswing of Peruvian cooking in the twenty-first century. "What Acurio did for Peru was amazing," said Zarate. "He made us feel proud about something for the first time."

With $30,000 of his own savings, Zarate took over a tiny stall in a run-down Latin American food court in the city's downtown garment district, which was as far from a foodie's destination for most Angelenos as Peru itself. The stall, which he called Mo-Chica, revolved around a concept Zarate called "Peru, Nice to Meet You," and the six-item menu was based on the favorite meals Zarate cooked at home, updated with the best ingredients he could buy. He sold stewed oxtail, chicken and rice, seafood stews, quinoa risotto, dried lamb, lomo saltado, and a number of fresh ceviches made with sashimi-quality fish purchased from his Japanese suppliers. "I didn't care about the money," he said. "I just wanted people to put one bite in their mouth and say, 'Wow!'"

Instead, no one said anything. The nearby University of Southern California students Zarate had counted on for business weren't interested in his offerings, and the Latin American garment workers found it too costly. Mo-Chica's sales averaged just $200 a day during the first month, and Zarate quickly fell into a depression. Then things slowly turned around. Word of exceptional Peruvian food in an unexpected place spread among adventurous diners, who began posting ecstatic reviews of the cooking (especially the ceviches) on the social network Yelp and their personal blogs. One day Zarate spotted a man who "looked like George Washington" taking photos through the window. Zarate asked whether he was a blogger, and the man gave him a bit of an obscure answer. When a review of Mo-Chica appeared in *LA Weekly* soon after, Zarate quickly realized the presidential mystery man had been Pulitzer Prize–winning food critic Jonathan Gold, the most powerful and respected tastemaker in the city's dining scene.

"Since Nobu Matsuhisa blew into town 20-odd years ago, high-quality Peruvian seafood has not been hard to find in Los Angeles, but this was somehow—earthier, more sensual, more Peruvian, speaking as much of the mountains as of the sea," wrote Gold in the review, referring to the namesake Japanese proprietor of the Nobu empire who had previously cooked in Peru and is credited with starting a trend of his own: the introduction of modern, global-fusion sushi dishes in the 1990s. "What Zarate is attempting is the professionalization of Peruvian cooking at popular prices, and the food he is turning out so far is sharper, more beautifully composed than any Peruvian food we have ever seen in Los Angeles."

Everything changed for Zarate with that review. Business tripled overnight, long lines formed outside Mo-Chica, the other local media outlets came calling with their own articles and reviews, and offers to finance more of Zarate's restaurants flooded in. "Jonathan Gold really saved my life," Zarate said, reflecting on his turn of fortune at the current Mo-Chica, which is a polished loft-like space in a revitalized corner of downtown that opened in 2012. "I will never forget that."

Ricardo Zarate's trendsetting ambition is based around popularizing his flavor profile. "The idea is to be a trend," he said, "to create something new but not extreme. Something familiar, but you don't see it right away." That profile is built on aggressive Peruvian ingredients, such as the spicy yellow pepper aji amarillo, the black mint huacatay, the whole grain quinoa, and the giant Amazonian river fish paiche. If he succeeds, Zarate hopes not only to open multiple restaurants in Los Angeles and in cities such as New York and Chicago but also that his success will spur other chefs to adopt and adapt the flavors he is popularizing, until every house in the country uses aji amarillo in their kitchens and throws alpaca steaks on their barbecues. "Peruvian food is a hard diamond that needs to be polished," Zarate told me with great hope.

All of this sounds preordained when Zarate predicts it through his wide grin, especially if you've just eaten a hearty lunch of his lomo saltado, a Peruvian beef tenderloin stir-fry laced with black peppercorns, garlic, and scallions, and washed it down with Chicha

Morada, a thick and intensely sweet purple juice made from a special strain of corn. But the road between a chef's lofty ambitions and their ability to successfully establish a food trend is long, twisted, and littered with the burned-out hulks of unrealized dreams, poorly timed schemes, and unfulfilled careers. Food trends don't just emerge fully formed onto the plates of the chefs who dream them up; they are as unpredictable as they are powerful, and they are more difficult to forecast than picking winning companies in the stock market. Each food trend that begins with a chef is the product of a number of disparate factors, from talent and personality to timing, luck, and media attention, all of which have to line up with near cosmic symmetry to allow something to take off.

First, you need a chef. They need to be talented, young (like musicians, older chefs are rarely trendsetters), independent, and just a touch cocky. "You need the conviction and balls to stand by an idea that no one else is doing," said Sang Yoon, a Los Angeles–based chef who takes credit for two other trends: the gourmet hamburger and the so-called gastropub (basically, a food-focused bar and grill), in the early 2000s. "Today, things either catch very organically, or they don't." A native of LA, Yoon had worked at some of the city's top kitchens, including Wolfgang Puck's Chinois and Michael's, a restaurant that was central to the development of California cuisine, but remained relatively unknown before he bought his favorite Santa Monica dive bar (a place called Father's Office) in 1999 with an eye on turning it into an authentic tapas bar.

"It was straight-up Andalusian tapas," said Yoon of the original menu. "Anchovies, chorizo, a cheese plate—basically anything that could be made in a kitchen the size of a phone booth." Business was brisk initially until the day Yoon's friend suggested he put a hamburger on the menu. Yoon is an obsessive chef who prefers to conduct meticulous research and experimentation in an isolated test kitchen where he hones his recipes. When he decided to put a hamburger on the Father's Office menu, Yoon set out to make sure it was the best burger on earth. He would deconstruct the idea of a hamburger down to its essential elements (beefiness, toppings, bun, cheese, flavor, texture) and then reassemble the disparate parts to highlight each element in perfect harmony. He began his research by keeping a hamburger journal, taking notes on over forty burgers he sampled over many months. Their qualities were eventually inputted into a spreadsheet, with the data ranked on criteria that reflected Yoon's own tastes. Then Yoon went to work, assembling the different parts of his perfect burger through experimentation and trial and error until he had what he felt was his perfect burger, which he introduced to his customers in 2001.

The beef was dry-aged scrap from a New York strip steak and ground up with fresh chuck, which gave the meat a funky, intense gaminess that was so flavorful, the patty could "stand up on its own," according to Yoon. Soft buns soaked up juices too readily and often fell apart, so Yoon commissioned a small French demi-baguette from a bakery, with a texture that could be toasted but would still yield easily with each bite. On top he put a pile of fresh peppery arugula because he knew the slightly bitter lettuce paired well with beef from his time at Michael's, the Hollywood restaurant he had worked at, which featured a steak and arugula salad. For cheese there was a mix of Maytag blue cheese and gruyere, which together hit with a one-two punch of creamy mouth-feel and sharp flavor punctuation. And all of it was topped with an onion compote that had crumbled bacon in it, which hit like a double exclamation mark!! Served in a basket with a mountain of thin-cut French fries, the salty, skunky, buttery juices of the Father's Office burger dripped down its diners' chins with each ravenous bite and right into their hearts (emotionally and arterially). Not only was it more expensive than most other hamburgers sold in bars ($10 initially, $12.50 today), but Yoon insisted, without exception, the Office Burger also couldn't be altered whatsoever. In Los Angeles, where people regularly order along the lines of "can you hold the cheese, but could I get lettuce instead of bread, and also, maybe fish instead of beef?" it was a move tantamount to declaring martial law. "People said, 'That's really ballsy,' and we got a ton of blowback," recalled Yoon, talking one evening outside the second location of Father's Office in Culver City. He stuck to his guns, though, and the Office Burger affected dining in several fundamental ways.

First, Father's Office kicked off an arms race in gourmet hamburgers that quickly spread from Los Angeles to New York, where French chef Daniel Boulud responded with the Original db Burger at his db Bistro Moderne restaurant. Ground prime rib was stuffed with a center of braised short rib, foie gras, and truffles and served on a parmesan bun, baked in house. An upscale shrine to American-style excess, Boulud's burger sold for $32 and set a gourmet burger frenzy in motion nationwide. Other restaurants followed, trying to outdo one another for burger decadence with increasingly outlandish interpretations, from caviar-topped burgers to an edible joke called the Douche Burger, sold for $666 in New York, with a patty wrapped in gold leaf. Even Burger King got into the game, launching a £95 gourmet burger at its West London location, made from Wagyu beef, white truffles, shaved Spanish pata negra ham, and onion tempura rings made with Cristal champagne (the proceeds for the publicity stunt thankfully went to charity).

Beyond the towering piles of luxury ingredient–stuffed gimmicks that Yoon's burger inspired, the overall quality of hamburgers everywhere began to improve as a result of all the attention. This food, possibly the most central to postwar American culture, had been so commoditized by fast food chains over the years that few put any thought into the burgers they served anymore. But with gourmet burgers now popping up on nearly every menu in the country, from fine-dining rooms to family restaurants, and with the press that they effortlessly generated, even the humblest bars and largest fast food chains began rethinking the quality of their hamburgers. Where previously chefs just used frozen patties to make hamburgers, now they experimented with house-ground combinations of various cuts, from skirt and short rib trimmings to aged sirloin and rump. They baked the perfect buns for these burgers and created whole new categories of condiments to top them. Hamburgers went from a maligned food to something worthy of culinary attention. Yoon realized the full impact of this when he visited Hong Kong a few years back and ate a gourmet hamburger in a mall food court there. "People were lined up for it," he recalled. "I think it's awesome. I planted a seed, and now I see the offspring everywhere."

More importantly, Father's Office demonstrated that great chefs could serve excellent food for reasonable prices in pretty much any setting that had a working kitchen. "That burger started a huge trend," said Yoon. "This was the first place where a pedigreed chef stepped away from a tablecloth restaurant to cook in a casual setting. I'm the first person to do that." Sure, other chefs may dispute Yoon's claim to being the inventor of both casual fine dining and the gastropub, but undoubtedly his burger's success and the format of Father's Office played a significant role in the emergence of one of the most significant changes in dining in the past century. In the decade since he opened up shop a generation of talented young chefs cast aside the confines of fancy, hierarchical, European kitchens in order to take an entrepreneurial stab at something smaller and more relaxed where they could cook the food they wanted to make. Whether it was grandma's spaghetti, perfect roast chicken, or artisanal pastrami, they got the same respect from diners and critics that was usually reserved for those serving refined tasting menus. Yoon's Office Burger proved to be the opening salvo in a revolution that democratized the way we eat in restaurants. No longer the province of hushed, suit-wearing diners and haute cuisine, the act of dining out has become a more expansive, even populist activity. Indirectly, Father's Office helped usher in popular restaurants like Chang's Momofuku Noodle Bar; Portland's Thai street-food mecca, Pok Pok; and San Francisco's permanent pop-up Mission Chinese. The success of these kinds of restaurants has been so conspicuous that the white tablecloth restaurant is now on the endangered species list.

One beneficiary of the rise of casual fine dining was another LA chef named Roy Choi. Choi's family, who were Korean immigrants to Los Angeles, had owned various small restaurants, markets, and liquor stores around the city, and Choi grew up around food. He worked in restaurants during high school and, later on, in his twenties, spent a number of years in New York, bouncing around kitchens at celebrated restaurants like Le Bernardin, and hotels in Los Angeles. He likely would have kept moving between various restaurants were it not for a stroke of fate.

In mid-2008, as the financial crisis hit the hospitality business, Choi was laid off from his latest job. Shortly after, he was approached by Mark Manguera, a Filipino who had married into a Korean family, with the idea to put Korean BBQ meats, such as sweet bulgogi, spicy pork belly, and crispy-thin short ribs, into tacos topped with Mexican salsas and kimchi, thus marrying two of Los Angeles's most prominent ethnic flavors. The two joined forces, commissioned a taco truck from a Los Angeles caterer, and launched the Kogi Korean BBQ taco truck shortly after Thanksgiving. They would park the truck in several different locations every day, each time posting their location to their Twitter feed in order to alert customers. The truck generated a fan base so devoted that it spawned the term *Kogi Kulture.* As Korean taco lovers chased the truck around the city like hippies trailing the Grateful Dead, lineups for the truck could stretch as long as eight hundred people who would stand patiently for up to two hours simply to eat a bulgogi taco on the curb.

Choi, who now has four Kogi branded trucks roaming Los Angeles and three sit-down restaurants, has been hailed as one of America's best new chefs by *Food & Wine* magazine and is an internationally known celebrity, said all of this happened over the course of a month. The idea came to Manguera, Choi whipped up the recipes, the truck hit the streets, and voilà! Two big trends emerged from the Kogi Korean BBQ experiment. First, Choi's Korean taco, like Yoon's burger, became a national phenomenon and quickly found its way onto menus far and wide. Other Korean BBQ trucks popped up within four months, and in less than a year large chains like California Pizza Kitchen, Baja Fresh, and even TGI Fridays were serving Korean-style tacos to mainstream Americans. More importantly, Choi provided the first high-profile example of a chef-driven food truck that could build a following through social media and eventually transform into a financially successful business. In Los Angeles budding cooks started taking to the streets in the months following Kogi's launch, buying old catering and taco trucks or commissioning gleaming new ones in order to sell everything from bacon-spiked snacks to Sprinkles cupcakes. Chefs in other cities took notice, launched their own trucks, and an entire industry of gourmet food trucks blossomed across North America and the world, upending the entry-level restaurant business in many cities and creating a whole new class of edible entrepreneurialism, with Kogi BBQ credited as its godfather.

∽

The difference between today's chef-driven trends and those from a generation ago has less to do with what's going on in the kitchen and more with how the media is covering it. No tastemakers are more reliant on the media's voice than chefs, whose craft is increasingly driven as much by personality and on-camera savvy as it is their knife and sautéing skills. As we saw with the great cupcake boom, the modern food media's innumerable messengers operate in a hierarchy of news, reviews, and looping feedback, whipping trends into a frenzy like summer winds spreading forest fires. They have transformed the very nature of chef-driven food trends, speeding up their evolution and changing the way chefs approach their cooking.

The modern food media is a relatively recent phenomenon. Craig Claiborne was the first editor of the *New York Times* dining section to move away from articles aimed at mostly female home cooks and to devoted journalistic coverage of restaurants, chefs, and the new flavors they were introducing. The starred restaurant review, which Claiborne introduced in 1962, added an element of competition to dining out. Suddenly, chefs were vying to outdo their competition for accolades, and the dining public responded, pouring favor on the highest-ranking restaurants. This often had the side effect of creating trends in their wake, as others emulated the favored menus, techniques, and flavor profiles. A few specialty publications, such as the now-extinct magazine *Gourmet*, wrote profiles of the men behind the stoves, but for the most part chefs were anonymous workers, emerging from the kitchen once in a while to pose for photos in giant white toques beside comically large buffet spreads. If they had tattoos, they hid them. No one called them celebrities.

In this climate chef-driven food trends took a long time to move beyond their restaurants and have a broader impact with the public. Someone would have to dine there, notice something extraordinary in a particular dish or technique, and spread the word organically, person by person, until a newspaper critic took the time to eat it. If the critic wrote for a large, well-read paper, such as the *Times* or the *Washington Post*, the restaurant review might have an impact beyond its particular market, spreading the trend to other cities. "It took two years for Paul Prudhomme's blackened red fish to make it upstream from New Orleans to Portland, Oregon, in the 1980s," recalled restaurant consultant Michael Whiteman over lunch at Rosemary's, a farm-to-table restaurant in New York's Greenwich Village. "Today it'd take about ten minutes."

Whiteman, who runs the restaurant consulting firm Baum + Whiteman, has created, nurtured, and tracked restaurant trends for over forty years. His partner, Joe Baum, was the mind behind legendary New York restaurants the Four Seasons, La Fonda del Sol, and Forum of the Twelve Ceasars and is regarded as the father of the theme restaurant, which broke the stranglehold that ostentatious French dining rooms and clubby steakhouses had on American dining. Baum and Whiteman were innovating with globally inspired tapas and classic cocktails twenty years before these trends caught on elsewhere, but since the late 1990s, as the media coverage of chefs and restaurants has exploded in both traditional outlets and online, Whiteman has seen the cycle of dining trends speed up exponentially. "The life cycle of a trend is interesting," said Whiteman as he picked at a kale and beet salad, which, he acknowledged, had become a mandatory appetizer on every farm-to-table restaurant menu in the country. "If Cajun blackening were invented today, you could easily call it a fad because it'd be gone in three years."

Chefs and restaurants today receive relentless media attention. There is 24/7 chef and food programming on two dedicated television networks (Food and its sister, Cooking), dozens of food shows on other networks (*Top Chef, Hell's Kitchen, Master Chef, The Chew, Cake Boss, Bizarre Foods, No Reservations, Diners, Drive Ins and Dives, etc.*), profiles and articles in the food sections of local and national newspapers, as well as a plethora of national and international food magazines (*Saveur, Bon Appétit, Food & Wine, Lucky Peach*), national food blogs churning out dozens of stories a day (*Eater, Grub Street, Chow, Serious Eats, Gayot*), hundreds of thousands of independent and specialized food blogs (on cupcakes, vegan chefs, recipes, dining out in Tucson, etc.), and a number of massive social networks, including Chowhound, Yelp, Citysearch, Urbanspoon, and countless other upstarts that are derived from recommendations and reviews that skew heavily to restaurants. Between all of these, every single minutia of our dining world is being chronicled, photographed, critiqued, and commented on in a relentless cycle that has no off switch.

Celebrity chefs have been compared, without a trace of irony, to geniuses and great artists. They are photographed by the paparazzi, dispense autographs like Hollywood hunks, and pen piles of memoirs and cookbooks each year. Celebrity chefs will talk about their "personal brand" regularly, with their faces appearing on cookware, clothing, and packaged foods that have been licensed by third parties. The top-tier chefs no longer cook nightly in restaurants—they build empires, with outposts in Sydney, Hong Kong, Singapore, Las Vegas that they visit a couple of times a year as they fly between their homes, TV shoots, and various charity events. Even the tier or two below the heights of A-list chefs like Mario Batali, David Chang, and Gordon Ramsay—the local young Turks, with their heavily followed Twitter accounts, and in-your-face menu items—are treated as sex symbols in their respective markets, doted on by the local media and the dining public. Once upon a time, if you were a chef, your greatest ambition was to own a restaurant. Now that's just a stepping stone to the true goal of global fame.

"There are large numbers of chefs who have set out already to be famous," said Whiteman, who blames the Food Network and the media for changing the way chefs approach their work. The attention has driven more and more chefs to focus on creating the next trend that the media will embrace rather than simply cooking good food for their customers. Young chefs are no longer content to work their way up through kitchens over the course of a decade;

instead, they want to create wild masterpieces the first day out of cooking school. "It's upped the ante," said Whiteman. "Because the media is voracious in scavenging things to write about, a chef says, 'You want something to write about? I'll give you a pastrami egg roll. You want something to write about? I'll smoke my meat over balsa wood with mussel shells ground into my smoking mixture!' I mean, why should the Kardashians have a monopoly on the bizarre? There's constant pressure on chefs' creativity to capture the media's attention."

The result, according to Whiteman, is food screaming out for media attention. The dishes these chefs create rattle around in the mouth and excite dopamine in your loins. The food clashes rather than harmonizes and disrupts rather than soothes. It's an oyster paste and blood sausage–stuffed, Sriracha-basted chicken, cooked sous-vide and then flash fried rather than a perfectly roasted chicken with fresh herbs and lemon. It is food that shoots for a trend and not often for the better. A city like Los Angeles, where Zarate has established himself, is highly susceptible to this. "In LA most of our restaurants are trend driven," said Leslie Shuter, the dining editor of *Los Angeles Magazine* and a chronicler of the city's extensive food scene. Shuter believes that when we're talking about restaurants and food trends, it is really driven by a small elite of foodies and bloggers who exert an outsized influence on the direction of popular restaurants; and those trends eventually filter down to the places where 90 percent of the public regularly eats. "The blogosphere changed everything," she said. Blogging is instantaneous, like an ongoing news ticker, and because of that, bloggers are only interested in what is currently trending. "If roasting whole goats on a patio is hot now, bloggers won't be interested in it in a year. They're not interested in consistency or longevity."

What results is a self-contained and highly predictable churn of trends. One outlet will write about a dish and then everyone will pile on in a sort of food media scrum, offering their own spin on the same story, whether it is gourmet hamburgers or food trucks or Peruvian cooking. Other chefs take notice and offer up their own interpretation of the growing trend because it will sell to the dining public and inevitably generate for that chef some coveted publicity. More stories are written about the trend around the city and, eventually, the country, culminating in top-ten lists of the best Korean tacos or the fifty hamburgers to eat before you die. Eventually the story can only be told so many ways, and the media moves on, openly declaring that trend dead even if the food in question is still delicious and many people still enjoy eating it. This is how we've arrived at a time when a restaurant can be absolutely packed to the gills seven nights a week, and six months later it sits empty, even while the food tastes exactly the same. The media trend cycle has chewed it up, digested it, and unceremoniously flushed it away.

∾

Two nights after my meal at Picca I returned there to attend a dinner the restaurant was hosting to preview its new menu for a group of journalists and bloggers. Ricardo Zarate and his partners were keenly aware of the media's power in shaping trends, and they frequently reached out to tastemakers in Los Angeles. An hour before they arrived Zarate sat at the counter by the kitchen with his business partner, Stephane Bombet, a French music producer who introduced himself to Zarate after tasting his ceviche at the original Mo Chica and left five hours later with a handshake deal to become the chef's business partner. "There are two types of chefs," said Bombet. "Those who are simply very talented," including many French masters like Paul Bocuse and Joël Robuchon, and those like Zarate, "who are leaders and create trends." Zarate had been working on the new menu for two weeks, and these new dishes would replace a third of the current menu's seasonal offerings. Most of these items began as an idea that Zarate jotted down on his phone, inspired by something he had eaten elsewhere, or an ingredient a supplier brought in. He scrolled through a list of random ideas, which read as recipe haikus, such as *grilled sous vide goose fat fennel* and *stuff yucca with octopus and parmesan aioli*. Head chef Ricardo Lopez kept sending dishes out of the kitchen for Zarate and Bombet to sample, as Zarate consulted photos on his phone of how he'd prepared them previously. "This one," Zarate told Lopez in Spanish, pointing to a plate of quinoa that looked too plain. "It should look like a quinoa salad but without the salad. *Comprende?*" He suggested they add to the dish a drizzle of chimichurri, a salty Argentinean steak sauce made from olive oil, lemon juice, and fresh oregano.

"When I build a menu I think about who my customer is, but I also throw three to five dishes in there for the tastemakers," said Zarate, looking over a plate of braised tongue in Peruvian romesco sauce that had been finished on the Japanese robata charcoal grill with a crisp char. "It should be something challenging. A big writer won't write about a chicken salad, but if you make every single bite a wow, there'll be no balance for regular diners. It's like a football team—you have to build around the stars." Zarate saw bloggers, Yelp reviewers, and other members of the digital food media as the advanced scouts for the city's foodie scene. They set in motion the buzz machine with their exclamation mark–laden reviews, and their #nomnom hashtagged Instagram photos, all of which eventually lure in more established publications and critics who could still cement a trend with the mainstream diner with far more authority than the more cavalier bloggers and online reviewers. It had happened once before at Mo-Chica with his ceviches, which brought them to the attention of Jonathan Gold, and tonight Zarate was looking to rekindle some of that magic. "I just hope that one of the dishes is a killer," he said. Clearly, he wanted to recapture some of his early momentum.

Within the hour a dozen people gathered upstairs in a private annex, along a rustic wooden table decorated with votive candles and giant, scattered, black and white Peruvian corn kernels. Some of the guests had their own blogs, whereas others wrote for larger food news websites or magazines, and a few were involved in public relations. Once everyone sat down, Zarate and Bombet thanked them for coming and began serving dishes, each of which Zarate explained in a very straightforward way. Every time something new hit the table, such as the lobster causa, everyone picked up their phones or giant cameras and bathed the food in flash photography, like starlets emerging onto the red carpet. "Are you familiar with causas?" asked Zarate, explaining that they were cold mashed potatoes seasoned with lime juice and aji amarillo. "Would you like a bit more light?" Bombet inquired, adjusting the overhead lighting as the bloggers clicked away.

I sat next to Matthew Kang, a writer for the LA branch of the national food website Eater who also owned Scoops, a local gourmet ice cream shop. Kang had been following Zarate's career since the original Mo-Chica, and he credited him with putting a spotlight onto Peruvian food, which had been dismissed as a cheap ethnic cuisine before he stepped onto the American scene. "That trend started with Ricardo," Kang said, diving into a fantastic, grilled branzino anticucho skewer, dressed in spicy huacatay butter and a tangy coleslaw. "He made it bourgeois, with small plates and people willing to pay $50 a person." Picca was the next step, a destination for diners that Kang not only put on par with the best and most unique restaurants in the city; he considered it a place where you could get food that no one else was serving in the entire country. "From a blogger standpoint, Ricardo Zarate is a chef that we can talk about on a national level. The entire blogging community is supportive of his places." Zarate's next venture, Paiche, a seafood-focused Peruvian Izakaya in the Marina Del Rey area, was already generating tremendous buzz even though it wouldn't open for another six months.

Despite all of this support and the accolades he received from the media and diners, Zarate had yet to see any of his dishes truly blossom into a trend. It was true that Peruvian cuisine was gaining greater international prominence, especially in Europe and Latin America, but most of that was credited to Gastón Acurio, and in America it hadn't really spread beyond Zarate's own restaurants. Tiraditos, causas, aji amarillo, and paiche were still far from household names, only appearing on scattered menus around the country. Although Zarate was undoubtedly a success—he owned several bustling restaurants that were packed every night of the week—his prediction, among others, that Americans would turn to alpaca as the new red meat had yet to materialize. Zarate himself didn't seem too concerned about this and wasn't in a rush to be crowned as a tastemaker. "I think it's a wave," he said during a break in the service. "This is just the beginning! You need another ten years to establish a trend."

Even if Zarate fails to ignite a national passion for his style of cooking, that may be a hidden blessing. Chefs who have established food trends are then saddled with their legacy, and often, that can be troubling. Your star rises on the back of a single item, flavor, or concept, and you are forever associated with it. At best it's a calling card, a high-water mark that establishes a chef's talents and allows them to move on. But it also has the danger of turning a chef into a one-hit wonder. "As a person, I'm proud of the Kogi taco," Roy Choi told me. "But as a chef, it took me a long time to get over being embarrassed by it. It's like having to sing 'Sweet Caroline' at every concert. Everyone looks at me, and all they think is kimchi tacos. Before that, I never worked with kimchi. It took me a long time to exorcise my own demons and have fun with it. It's a tough thing, man. It's tough to create something that's become iconic. It's tough because it's not everything you are. The person I was when I made that taco is not the person I am now. But people are just starting to catch up to it and just finding out about it, and I have to relive that moment over and over again. It's a trip."

Momofuku's David Chang, whose stratospheric success launched a thousand pork belly–stuffed buns, hip ramen restaurants, and kimchi-topped dishes, found his early realization that he was a trendsetter profoundly unsettling. Chang would walk into a new restaurant in Denver and find himself face to face with nearly half of his menu and the same minimalist plywood décor that he'd used at Momofuku Noodle Bar. "I try to take it with a grain of salt," he said. "I try not to eat at those restaurants. I try to avoid them. It would be like watching the cover band of the band I wanted to see. It's too meta-fucking-weird." For a while Chang resented the trends he started and all that they had spawned, but as he has matured and his restaurant business expanded, Chang realized that his power as a trendsetting tastemaker was actually liberating. "It allows us to do other things," said Chang, "to finance and pursue new flavors and more interesting projects. I fully embrace it, and I want to serve the best buns, the best ramens, the best fried chicken of all time."

Chang also worried that the increasing importance of food trends for chefs and the restaurant business was skewing the priorities of young cooks, who are less interested in learning the fundamentals of the classical kitchen than they are with whipping out a bag of edible fireworks, as Michael Whiteman explained. He also has a deep problem with appropriation, which has increased in pace dramatically now that the minutia of every single menu is posted online almost instantly. When Chang first heard about Catalan modernist chef Ferran Adrià, who operated the surrealist restaurant El Bulli in northern Spain, he had no idea what was being described, how the dishes looked, let alone how they were made. Those who wanted to find out had to travel there, work in Adrià's kitchen, and pick up the knowledge by hand. "But now with the Internet, cooks don't have to travel and see how something is done." They can just replicate it from photos and recipes posted online. "Food trends are a very dangerous thing," Chang warned me. "They can spark innovation but also kill innovation."

Chang acknowledged that food culture is an evolution, and even the foolish trends are what push our culture forward. No one creates their ideas in a vacuum. Even when it seems like someone is putting one more molten chocolate cake on their menu, if the chef is tweaking it in any way by, say, adding Mexican-style chilies and cinnamon to the chocolate or making it with something crazy like pig's blood (something I tried once, and actually liked), it opens up another road for our taste buds to venture down. Trends are the process of a feedback loop, of competition between talents, and they are a balance between following the herd, pleasing customers, and letting creativity flow. Without them restaurants would serve the exact same dishes they did forty years ago—we'd still be eating roast beef, mashed potatoes, and frozen vegetables night after night after night.

Zarate was doing his best to break that loop or, at least, inject his own influence into it. Whether something from his kitchen becomes a trend will be up to fate as much as his own kitchen magic.

After eighteen courses the table of bloggers and writers were served Maine lobsters that had been split in half and stuffed with lobster meat, aji amarillo béchamel sauce, and an herbed-panko breading. "It's like a Peruvian lobster thermidor," said Kang aloud as he took his umpteenth photo of the night. "Yeah, you got it," said Zarate, watching as everyone put down their phones and took their first bite. The lobster was fantastic. It was buttery, tender, and just spicy enough that it cut through the richness of the béchamel. The table was littered with the debris of Zarate's various attempts at impressing the crowd, and everyone was so full that they refused dessert, an action I found unconscionable, but it was apparently par for the course among Los Angeles foodies, who always seem to be following the latest diet trends, which, in many ways, are even more powerful than chef trends.

Satisfied, Kang put down his napkin and delivered his verdict to me: The meal was great, but "I don't think he has that killer dish yet," he said. "You need that pork bun."

4

HEALTH

TAKE TWO CHIA SEEDS AND CALL ME IN THE MORNING

"Gluten is just a term for things that are bad for you. Like calories or fat, that's all gluten."

—Seth Rogen

"As far as vitamins go, if I take a few with each meal, over time I can usually get in quite a lot before the latest study confirms they're worthless."

—Woody Allen

The morning after my marathon dinner at Picca I drove up into the mountains north of the city to the suburb of Westlake Village and the manicured headquarters of the Dole Food Company. Dole is the biggest produce company in the world, a corporate juggernaut that dominates whole swaths of the fruit and vegetable trade, in everything from bananas and pineapples to plastic fruit cups and ready-to-drink smoothies. I waited in a soaring lobby, decorated with three-story murals of abundant fields overflowing with fresh fruits, detailed models of Dole's shipping fleet, vintage Dole advertisements, and every painting of a pineapple ever produced. A huge pineapple sculpture anchored the center of the room. It was encased in glass, like a precious gem.

Marty Ordman, the company's vice president of marketing and communications (who bears a striking resemblance to the comedian Tom Smothers), came out to meet me. We walked to a large events room in the building's rear where the Dole Healthy Lifestyle Blogger Summit was beginning its second day. Over a buffet breakfast of mimosas, coffee, Dole fruit platters, and blueberry scones, ten bloggers (all women) were talking about last night's dinner. They ranged in age and background, from Los Angeles–based wellness blogger Erin Haslag and Arizona grocery chain dietician Barbara Ruhs, to Chicago's Jennifer DaFonte, who writes the Mom Spotted blog. Dole had flown everybody out and put them up at the nearby Four Seasons for two nights, though none of the bloggers were being paid for their time and they weren't obliged to write anything about Dole.

After breakfast everyone walked to a small windowless test kitchen in the middle of the building. With its beige laminate cupboards, white electric appliances, shelves lined with canned pineapples, and fruit wallpaper trim running around the perimeter of the drop ceiling, it felt like a slice of 1980s suburbia. The group gathered around a large butcher block–topped island as a procession of Dole product managers demonstrated new products, recipes, and gadgets, ranging from chicken breasts marinated in mango and orange juice (they didn't taste like much); a healthier version of Dole's classic pineapple upside-down cake, Yonanas; a machine that pureed frozen bananas into something resembling ice cream; and a new line of frozen, chocolate-dipped banana slices that was a particular hit with everyone.

Midway through the morning Naomi Hanson, a fit, confident product manager for Dole's new Nutrition Plus line of products, stepped up to the counter and laid out her case. "Have you all heard of chia?" she asked. "And not just the toy." Everyone laughed as the Chia Pet's unforgettable "ch-ch-ch-chia" jingle sprung up in their heads. Hanson was here to talk to the group about eating chia seeds, which the Dole Nutrition Plus brand had been launched to promote. There were canisters of whole chia seeds and milled chia seeds, small single-serve packages of chia seeds that could fit into a purse or a pocket (chia dime bags, essentially), and chia-and-fruit clusters, which baked chia seeds into sweet, bite-sized crunchy snacks that came in mixed berry, cranberry apple, and tropical fruit flavors and were seriously addictive. Everyone in the group passed around the different Nutrition Plus products.

"I'm kind of put off by people making all sorts of crazy claims in this category," one of the women in the group said. Especially if she or her readers didn't regularly shop at places like Whole Foods.

"Well, there's a lot of misinformation, rumor, and myth around these foods," Hanson replied.

"What I had always been led to believe was that chia was better than flax seed because you don't have to mill it," said another.

"What about milling it in your teeth?" asked Nicole Presley, an East Los Angeles–based food blogger. "I know it's popular in Latin culture to make chia lemonade with whole seeds. They make a kind of gel out of it."

"Honestly," said another woman in the group, "I've never heard of this before."

Hanson began to rattle off the chia gospel in response: chia seeds had twice the Omega-3 alpha-linolenic acid (ALA) of walnuts, twice the fiber of oatmeal, three times the calcium of cottage cheese, and 68 percent more than a glass of milk. A single serving of chia boasted nearly the same protein as an egg and as much iron as spinach. "You can put it in smoothies, breads, anything at all," Hanson said, growing more animated as she reeled the group in. "You could sprinkle it onto a salad, into pasta sauce, into a meatball!"

"I'd buy this stuff today!" one of the women blurted out, instantly convinced.

Ordman passed around a tray with cups of Dole pineapple juice mixed with chia seeds, which had expanded to form a tasteless, gray sludge floating in the mix. "It's not the prettiest color," Hanson said. "And the whole seeds get this frog egg look to them, but it tastes just like pineapple juice." She was right. The chia, which is an entirely flavorless and odorless grain, was more of a textural addition to the juice, a slimy crunch that you could detect, but it didn't really change the taste at all.

"There's some beautiful chia recipes on Pinterest," said Ruhs, who had already tested a mango chia smoothie, chia-fortified pancakes, and a chia pudding over the past few months.

Hanson interjected to let the group know that Dr. Oz, Oprah Winfrey, and Martha Stewart's websites already featured chia recipes. "Lots of people are getting into chia," she said with a salesman's knowing grin.

∽

Eat more fiber, but be sure to eat less carbs. Drink three glasses of milk a day, so long as you avoid lactose and dairy. Beef is filled with much-needed iron and protein, but you should steer clear of red meat entirely. Eat fish, unless it (almost certainly) contains mercury. Margarine is the evolutionary replacement for butter, although it turns out margarine should be avoided like the plague, so how about some more butter? The perfect food is açai, bananas, blueberries, bran, coconut water, flax seeds, and goji berries, so be sure to eat as much of these as possible, as well as chocolate and red wine, too (not too much of any of them . . . but enough that it will make a difference, which is too much). Eat donuts and organ meats, and especially bacon and eggs for breakfast. Avoid white foods, brown foods, and anything that aggravates the blood, as it leads to disorders like masturbation and blindness. Eat whatever you want. But don't finish it. And make sure it contains no gluten, because gluten is certain death. Be sure to read the labels on your food, but do not for one second trust the information printed there. You really shouldn't be eating foods that come in boxes anyway.

In the dizzying world of food trends, there are perhaps none more compelling and confusing than health and diet trends. Compelling because they hold the promise of a longer, happier life simply through the foods we eat, and confusing because they seemingly shift with the tides, vacillating from salvation to damnation. For as long as human beings have had enough to eat, they've worried about eating the right thing and have tackled that anxiety by devising diets and exalting certain foods. Chinese emperor Qin Shi Huang, who ruled in the second century BC, died after eating mercury pills made by his court's alchemist to provide immortality. In the eleventh century obese English king William the Conqueror took to bed and consumed nothing but alcohol to shed pounds, a practice many of his countrymen seem to continue to this day. Around the same time Persian physician and philosopher Avicenna advised the fat to eat a bulky diet with little nutrition so they'd have to work extra hard to expel the constipating mass stuck in their bodies (the Four-Hour Crap Workout!). Sixteenth-century Italians advised drinking more wine than eating food, and the low-carb and -sugar diet in vogue today was initially heralded by Jean Anthelme-Brillat Savarin, a French lawyer and politician who is regarded as the father of modern foodies and who regularly consumed great quantities of fowl and ale with the ostentatious greed of the Coney Island Hot Dog Eating Contest.

For as long as we've been foraging, humans have been trying new berries, leaves, potions, herbs, and more, all in service of the special cocktail that would make us well. Doctors or pharmacists originally devised Coca-Cola, Dr. Pepper, Dr. Brown's Cel-Ray, 7-Up, and pretty much every major soda on the market as health tonics, claiming they would cure everything from hangovers and depression to malnutrition and nausea, and, in the case of Schweppes Tonic Water, to preventing malaria. Since the late nineteenth century, diet and health trends have increasingly focused on weight loss and vitality. They've ranged from the Fletcherizing diet, which advocated chewing each bite of food thirty-two to eighty times until it was a suitable mush, to the Paleo diet, which theorizes that we really haven't evolved since our knuckle-dragging days and should basically eat as much grass-fed meat as possible. There are grapefruit diets, cookie diets, graham cracker diets, martini and steak diets, cabbage soup diets, macrobiotic diets, extreme calorie reduction diets (which is really just starvation), and a diet that advocated consuming a live tapeworm, which, the theory went, would literally suck your pounds away. People move toward diets in herds. For ten years a significant percentage of my friends and family suddenly discovered they were lactose intolerant and went out to buy Lactaid-brand pills, lactose-free milk, and other products. Now those very same individuals have switched to eating gluten-free, buying gluten-deprived breads, flours, and pastas as well as products that haven't changed but now label themselves as gluten-free, like orange juice, simply because it sells more cartons. Of all of these acquaintances, only one of them actually has celiac disease, the disorder in which the body cannot process gluten. The rest have adopted the diet because they believe it will help them shed pounds, gain energy, clear their skin, and, in one case, have an easier time becoming pregnant.

Each new diet or health trend plays off the emotions of consumers, who are driven by powerful feelings of insecurity, hope, and fear over their bodies and look to the market for answers. Over the years I've watched my father endure dozens of weight loss diets. He's a fit man who eats well, works out regularly, and bicycles over a hundred miles a week, but he also has a fondness for donuts and hamburgers and is consistently trying to shed a few extra pounds. He has tried Weight Watchers, the Atkins Diet, the South Beach Diet, the All-Bran diet (in which you basically load up on so much fiber that you live on the toilet), diets that required special shakes, and diets that required calorie calculus. He has also embraced new health trends with particular zeal. He boiled pungent Chinese herbal teas for asthma; switched from sugar to aspartame, to honey, to agave; and spent a few years eating a lactose-free cheese that even our golden retriever wouldn't touch. One day I'd find the fridge filled with bottles of cranberry juice, a year later it would all be replaced with bottles of pomegranate juice, a year after that it would be brimming with Greek yogurt. One day he'd be eating boiled eggs, and the next he'd be microwaving egg whites. Partly this was for weight and partly for heart health, but the health trends swung with each season, as the stash of discarded bars, powders, and diet snack products in the basement pantry gathered dust in an increasingly large pile.

My late father-in-law was even more devoted to health trends, especially after he was diagnosed with prostate cancer in his fifties. He only ate organic products and supplemented heavily with "ancient grains" like amaranth and quinoa. He once boiled a sea turtle to make soup, which supposedly stank up the house so badly that my wife and her siblings slept over with friends for a week. When his cancer returned a decade later he sought treatment at a Florida health spa that advocated a raw vegan diet, centered on a round-the-clock regiment of wheatgrass juice shots. Suddenly, the house filled with bags of sprouted mung beans and jugs of steeped almond milk as a dehydrator rendered vegetables like carrots and kale into jerky. The fridge burst with bags of wheatgrass—it basically looked like someone had emptied the lawnmower each day—and the pungent, intense shots they produced tasted like bottled chlorophyll. We dined out regularly at a number of newly opened raw restaurants, a budding diet trend, where we ate raw "lasagna," raw "hamburgers," and raw "cheesecake," made by dehydrating, emulsifying, pressing, and reforming everything from coconut milk to cashew butter to thinly sliced zucchinis.

My father-in-law's friends, family, and physicians initially dismissed each of these health foods he embraced as fringe hippie fads, only to find them make their way into the mainstream of health and diet trends sooner or later. A decade and a half ago he had to go to patchouli-scented health food stores and seasonal farmers markets to procure organic lamb and beef from the freezer case. Today, you can buy organic meat at nearly every supermarket. Wheatgrass juices are now available prebottled and ready mixed in delicious flavors, and there are hundreds of raw snack bars, cookbooks, and restaurants out there, with more opening each day. Because health trends are so powerful in their message and motivation (i.e., if you don't eat this, you'll die), the successful ones find their way into the mainstream in a big way. Food companies take notice and adapt to service these trends, whether they do it with a menu item (the McLean hamburger, from McDonald's) or a consumer-packaged food (eggs, Tropicana Orange Juice, and granola bars fortified with Omega-3s).

Health trends can create tectonic shifts in the way we eat. When I was writing a book on the Jewish delicatessen business a few years back, deli owners charted their fortunes on which diet was in fashion over the decades. The low-fat movement of the late 1970s and 1980s was a serious blow to the full-fat corned beef and pastrami sandwiches that defined these businesses. Sales plummeted, and in response, Jewish delis upped their offering of low-fat turkey and chicken options. Customers were requesting lean and extra-lean corned beef, and so the delis not only trimmed the fat but also asked their suppliers to send only lean briskets. The suppliers, seeing this shift in demand, passed along requests to the ranchers, who began raising leaner cattle. When the low-fat diet trend faded and was replaced by the Atkins diet craze, which identified carbohydrates as the devil, the delis began selling lettuce wraps and thin burrito-style wraps with their sandwiches. These same customers complained that the meat was too dry—because it had been shorn of its succulent fat—and that the delicatessen was no longer as good as it once was. Thousands of delis shut down during this time, and many of the owners blamed health and diet trends for this. Today, these same delis are scrambling to recast dishes like cabbage rolls as gluten-free options and are tinkering with how to make matzo balls without the matzo.

Today, the big driver in health trends is single ingredients. These so-called superfoods have an advantage over more complicated dietary regimens, which prescribe a balance of certain foods at the expense of others. Superfood trends come with a simple message: This one thing is so good for you that you basically need to eat as much of it as possible. The term itself is fairly recent, popularized in 1998 by the nutrition writer Aaron Moss, who wrote, "Humans have many options when it comes to fueling their bodies, but the benefits of some options are so nutritious that they might be labeled as superfoods." The term, which is no more than a brilliant spark of marketing speak, quickly spread through the food world, as various diet practitioners, nutritionists, and food companies used it to sell their products and services. In 2004 Dr. Steven Pratt published his book *SuperFoods Rx: Fourteen Foods That Will Change*

Your Life, furthering the definition by claiming that a superfood had three qualifications: (1) it is readily available to the public, (2) it contains nutrients that enhance longevity, and (3) its health benefits are backed by scientific studies. Salmon, broccoli, spinach, berries, and green tea were among his favorites because "they contain high concentrations of crucial nutrients, as well as the fact that many of them are low in calories." Pratt's website, SuperFoodsRx.com, claims that "foods containing these nutrients have been proven to help prevent and, in some cases, reverse the well-known effects of aging, including cardiovascular disease, Type II Diabetes, hypertension and certain cancers." The nutrients these foods contain have become household names in their own right: flavonoids, Omega-3 fatty acids, polyphenols, and, of course, antioxidants, which have been held up—by those trying to sell them to you—as the best defense against cancer.

Even with so many conflicting health trends already around, we never seem to lose our appetites for new ones. Chia seeds are the latest and greatest "superfood." The plant *Salvia hispanica L.* is an herb, related to mint, which was originally found in central and southern Mexico and Guatemala and later cultivated in other areas of Central America. For thousands of years it was central to the Aztec and Mayan diet as a staple food, in which the small black seeds were ground for flour, pressed for their oil, or simply mixed with water and drunk straight. Aztec rulers received chia seeds in tribute from their subjects, and the seeds were incorporated into religious ceremonies. After the Spanish conquest of Latin America, chia's use declined in all but a few areas, as the Christian conquistadores banned it for use in religious ceremonies, and the imported European flours, grains, and foods overtook it in the Latin American diet. In Mexico people still made *chia frescas* (a sugary limeade with chia seeds in it), but for the most part chia was forgotten as a food, cultivated in only a handful of farms. Chia was so undervalued, in fact, that it was used as a decoration by artisans in Oaxaca, Mexico, where the moistened seeds were spread onto terra cotta figures and molds. As they sprouted, a garden of green hair seemed to grow from the figures. In 1977 Joe Pedott, an American marketing and advertising maven, came across the chia figures at a trade show and acquired the rights, rebranding them as Chia Pets in 1982 and adding the ubiquitous "ch-ch-ch-chia" television jingle that assured their fame. His company, Joseph Enterprises (which also produced the Clapper), built a multimillion-dollar business off the verdant backs of Chia Pets, which have included molds in the guise of Elmer Fudd, Hello Kitty, and two different versions of President Barack Obama as well as his electoral rival Mitt Romney. No one ever thought to eat their Chia Pet, however.

The father of the chia diet trend is Dr. Wayne Coates, a professor of agricultural engineering at the University of Arizona. A marathon runner with an interest in health foods, Coates's research had focused on cultivating new crops from various sources over the years, including many from Latin America, such as quinoa, amaranth, and various strains of lettuce. In 1991 he was working in partnership with other academics in the northwestern provinces of Argentina, trying to introduce to poor farmers there more lucrative crops beyond the traditional staples of corn and beans. A few small farms in Guatemala and Mexico were still cultivating chia seeds, but someone on the team suggested they try them in Argentina, so in 1992 chia was planted as part of the program on thirty-five acres of land in the province of Catamarca.

"The initial work we did was feeding it to chickens to make Omega-3-enriched, healthier eggs," recalled Coates. "That's how it started." Omega-3 fatty acids were becoming a big driver of health trends at the time, and so Coates and his team focused their research on the effects of feeding chia to chickens, pigs, and dairy cows as well as laboratory rats. After a few years they began looking at chia as something humans should be consuming directly. Coates began working with others to identify additional health benefits, isolating chia's antioxidant, fiber, and protein attributes in various studies he and his Argentine partner in the project, agronomist Ricardo Ayerza Jr., conducted. The Omega-3 acid levels in chia were particularly high, and the more Coates and Ayerza studied the seed, the more they realized what a potential gold mine they had unearthed. Chia seed stored easily, and unlike flax, it never went rancid once it was milled, which meant it wasn't perishable. It had no discernible taste and could hold up to heat of various types, so it could conceivably work in everything from baked goods and meat dishes to heavily processed food products. In 2005 Coates and Ayerza published *Chia: Rediscovering a Forgotten Crop of the Aztecs*, a book that summarized their research and passion about chia and strongly evangelized for its consumption. It coincided with Coates's efforts to sell chia seeds in the North American market. He received approval for its sale by the Food and Drug Administration, who certified it was safe to eat, and Coates sold the seeds online and to health food stores around North America.

Around the same time a Toronto health food entrepreneur and self-confessed jack-of-all-trades named Larry Brown was launching his own chia seed business. Brown had been selling various whole grain breads to Canadian health food stores since the mid-1980s and had occasionally heard about chia seeds. "I remember reading a book in a health food store called *All About Chia* in 1972," recalled Brown, sitting at a Starbucks near his house one day. "But you could barely find it. It was sometimes in health food stores in little plastic bags with twist ties on it and a handwritten paper label." Brown's sister Trudy searched online for someone who could procure chia seeds, and they came across a family of farmers in Argentina who were using it as chicken feed (and likely got their start from Dr. Coates's project). Brown showed some of Coates's preliminary research to a friend who owned a health food store. "This will change the world," Brown recalled the friend saying. "But you need to do research."

Brown took a small bag of chia seeds to Dr. Vladimir Vuksan, a highly respected professor of nutrition at the University of Toronto, and literally knocked on his office door, asking whether the professor would study the seed. "You don't just walk in off the street," Vuksan shot back. "I don't even know you." But Brown, a persistent salesman, convinced Vuksan to keep the seeds and take a look if he was interested—no obligations or questions asked. Five days later Vuksan called Brown back and told him it was the most nutritious food he'd ever seen. He began conducting his own studies, which showed that salba seeds (he and Brown didn't use the name chia because of associations with the Chia Pet) were beneficial in reducing blood glucose, blood pressure, body inflammation, and fibrinolysis, especially in patients with type 2 diabetes. Vuksan and Brown dug into the different strains of chia seeds out there, including white chia, red chia, and black chia, as well as the various attributes of seeds grown in different regions. Eventually they identified the two strains they felt were the most consistently nutritious, and in 2002 they filed provisional patents for *Salba Hispanica L.* (basically chia seeds) as a medical treatment. Brown set up the Salba company and released the first branded strain of chia seeds to the market in the early 2000s. As sales slowly grew in the health food community, Brown reached out to a Denver-based company, operated by a man named Rally Ralston, that made tortilla chips and other products with whole grains. Ralston and his brother had been looking into chia seeds since 1999 and soon began working with Brown to develop chia-fortified chips, salsas, pretzels, and snack foods under the Salba brand.

Other companies started popping up, particularly in Toronto, which became a sort of chia mecca in the trend's early years. Press followed as well. In 2005 the *Saturday Evening Post*—which, almost two hundred years old, now targets a geriatric audience—wrote about chia seeds as a returning "supergrain," quoting Dr. Vuksan and his research extensively. Margaret Conover, a Long Island botanist and science educator turned chia blogger, was shocked when her eighty-year-old mother baked salba muffins for her family reunion after reading the article. "'Yeah, they're these miracle seeds I read about in *Saturday Evening Post*.'" Conover recalled her mother saying. "'They do blah blah blah . . . and I paid thirty-two dollars a pound.' My mother doesn't pay thirty-two dollars a pound for anything!" Conover said. "I was just flabbergasted. She was the first person I'd ever heard of outside the chia world who bought it, and she bought it through mail order." A year later Dr. Andrew Weil wrote about chia seeds on his website, which is one of the most read wellness and nutrition publications in the world.

As word spread, around 2007 and 2008, more chia suppliers began entering the market, and more chia products (drinks, bars, supplements) began appearing on health food shelves. Because chia wasn't a widely traded commodity, the price and quality fluctuated unpredictably. It was the Wild West: a constant influx of new players, each staking their claim to some previously unnoticed corner of the market, with no one really able to guarantee anything. Brown and Ralston got into a disagreement over the direction of Salba's business and split ways, though not before heading to court with each other and the Argentinean suppliers of the seeds over who could use the trademarked name of Salba (essentially, Ralston won the rights). Wayne Coates worked with a Florida company called Lifemax to develop the Mila-branded mix of chia seeds, which Lifemax then distributed through a sort of Amway-style direct marketing model, in which users sold bags of seeds to their friends and recouped a share of the profits. Mila is priced several times higher than other chia products, and many in the chia community (yes, there is a chia community) have complained that it is nothing but a pyramid scheme. On her chiativity.org blog Conover reported that Lifemax was rumored to have published a study written by an "expert" serving time in federal prison and that Coates claimed that the Lifemax people owed him money, and this is why he left the company.

Then, in 2009, author Christopher McDougall released the book *Born to Run* about the reclusive Tarahumara Indian tribe in Mexico's Copper Canyons who are reputed to be the world's greatest long-distance runners. They run in thin sandals, avoiding the injuries that plague most joggers, and they eat chia. Though McDougall only mentioned chia seeds a few times in the book, he did so with the zeal of a missionary, spreading a powerful gospel to fresh converts. "If you had to pick just one desert-island food, you couldn't do much better than chia," McDougall wrote, "at least if you were interested in building muscle, lowering cholesterol, and reducing your risk of heart disease; after a few months on the chia diet, you could probably swim home." *Born to Run* quickly became a global sensation, selling millions of copies and igniting a fever in the jogging community. I remember being on a book tour in Buffalo, New York, and my chaperone was an enthusiastic jogger who couldn't stop talking about the book. He had tossed out his running shoes and had begun running in minimally supportive "barefoot" sandals (an entire industry that sprung up in the book's wake), and as I sat eating chicken wings at the Anchor Bar, he stirred a spoonful of chia seeds he kept in a plastic baggie into a glass of water and told me how I really should have written a book about running instead. Runners' message boards and websites filled up with enthusiastic discussions on chia seeds, and their use began growing in other athletic communities, which are early adopters of many health trends.

After *Born to Run* the market burst open with chia entrepreneurs. Janie Hoffman, an upbeat avocado and pineapple farmer from Southern California, heard about chia seeds from her personal trainer, who was using them instead of flax seeds because of their longer shelf life. She bottled chia fresca drinks (basically chia lemonade) and brought them to her yoga students, who couldn't get enough of them. In 2010 Hoffman launched the Mamma Chia line of beverages, promoting them with the above quote from *Born to Run* posted prominently on her website. Mamma Chia's first customer was all the Whole Foods stores in the southern Pacific region of the United States, where they sold so well that within a month they were distributed nationally throughout the chain—a major coup for any company, let alone a startup. Mamma Chia drinks are now available in thousands of stores around North America, including mainstream grocery retailers like Wegmans, Kroeger, and Safeway. A year after Mamma Chia's launch, Dan Gluck and Nick Morris, two young hedge fund financiers in New York with a passion for intense workouts, got into the business with Health Warrior, which marketed whole chia seeds and chia energy bars, initially to other type-A athletes who worked in finance. They sponsored 5 a.m. power workouts in Central Park, where they served chia drinks, granola with chia, and their Health Warrior bars. Wall Street traders got hooked on it and brought Health Warrior products to their offices, where they began leaning on chia as an energy boost during frantic days on the market—popping a handful of seeds or a Health Warrior bar to stay alert during marathon sessions of shorting derivatives like their predecessors had once done with coffee, Red Bull, and cocaine. Even the folks behind Chia Pet got into the act, launching a line of ch-ch-ch-chia Omega-3 seeds with their particular brand of low-budget, catchy TV commercials.

All of this threw the chia market, which had barely existed a few years before, into a frenzy, as increasing numbers of distributors, importers, and producers began buying up a finite amount of chia seeds. Sandra Gillot, the CEO of Benexia, a Chilean-based company that is one of the largest chia seed suppliers on the market, said that the demand went from "zero to a market that could take ten thousand tons of seeds, and the supply is only six thousand tons in a year." Several droughts and weather events affected chia crops in South America during these prime years, and chia's price, correspondingly, shot through the roof in 2012. With chia seeds selling for more money per pound than filet mignon and, in some cases, rising up to 30 percent in a few months, new suppliers rushed into the fray to try to capitalize on the chia boom. People began planting chia wherever it could grow, from countries like Peru and Bolivia to experiments in America and the Philippines. One of the largest growers to emerge was the Chia Co., which only began cultivating chia in Australia in 2003 when the company's founder, a fourth-generation Western Australian grain farmer named John Foss, discovered chia while studying global health food trends.

Dole came late to the chia market, but as often happens along the progression of food trends, their entry was a game changer. Prior to the slow launch of the Dole Nutrition Plus label, in late 2012 the players in chia products were relatively new entrepreneurs, like Mamma Chia, or natural foods specialty brands, like cereal maker Nature's Path and Hain Celestial, which mainly sell at health food stores and higher-end retailers, like Whole Foods. The Dole Food Company, in contrast, is a $7 billion, publicly traded juggernaut with operations in ninety countries and more than three hundred products sold globally in pretty much every supermarket and corner store. When a company like Dole dips their toe into chia, even tentatively, it's a clear indication that the trend has entered the mainstream. As recently as 2007 Larry Brown and his partners at Salba were banging on the doors of companies like Chiquita Banana and

General Mills to put chia into their products, without any luck. Now, if Dole succeeded with it, everyone else would surely jump aboard.

∾

A few weeks before visiting Dole's headquarters in California, I had flown to Kannapolis, North Carolina, a former mill town outside Charlotte that was best known as the home of the Earnhardt NASCAR racing dynasty. Since 2008 it has also been the location of the North Carolina Research Campus, an array of massive regency buildings where universities, big food corporations like General Mills and Monsanto, and healthcare organizations conduct research into health and nutrition. It was largely paid for by David H. Murdock, the ninety-one-year-old CEO and chairman of Dole, who plans to live well into his hundreds and has committed millions of dollars to finding a fountain of youth in the vegetables and fruits he sells. His eponymous research institute is the core of the campus, and there is significant space devoted to Dole's nutrition research laboratory, where the company conducts most of its studies on the nutritional content of the products it sells, from fruits and vegetables to more processed foods. Everything, it should be said, is decorated in Murdock's style, which is a mixture of oversized colonial architecture, golden elephant statues, and gigantic sun-drenched murals of fruit and vegetable spreads, including a rotunda with an eagle soaring through it—almost like a cross between a WPA food poster and a gaudy Macau casino.

Marty Ordman met me there, along with Nicholas Gillitt, a British scientist who heads up Dole's nutritional research laboratory, and Brad Bartlett, the company's vice president of packaged foods. A native of Virginia Beach, Bartlett had the broad shoulders, confident demeanor, and pencil-thin mustache of a major league baseball manager, which was common among food industry big shots, and he'd invited me to visit the facility to illustrate a key point in the chia trend's evolution. "It's one thing to show a nutrient in a fruit or vegetable," he said as we sat down at a conference table piled with Dole Nutrition Plus chia products, "but it's another to show how it changes health." Chia had grown to this point thanks to an aura around its purported benefits, but with Dole Nutrition Plus, the company was committed to backing up every single claim it made with its own scientific studies. "You get this mystique behind something without evidence, but then with research, it becomes true."

Gillitt began going through the results of his research so far, which had demonstrated that Omega-3 ALA levels (believed to control inflammation) had only gone up in subjects when the chia seeds were milled into a powder. Whole chia seeds were statistically no different in their effect from whole poppy seeds, which meant that milled chia was more nutritious for consumers. Another study showed that ALA levels in the blood peaked two and a half hours after eating milled chia and left the body six hours after consumption. Gillitt theorized and was trying to prove that this was converted to energy during the time it was in the body, lending evidence to the folklore that chia provides a natural sustained energy boost—something Bartlett said the company could easily market in products like squeeze packs, juices, and energy bars targeted to marathon runners, long-distance cyclists, and other athletes. These studies were the core of chia's future with Dole, and Gillitt wanted to have a new study constantly ongoing in the wings, waiting to be released in order to stoke fresh demand for the company's chia products and the trend.

Chia represented what the food industry calls a functional food, a growing segment of ingredients with purported health benefits, a food that can drive sales when integrated into other food products. Several years ago I visited a complex at the University of Manitoba in Winnipeg that dedicated itself to discovering and working with functional foods. At the time they were conducting large-scale trials on behalf of the Unilever margarine brand Becel, which was releasing a margarine with added plant sterols, a naturally occurring substance in vegetables that researchers believed could lower cholesterol. Test subjects came to the university each day to eat breakfast, which always included foods made with the sterol-fortified margarine (unless they were in the control group, who just got regular margarine). The study, which cost hundreds of thousands of dollars, measured the cholesterol levels of the subjects over various periods of time to see what effect the margarine would have.

This one study represented a minute fraction of the studies food companies were conducting around functional foods all over the world. Though most took place at universities in the name of health science, all of them were driven by the search for increased profit margins of the food companies who funded them. The increased awareness around chronic health problems, such as heart disease, diabetes, and cancers, had created a tremendous amount of confusion with consumers, who wanted to do something to improve their health but didn't necessarily know what. If a company could convince them that their product, whether it was Dole's chia clusters, Becel's proactive margarine, or the latest flavor of Vitamin Water, would make them healthier, they would be more inclined to buy it—and pay a premium while they did. Bartlett estimated that a product with functional ingredients could sell anywhere from 10 to 30 percent more than a similar one without, and in an industry in which careers were built on wrestling away fractions of a percentage from your competitor's market share, that advantage meant the world to grocery-shelf warriors like Bartlett. "We chose chia because of its nutritional versatility," Bartlett said. However, "to get big, chia has to go through the food supply more. It needs to be in chips, cereals, energy bars, clusters, squeeze packs," all of which were relying on the results of studies to drive consumers their way.

Food companies have relied on studies and science to take advantage of health trends for many decades. In the 1920s the Beech-nut Packing Company, one of America's major food producers with a big share of the bacon market, was concerned that Americans were eating lighter breakfasts, typically coffee, orange juice, and toast. To deal with this they contracted Edward Bernays, the so-called father of public relations and a master of marketing schemes. Bernays surveyed a number of doctors on whether they recommended a light breakfast or a hearty one that included bacon and eggs, and though the survey wasn't scientific (and Bernays had hand-picked the doctors), the hearty breakfast won out. Bernays then contacted scores of newspapers, which wrote stories about the medical "findings."

The resulting change—and not just for Beechnut—was that Americans read these stories and began eating bacon and eggs for breakfast so enthusiastically that their collective behavior changed to the point at which bacon and eggs is now the prototypical American breakfast meal. In her monumental book *Food Politics*, Marion Nestle, arguably the country's preeminent academic figure on nutrition and food policy, detailed the modern ways that large food companies have used studies and science to support questionable claims in order to sell products. In 1984 Kellogg's implied in ads and marketing material that its All-Bran cereal, which was high in fiber, could reduce the risk of cancer, resulting in a nearly 50 percent rise of All-Bran's market share, the supermarket equivalent of a lottery win. Gum makers claimed chewing gum cleaned teeth, Quaker had mustachioed actor Wilford Brimley scare the crap out of TV viewers as he admonished them to eat their oatmeal and prevent heart disease, and Tropicana claimed its calcium-enriched orange juice would build stronger bones in children and adolescents.

One of the best-publicized examples of a food company wielding studies to create a new health and diet trend is the case of POM Wonderful, a California company that turned the previously underappreciated pomegranate into a must-have life tonic for Baby Boomers and the health conscious. POM was the brainchild of Lynda Resnick and her husband Stewart, a pair of fantastically successful entrepreneurs who owned the Teleflora flower delivery company as well as kitsch emporium, the Franklin Mint, and later, Fiji Water. In 1987 Stewart had acquired a hundred acres of pomegranate trees in California and planted hundreds more over the years, selling most of the crop to California's Middle Eastern population, who used pomegranates for cooking and holiday decorations. The Resnicks wanted to increase the pomegranate's reach, and seeing the growth of the functional food market and health trends, they commissioned costly studies at universities in America and globally to isolate the health properties of pomegranates. In her memoir, *Rubies in the Orchard*, Resnick recounts the results of the early studies, stating it was "jawdropping. Among the first findings: pomegranate juice inhibits inflammation and pain. In addition, pomegranates turn out to be astonishingly rich in antioxidants, which inhibit oxidization of the body that can damage cells." Pomegranates contained more antioxidants than "just about anything else known to humankind. In addition, the fruit was shown to reduce arterial plaque and factors leading to atherosclerosis. Subsequent studies suggested that pomegranates have a powerful effect against prostate cancer." Further studies the company commissioned showed positive effects that could even impact diabetes, erectile dysfunction, and other ailments.

The company took these studies and turned them around, using the preliminary findings to heavily promote POM brand juices, antioxidant teas, supplements, energy bars, iced coffee, and fresh pomegranates with a flurry of advertising and far-reaching promises. I remember seeing posters in the New York subway all the time with slogans like, "Cheat Death," with a torn noose around the telltale curvaceous bottle's neck, "Death Defying" as the bottle straddled a tight rope, and "Life Support," with the bottle feeding an intravenous line. Another had the bottle rocketing through the sky, like a comic book superhero, claiming, "I'm off to save PROSTATES!" an ad that included a small link to the actual study itself. Suddenly POM juice, pomegranates, and antioxidants were everywhere, as the Resnick's turned the fruit into a multimillion-dollar business, unleashing dozens of pomegranate-hawking competitors. For several years, when I went to my parents' house for dinner, there was invariably a bottle of POM in the fridge and pomegranate seeds sprinkled over the salad. Chefs were basting chicken in pomegranate syrup, and bakeries were flavoring muffins with it. Everyone, from those selling pomegranate-flavored products to those eating them, boasted of its antioxidants and benefits, which expanded the trend to other fruits and foods as produce growers, importers, and distributors sought a slice of this fast-growing market.

Then Chinese goji berries were added to cereal and candy, and an entire industry sprang up around the exports of Brazil's açai berry, a bitter purple Amazonian fruit pronounced *ass-eye-E*. I had lived in Rio de Janeiro for a couple of months back in 2005 and ate bowls of sweetened, frozen açai slush for breakfast after surfing, but when I returned to Canada that same year it was basically unknown. Fast forward three years, and açai was everywhere—in juices, in granola bars, in pills and powders, and even at the hamburger chain Wendy's, which featured a salad dressing with açai juice in it. Maine blueberry farmers rode a surge of demand from studies that showed blueberries were antioxidant rich, and everyone from Ecuadorian goldenberry exporters to California's Walnut marketers tried to get a piece of the antioxidant action by tying their product marketing to health claims (remember Glenn Roberts talking about the antioxidant potential of China Black?). The market research group Packaged Facts estimates that by 2016 the American antioxidant product market, ranging from pomegranate juices and snack bars, to açai-flavored cosmetics and supplements, will be as big as $86 billion in annual sales

The media has played a tremendous role in growing the "superfood" trend through a fairly predictable cycle. Someone like POM, Kellogg, or Dole would submit a food to a study, and the results of that study would be distilled down to a press-friendly message, which newspapers, magazines, blogs, and morning news shows would deliver verbatim. Studies show that pomegranates contain X and other studies show that X can possibly help with Y, therefore, pomegranates/açai/blueberries/chia could help—hey, maybe even cure—Y. No one traffics in this type of messaging as enthusiastically or successfully as the celebrity physician Dr. Mehmet Oz. The cardiac surgeon began combining Western medical advice with naturopathic therapies in the 1990s and first authored a book on the subject in 1999, advocating a balanced lifestyle of exercise and diet to help with common chronic health problems. He became a household name as a regular guest on the *Oprah Winfrey Show* and *Larry King Live* and has hosted the highly rated *Dr. Oz Show* since 2009. It is almost impossible to walk by a supermarket checkout and not see his handsome face, dressed in dark blue scrubs (with plunging v-neck collar), grinning down from a national magazine cover, including his own magazine *Dr. Oz: The Good Life*, which launched earlier this year.

More often than not his show's viewers will find Dr. Oz talking about the top five, ten, or fifteen superfoods we need to be eating to stop aging or cancer or heart disease, sometimes by himself, and sometimes with regular guests like Dr. John La Puma, his superfoods guru. Oz has pumped up pumpkin seeds ("A food rich in magnesium that helps lower blood pressure and reduces your risk for heart attacks or stroke"), lobbied for leeks ("Just about any part of the allium family has been shown to reduce various types of cancers, including stomach and colorectal cancer, prostate and breast cancers as well as a number of other common cancers"), and touted tahini ("Tahini is made from sesame seeds, a rich source of zinc. And zinc may increase the production of leptin, a hormone that improves metabolism and curbs appetite.")

He has also cheered for chia. In 2008, appearing on the *Oprah Winfrey Show*, Dr. Oz told women to include chia seeds in their diet (in this case, baked into pumpkin muffins) for their fiber, magnesium, calcium, and Omega-3 fatty acids. In 2011 he said, "chia can substitute for whole grains in your diet . . . which helps stabilize blood sugar levels in your diet," and in 2012 he said, "this is the year when you must add chia to your diet," calling them the "latest superseed" that are a "must-have supplement to your diet" and asking, "is it possible chia seeds have superseded other superfoods?" The effect Oz's endorsement has had on the chia trend can't be understated. He is to superfoods as his mentor Oprah once was to books: If Dr. Oz tells his audience to eat chia, you can bet they'll go out and buy chia seeds the next day. "Without a doubt he's done a lot to elevate the awareness of chia," said Mamma Chia's owner, Janie Hoffman. "I can't tell you how many people said, 'Oh yeah, I heard Dr. Oz talk about this!' Even more than *Born to Run*, he's been the most instrumental in this. He moves needles, without a doubt." Dole has approached Dr. Oz's people to see whether he will promote the Dole Nutrition Plus product line on his show, and seed-exporter Benexia has also worked with his production company to increase the seed's visibility through his endorsement. In the health world today he is the single-most important tastemaker in setting trends.

Inevitably, this has led to substantial criticism about the credibility of Dr. Oz's pronouncements and, indeed, the veracity of the whole notion of superfoods. To many, what Dr. Oz and other superfood proponents are promoting is ultimately for the greater good: By emphasizing particularly healthful whole foods, they are encouraging people to eat better and more consciously. With so many people in Western countries eating too few fruits and vegetables and too much processed packaged snack foods, the downside from Dr. Oz telling you to eat more chia is far outweighed by the good he's doing. But the idea that there are foods so fundamentally nutritious that they should be eaten in tremendous quantities worries many in the nutrition field. "It's a marketing device," Marion Nestle told me in an e-mail when I asked her about superfoods. "Nutritionists like me don't recognize any one food as especially super. All unprocessed foods contain a huge range of nutrients but in varying proportions. That's why healthful diets are supposed to contain a range of foods with complementary nutrient contents. The 'super' designation usually depends on one nutrient or a category of nutrients (antioxidants are a good example). All fruits and vegetables contain antioxidants, so by that standard all are superfoods. This is about marketing, not health."

We also buy into a narrative, present in each of these health trends, that simplifies a complicated lifestyle down to a single ingredient. The seductive power of many of these superfoods lies in their place in remote, somewhat mystical cultures. Whether it's the longevity of Greek goat herders, Okinawan fishermen, Amazonian tribesmen, or Mexican tribal joggers, the tremendous difference between their health and ours has a hell of a lot more to do with the fact that we drive cars, sit at computers, and have access to super-sized sodas than the fact that they eat yogurt, salmon, açaí, or chia. (It is also much easier to romanticize these exotic lifestyles rather than, say, actually herd goats every day.) Superfoods exist simply to sell more pomegranates, chia seeds, or other foods that are good for us, even if they are not the fountain of youth. And the inevitability with any of these labels is that they are abused.

POM's boastful claims about the power of pomegranates eventually led to a massive lawsuit from the Federal Trade Commission, which ruled that they amounted to false advertising, a case of pure chutzpah extrapolating weak science in order to push more bottles of juice. "The greater weight of the persuasive expert testimony demonstrates that there is insufficient competent and reliable scientific evidence to substantiate claims that the Pom products treat, prevent or reduce the risk of erectile dysfunction or that they are clinically proven to do so," a federal judge wrote in his 2012 decision in issuing a twenty-year cease-and-desist order on the type of advertising POM had used to build their market. The European Union went a step further, in 2007 banning outright the use of the term "superfood" unless it is backed by a specific authorized health claim explaining why the product is beneficial to the health of consumers and making clear the effect of other ingredients as well.

If that sounds draconian, keep in mind that most of us know very little about the science behind nutrition and so these buzzwords are powerful drivers. When you have a half-hour to buy groceries, and your kid is screaming in the shopping cart, you're not going to search a number of peer-reviewed studies on your phone while debating what cereal to buy. More likely, you'll pick up the one that says it's enriched with antioxidants or chia, because you heard somewhere those are superfoods, and you don't want to die of cancer, right? Which is how something like clinical research into the effects of antioxidants on various ailments turns into a trend and filters down the food chain until you get a product like 7-Up Antioxidant Cherry, which contains no juices but the same massive amount of refined corn syrup as regular 7-Up. Yes, that is a real product, launched by beverage maker Dr. Pepper Snapple Group in 2009 and removed from shelves in 2013 in the face of a class-action lawsuit alleging false advertising.

"Consumers believe that food is medicine or food can be a silver bullet that cures what ails them," said Dr. Bruce Chassy, professor emeritus of food science and human nutrition at the University of Illinois and a fierce critic of the superfoods trend. "They're looking for a magic food to make them healthier, happier, wealthier. Those foods probably don't exist, and while diet changes can help you, I doubt chia or any other food can have any more than a marginal effect. It's no different from nineteenth-century snake oil salesmen. It's got a better coat of varnish on it, but no different."

"From a nutrition educator's point of view, it's 'Here we go again,'" said Chassy regarding each new health and diet trend that emerges. "The message is: eat a balanced diet in moderation, which is totally counter to the message of a superfood, which is basically saying, 'eat one thing as much as possible.'" We want to have our cake and eat it, too, and now with chia flour cake mix (selling at twice the price of a normal cake mix), we can eat it without feeling guilty. "What Dr. Oz is doing is very, very bad because it reinforces the mistaken belief that there's a magic answer. The magic answer, you've heard it all! Get sleep, exercise, get a balanced diet. That's what the scientific literature supports. Every time Dr. Oz sells you blueberries and pomegranates, he's selling you snake oil."

University research into superfoods, whether Dole's work with chia or others looking into olive oil, Greek yogurt, or apples, is diverting attention and resources away from more pressing problems, basically wasting the time of nutrition faculties who gladly accept the funds to conduct studies into margarine's efficacy in lowering cholesterol. It is research that will not fundamentally help humanity aside from those who own shares in Unilever or Kellogg's. Chassy even questioned the value of antioxidants, which may ultimately have some benefit to human health, but this has not been proven in a way that justifies their widespread adoption as a health trend. "We're so used to antioxidants being added to products by producers who believe it'll sell . . . it becomes part of the food culture. Even though the science hasn't continued to point to real efficacy, it just becomes a matter of fact."

Back at Dole, Bartlett and Gillitt are fully aware of this, and they are as disdainful of the superfood label's overreach as anyone else. For now Dole is proceeding with caution around chia, rolling it out in the rather reserved Dole Nutrition Plus line and only making specific claims that the studies they've conducted in house can back up. They're not going to claim Dole's chia clusters are curing cancer anytime soon or that they'll allow you to run a marathon. The market will dictate chia's adoption on a wide scale, both at the supply level (prices remain high and the crop is in such demand that Dole is experimenting with growing their own chia on banana plantations) and at the consumer level, at which people are only willing to pay so much extra for their food. Down the road that might mean that Dole has to put out products with lower levels of chia in them in order to achieve a realistic balance between effective amounts of the seed (which can have a measurable effect on the body) and an amount that won't make their products too expensive for consumers. The danger is that other companies come in and sprinkle a bit of chia seed onto their products to boost sales. Already, ConAgra, the largest processed food manufacturer in the world, was selling an ancient grain flour with chia seeds, and consumer research group Mintel reported a 78 percent increase, compared to the year before, in products with chia in 2012. Though the market at that point was just over $10 million in the United States, Dole already controlled 14 percent of it, and competition was only going to increase as companies piled on to the chia trend's bandwagon.

"It gets saturated at some point," said Barlett. "When Coca-Cola puts it in their drinks, you're probably done. You hate to see it. It creates confusion and draws other products into question. If chia really takes off, the odds start moving that way."

With so much of the American population eating poorly and lacking in even basic nutrition, Dole's success with chia could hopefully encourage more people to be conscious of what they're ingesting and maybe even introduce some better eating habits. "Now only three percent of the US population has tried chia," Barlett said over lunch at a nearby health food restaurant owned by David Murdock, and he believes that even if it takes off as a diet trend in the way that flax did, the price will ensure it will remain a niche. "It is a wonderful, versatile, truly super food, but it is not like you can't get Omega-3, fiber, iron, and calcium from a lot of other less expensive food products. "

Barlett is reassuringly careful. But listening to Chassy, Nestle, and others, I have a hard time not sneering at chia or the latest diet trend. The constant parade of special ingredients and the back and forth between theories so often disproven is exhausting, and maybe the most valuable lesson of goat herders and desert runners and fishermen is that they eat real foods and balanced diets that include—gasp!—things like gluten. It is not a matter of antioxidant-enhanced soda but an actual piece of fruit that just happens to contain antioxidants. Yet when we go back to the grocery store, there are all the latest fads, exerting their pull on our brains.

PART II

HOW TRENDS BREAK OUT

5

SALES

AWARDS NIGHT

T
he crowd on the narrow balcony, high above the ballroom of the Walter E. Washington Convention Center in Washington, DC, was milling about nervously, like a living pantry. New York picklers in jeans and T-shirts were talking with Italian balsamic vinegarites in tuxedos. A baker of sweet potato crackers, dressed in cargo shorts and a Hawaiian T-shirt, was sipping a beer next to Carrie Morey, a blonde biscuit maker from Charleston, South Carolina, who had just changed into a form-fitting cocktail dress and put on makeup as though this were prom night. "I'm nervous," Morey said. "Definitely I've got some butterflies going on."

"I feel like a kid," said Juan Figueroa, a Spanish cheese monger, dressed in finely pressed linen slacks as though he was about to board a yacht. "I'm so nervous, I'm shivering."

In a quiet corner, thirty-year-old married couple Louisa Conrad and Lucas Farrell, goat dairy farmers from Vermont, were the impossibly cute poster children for sustainable agricultural idealism. They gazed over the balcony at the sweeping red carpet cutting through the ballroom. At its foot rose a grand stage topped by the giant golden figure of a sculpted chef with a chafing dish, flanked on both sides by rows of smaller statues, each cast in the same image. Louisa looked down at her phone, flipping through photographs of her goats, as Lucas chatted with Sanjog Sikand, an Indian food magnate from San Francisco who wore a bright blue sari under her orange T-shirt, which was splashed with the logo for Sukhi's, the company her mother had founded.

The hundred or so people on the balcony were all nominees for the sofi™ awards, a distinction that stands for specialty outstanding food innovation, and receiving one is the highest honor the specialty food industry bestows on food products. Conrad and Farrell were here because the gooey, lush goat's milk caramels made by their new company Big Picture Farm had been selected from thousands of entries submitted from around the world to compete for a gold sofi in the confection category. They faced off against Theo Chocolate's artisan caramels, Indie Candy's mango-flavored "Jackie Lanterns," and mints in tropical mango flavor served in something called an "Eco Twist Tube" from Sencha Naturals.

"We haven't slept in weeks," said Conrad, who is a slender, freckly redhead with J.Crew catalog looks, as she nervously peeled the label off her beer bottle. "Just producing enough caramel for this event was a lot." Her arm still ached from hours of hand stirring in addition to all the milking, herding, wrapping, boxing, and shipping they'd done in preparation for this weekend. "Well," said her equally hunky husband, Farrel, "the goats bore the brunt of it."

Just then the ballroom's doors opened, and hundreds of friends, supporters, and spectators filed in and took their seats as the band kicked up a furious set of smooth, elevator-approved bossa nova. An announcer stepped to the podium, welcomed everyone, and asked that they turn their attention to the rear of the hall and give a big round of applause to welcome the 2012 sofi nominees. Ushers with headsets began signaling everyone on the balcony that this was their moment, and as the assembled nominees descended the two curved staircases and made their way down the red carpet to vigorous applause (plus a few catcalls and wolf whistles), they looked like a graduating class heading out to conquer the world.

☙

Every industry in America, from carbon trading to magazine publishing, hosts its own back-slapping awards night. These boozy events, complete with Oscar-inspired statues and contrived glamour, rarely matter much to the world outside. The sofi awards, which happen during the final night of the Summer Fancy Food Show, an annual trade fair for fine food producers and buyers put on by the Specialty Food Association (formerly the National Association of the Specialty Food Trade), at first glance appear to be no different. But as gourmet food trends increasingly shape what we're finding in mainstream grocery aisles—a cupcake in every oven, a chia seed on each plate, so to speak—the sofis have become a kind of fancy foods kingmaker, a gateway to the aisles of grocery stores and, ultimately, your dinner plate. A sofi win now brings instant credibility and brand recognition to a food product and its producer and, most often, a corresponding increase in orders from retailers as well as a lift to similar products in that category.

The Specialty Food Association, which is based in New York, is a nonprofit trade group that is over sixty years old. It represents both producers of specialty packaged food and beverages (like teas and chocolates) as well as the stores that sell them. The first Fancy Food Show took place in 1955, with a small number of visitors showing off mostly imported European goods. Because specialty foods are a business dominated by small, independent producers and small, independent stores, the show provided a valuable service by gathering everyone in one place, streamlining contact between buyers and sellers while also allowing the industry to network. It was a relatively rarefied affair, as boutique producers of cheeses and chocolates sold to the select fancy markets that carried their products. These foods were called "specialty" for a reason; they were almost exclusively eaten by well-traveled and well-financed eaters who knew their French wines by region, their cheeses by scent, and their personal chefs by name. They were the gourmands, a small, often insufferable subspecies of Western civilization, prone to ascots and general snobbery. If they weren't European by lineage, they were by association. Real North Americans (with the exception of Quebec and Louisiana) didn't fret about food; instead, they drank cold beer and liked big steaks. Anyone else was referred to, with no small dose of derision, as "foodies," usually preceded by the word "fussy."

Ever since the 1980s, however, this began to change, as the culture of specialty food, and that of the foodies who drove it, became more and more mainstream. Thanks to increased travel and immigration, culinary influences and flavors from beyond continental Europe began occupying an increasingly prominent place on the North American dinner plate. Sushi began as a rare, often terrifying luxury and evolved into a casual meal and style of preparation that soon blanketed global menus. Bold ingredients like wasabi, soy sauce, curry, and jalapeño soon became commonplace. Driven by California's posthippie farm movement, freshness and seasonality eventually became buzzwords that found their way onto fast food menus as big as McDonald's. Salads went from a wedge of iceberg with bacon and Thousand Island dressing to a multibillion-dollar organic mixed greens industry, turning balsamic vinegar and extra virgin olive oil into all-American condiments that were mandatory on every table. By the first decade of the twenty-first century, the foodies had shed their exclusivity along with their bowties and then conquered mass culture, as popular television chefs like Anthony Bourdain, Emeril Lagasse, and even Guy Fieri made it socially acceptable for men to sit around a campfire, talking about the proper way to brown meat for a stock.

Today your average suburban supermarket now carries a vastly greater variety of foods, flavors, and products than it did just two decades back. Just think of the selection of barbecue sauces in your local supermarket or the size of the mustard section, and you have an inkling of how much specialty food has penetrated your palate. Where once stood the single, perfect variety of Heinz ketchup, today you'll find balsamic, jalapeño, organic, salt-free, reduced sugar, and all-natural varieties from Heinz in addition to the other ketchup competitors that have sprung up in flavors ranging from curry to cranberry. These aren't just sold at specialty shops like Dean and Deluca; they're in average supermarkets like Ralph's, Wegmans, Safeway, and even big-box fixtures like Walmart and Costco, which even carries its own brand of single-malt scotch.

In the United States the specialty food market is estimated to generate over $80 billion in sales a year, according to the Specialty Food Association's own figures. And although that is still less than Proctor and Gamble's annual revenue, specialty food experienced sales growth of over 20 percent between 2010 and 2012, in an industry in which category growth rarely edges out of the low single digits. Specialty food brings in the hottest elements of the business, from local, natural, and organic products to health and diet lines, ethnic imports, and energy drinks. It's the elite of your shopping cart, the cool stuff that you really want to buy while you're stocking up on bananas and milk and eggs, but it has now profoundly affected every aspect of our food culture. When conservative, blue chip–packaged food companies like Kraft have spent untold piles of cash making their processed luncheon meats look more "natural" by engineering ways to make turkey slices appear as though they were hand carved, specialty has become every day. Where it once would have taken the better part of a decade for these niche foods to trickle down from the specialty food stores to the mainstream supermarket customer, the increased competitiveness of the grocery business coupled with the rapid spread of foodie culture has sent the big grocers deeper into the world of specialty foods, looking for the next trend to sell to their customers. They want something different, something that will drive shoppers into their stores. And so each summer these buyers come in great numbers to the Fancy Food Show, where the grocery business spends three days filling their carts with what will eventually appear on their shelves. It's where the supermarket goes to shop for food trends.

During the 2012 Fancy Food Show (which took place in DC because the show's usual home in New York was undergoing renovations) 2,250 specialty food purveyors from around the world filled a convention hall the size of several city blocks, offering samples of over 150,000 products. Turkish olive oil farmers, corporate Greek yogurt salesmen, and praline cookin' Texas housewives spread out over 700,000 square feet, vying for the attention of distributors and retailers ranging from independent stores, like Liberty Heights Fresh in Salt Lake City, to national chains like Costco. Attendees tasted products ranging from grapefruit campari sorbet, organic pistachio butter, and oat breakfast drinks to a tonic water specifically formulated to go with premium vodka, along with countless fine cheeses, heritage hams, and every single possible variant of chocolate.

The floor of the Fancy Food Show is a veritable orgy of food trends on the market and in the making, each thrust at you by their eager backers, who insist that their product is the thing that is going to change the way we eat. Inside a thirty-foot radius you can put the following items into your body in under a minute: duck prosciutto, Haribo gummy bears, a shot of espresso, aged blue cheese, a shot of raspberry kombucha, four different Argentinean olive oils, dried Spanish figs, kale chips, cayenne shortbread, a spoonful of red pepper–flavored Greek yogurt, and a boozy whisky gelato ice pop. You've hardly noticed one exotic bite before the next pops up before your eyes, like a tasting menu served at warp speed, with barely enough time to swallow in between. It is like nothing I have ever experienced as an eater—and trust me, I have been eating my whole life.

In many ways the Fancy Food Show is a giant science fair for food trends, past and present. There were hundreds of hopeful, independent startups, premiering their wares for the first time to a vast audience, hoping to land a big account and see their idea take off into a trend. They tended to have the smallest booths, often in the crowded centers of the aisles or off in the corners of the basement, where the lighting was dim. Some had hand-drawn signs and decorations they'd made themselves, but what they lacked in polish they made up for in enthusiasm and pie-eyed hunger. They sold products that included iced rice teas and gourmet jerky, beer-flavored crackers and Himalayan salt shot glasses. Shortly after arriving I met first-time show attendees Back to the Roots, an Oakland, California, company that was selling grow-your-own-mushroom kits with more vigor than a carnival barker. Nikhil Arora and Alejandro Velez started the company when they were seniors at the University of Berkeley. After hearing in a lecture that it was possible to grow gourmet mushrooms out of used coffee grounds, the two began growing mushrooms in their frat house kitchen. Though Arora and Velez were destined for consulting and investment banking, after nine months of experiments they abandoned those certain futures for fungi. "It was awesome," said Arora with a huge smile as he held up a box of mushrooms for anyone who walked by their booth. "I mean, we walked the first bucket of mushrooms we had into Chez Panisse and Whole Foods when we were still students." Back to the Roots had been nominated for its first-ever sofi award, in the Best Gift category, and Arora was proudly displaying the silver statue all nominees received (gold statues are awarded to winners on the final night of the show). "It adds legitimacy right away. We're not just two crazy kids selling shrooms," he said, making sure I knew just how pumped he was for the awards ceremony.

The goat caramel couple, Louisa Conrad and Lucas Farrell, from Big Picture Farms, had their table in an aisle with other Vermont producers. Their exquisitely soft goat's milk caramels, in vanilla bean and chai flavors, were cut up into little cubes and displayed on dark wood boards, which they'd stained themselves. On the table behind them sat a mix of homespun decorations, from tin milk pails to portraits of their goats that Conrad had illustrated by hand. The two had met at college in Vermont back in 2000, and after graduating they remained in the state, where Conrad pursued a successful career in photography and fine art while Farrell wrote poetry and taught at a nearby college (sigh). Though Conrad was raised on the concrete pastures of New York's tony Upper East Side, the two began an apprenticeship at the goat farm of one of Farrell's students and quickly fell in love with it. In 2010, after their wedding, they acquired some property and three goats (they put milking equipment on their wedding registry) and began making cheese from the milk. Shortly after, they began experimenting with goat's milk caramels, which are common in Mexico but almost entirely unknown in the United States. With their rich, creamy texture and clean, sweet flavor, Farrell and Conrad believed that the caramels they made were simply the best in the world, and this was their first time at the Fancy Food Show—or any food show, for that matter— as well as the first time they were nominated for any award. Less than a year before, Farrell and Conrad had been cooking their caramel in their home kitchen, hand stirring a pot for hours on end and delivering the final product to five local customers. Now they had fifty customers around the region and were at the show to see whether there was more interest for their caramels, which they still wrapped by hand. "We're limited because we only have twelve goats now," Conrad said, talking sweetly about each of their personalities like they were her children. The company's silver sofi award was displayed proudly next to the caramels, and Conrad and Farrell were nervously awaiting the results of the gold awards later that night. They had already used the nomination to help secure a USDA loan to purchase their farm, which they were closing on in ten days. If they could clinch the award, the future was bright. Theirs was a Cinderella story in the making.

∾

Based on the backgrounds of many new companies at the show, selling everything from chia seed cookies to fine cheeses, a prior career in corporate law or investment banking seemed to be the main prerequisite for starting a specialty food company. The dynamic at play was the same one that saw so many cupcakeries popping up in the wake of the financial crisis, helmed by corporate refugees with Ivy League degrees. The attraction to the food business, though difficult, costly, and cutthroat, is that it is also incredibly fun, and if you have an idea that people will eat, the potential is limitless. The Fancy Food Show was where these dreamers could look across the aisle and see those who had once been in their shoes, had succeeded in establishing trends, and were now market leaders with billions of dollars in sales each year. Companies like Jelly Belly jellybeans, Fage Greek yogurt, and Kashi grains didn't just have their food displayed at booths for the show; instead, they had erected entire pavilions, complete with custom carpeting, arrays of televisions, lounge seating, and dozens of company representatives in matching polo shirts or suits, there to handle every sales inquiry and opportunity from buyers all around the world.

Of course, this is the era of global trade, and the international community brings its own flurry of activity to the Fancy Food

Show each year, paid for by the governments of nearly every food-producing country and region, aiming to entice North American buyers. These range from small booths displaying the seeds of an obscure African country, such as Zambia, to massive pavilions like Chile's, which featured a lounge with dozens of companies selling everything from wine to oil to pisco mix and a huge food truck dispensing Chilean meals. Not only did each nation's presence reflect their spot on the global hierarchy of food trends; they were also a mirror into their culture, like food-based exhibits at Disney's Epcot Center. The first one I encountered was Canada, my home and native land. Despite the abundance of terrific specialty food companies here, producing everything from craft beers to salad dressings and artisan breads, my government decided to showcase unprocessed hemp seeds from Manitoba and a company selling glass containers. In fact, one well-known Canadian cracker company took a booth far away from the Canada pavilion so they wouldn't be associated with our country's milquetoast effort. Nearby, in Mexico, salsas, tequilas, and minitacos freely flowed from big, colorful booths, and Mexican producers clearly believed there were few products that couldn't benefit from a tightly clad, attractive, female spokesperson. The Brazilians were still pushing the açai health trend hard, displaying it in candy, drinks, liquor, and cereal, even though much of the American market had already moved on. Over in Argentina a smattering of booths promoting chia seeds, olive oils, and dulce de leche were left unmanned for long periods of time as the Argentines observed their customary two-hour lunch.

Most countries seemed almost to be courting their national stereotypes, especially the Europeans. The United Kingdom booth was set up with understated displays of shortbread cookies, cheddars, and other finger foods from her majesty's island, accented by a pile of Wales/USA friendship flag pins. Germany's precision engineering was on display in perfect arrangements of Ritter Sport chocolates and erectly postured trade representatives sitting in sharply tailored suits and with modern, angular glasses. The financial crisis hadn't really affected the Greeks, whose bounty of olives, oils, and stuffed grape leaves attracted constant activity as other Greeks popped by for samples like it was a village market. Next in store was Italy, usually the strongest pavilion in the hall of nations (the Italians basically established the specialty food market in America), with the country's gorgeous men and women sporting pristine suits as they poured out shots of limoncello and carved huge chunks off parmesan wheels. Then, on Sunday afternoon, when it was time for Italy to play Ireland in the Euro Cup, all the men disappeared to a booth in the rear with a large television, leaving their women, once again, to do all the work.

Portugal's austerity in the wake of the Euro crisis must have had an impact on their presence, because they ended up with one unaffiliated booth decorated with a homemade flag—even the Palestinians outdid them. No one in Africa or the Middle East outdid Morocco, however. Among that country's plushly carpeted lounges was a bevy of TVs that didn't show anything and several ornate fountains like you would find in the courtyard of a palace but dispensing fresh pear juice. The Japanese, it seemed, were out to create a parody of Japaneseness, with samples of sake, beer, and kangaroo-shaped cookies displayed like objects in a museum. Many of their vendors wore traditional robes, and the whole Japanese pavilion was being filmed, constantly, by enthusiastic Japanese TV crews. Thankfully, they weren't too close to their South Korean rivals, who brought their Fancy Food A-game, offering up freshly fried persimmon jam–stuffed donuts, bulgogi sliders, and flavored dry seaweed snacks thrust into every hand and bag from promoters who fanned out all around the show.

By far my favorite section belonged to China, simply for its sheer disconnect with the audience at the Fancy Food Show. Despite China's glorious food culture, its booth seemed to reflect almost no taste at all. The largest international contingent by far, spread out over four separate areas, China's delegation featured companies with incongruous names like Ningbo Glory International Corporation and Shaanxi Yiyexuan Ecology and Science and Technology Co. Ltd., all of whom occupied tables and chairs in sparse booths. These were decorated with photographs of factories and stock pictures of food products (grains of rice, a tanker ship), additives, and, in one case, a tribute to Lei Feng, apparently a People's Liberation Army hero and icon of the Chinese Communist Party who died at twenty-two when he was struck by a falling telephone pole and was so beloved by the booth's sponsor that he had dedicated his entire space to him despite the fact that Feng had absolutely no connection to food whatsoever. Chinese samples were sparse and unappetizing—a few nuts in a bowl or some unlabeled candies—though my favorite was a large baking sheet, covered in tomato paste, with a single plastic spoon resting in it. "Please," the tray practically beckoned, "enjoy all the tomato paste from Ghanzhou Trading and Chemical Corporation you can eat. Now 98 percent formaldehyde-free."

In Ecuador's brightly colored area I met up with David Bermeo, who had recently taken over his family's fragrance and ingredient business, which had lost its biggest account when Nestlé moved its regional soup production to Chile. Bermeo had repositioned Terrafertil to exclusively sell dried fruits and was here at the Fancy Food Show to talk up the potential of the goldenberry. Grown in the Andes and also known as the *uvilla*, or Peru cherry, goldenberries are best known as the deep yellow, perfectly round, tart fruits with the papery husk that regularly garnish molten chocolate cakes and other wedding desserts. Bermeo believed that dried goldenberries had the market potential to become the next cranberry, and he saw his company's future as a goldenberry version of Ocean Spray, sold under the name Nature's Heart. Terrafertil already owned 90 percent of the world's goldenberry market share, but people weren't going to buy them in the volume he wanted unless they believed goldenberries were good for them. In other words, Bermeo needed to create a health trend. Already they had hired PR firms in the UK to pitch the goldenberry to press, and in 2011 Dr. Oz had mentioned it on his show. That had raised awareness in the United States significantly, and sales had tripled since, which is why Bermeo was here, trying to capitalize on that momentum. "You can spend millions on PR for these products," he said, pointing out one of the roving teams handing out Korean seaweed snacks, "and it still tastes like seawater. In agricultural products it's not like selling iPhones. You want to take it step by step."

❦

Every exhibitor at the show, whether they were mom-and-pop startups like Big Picture farms or international market leaders like Twinings Tea, were there to attract the attention of the tastemakers in attendance. These include restaurant consultants, corporate chefs, and distributors. There were also representatives from large food corporations, such as Kraft and Proctor and Gamble, who came to encounter the latest trends, assess potential companies they could acquire, and find ideas that they could emulate. The show is covered by hundreds of reporters ranging from mainstream culinary magazines like *Food & Wine* and *Martha Stewart Living* to national outlets like CBS, NPR, and the *New York Times* as well as plenty of trade industry publications, including *Food Safety Magazine* and *Candy Industry*. Overwhelmingly the most important and numerous tastemakers at the show are the buyers from grocery stores. They walk the aisles, looking for new products and ideas, almost as though they were cruising their own stores with a shopping cart, plucking the latest trends off the shelves.

As I waited to enter the show on the first morning, I bumped into Sergio Hernandez, an acquaintance who owns BKLYN Larder, a small but well-known specialty food store in Brooklyn. On the train ride down from New York that morning Hernandez had gone through the list of vendors with his partner, Francie Stephens, flagging those they already sold and those they were interested in checking out, based around products they needed in certain categories (e.g., a new chocolate or olive oil). "Once we get inside, we start walking the aisles," Hernandez said, setting off toward an Italian importer to taste a dozen fruit vinegars. Omnivorousness was helpful, but Hernandez had to be discerning. "You can systematically walk up and down every single aisle, but you'll be exhausted and taste stuff you don't like." Later on I met up with Ari Weinzweig, one of the cofounders of Zingerman's, a specialty food empire in Ann Arbor, Michigan, who had been coming to the show for thirty years, looking for the full-flavored, traditional foods his stores, restaurants, and national mail-order business built its reputation on.

"With the web and e-mail, this show is a lot easier to navigate," Weinzweig said, striding briskly through the aisles on his long legs. As he went by, people called out to him from booths left and right, and occasionally he'd stop to grab a sample or take a small bite, but most of the time he just kept on moving. "My method is to start on one end and take notes till I run out of time. You have to suspend all eating convention. It's not a good way to do it, but it is the only way to do it." Finally, he planted his feet at the booth of Taza Chocolate, a Massachusetts company that specialized in Mexican-style stone-ground chocolates. "Where's the salt and pepper one?" Weinzweig asked the woman behind the booth. "I've tried it before, but I want to try it again, even though I sell their stuff. With chocolate, you have to taste it, because like olive oil, everyone pretty much says the same thing to describe their product." Companies will tell Weinzweig something is "artisanal" and "traditional" and "handcrafted," but rarely do they actually tell him how it tastes. The salt-and-pepper chocolate tasted just as you'd expect . . . like you'd sprinkled salt and pepper on a good-quality chocolate bar, which was too jarring and confusing for me, but Weinzweig swore there were people who wanted that.

Each buyer on the floor was out there, tasting and sampling and schmoozing so they could identify the next trend that would appeal to their customer base. People like Hernandez and Weinzweig looked for small, independent producers who could offer completely unique tastes, because the people who shopped in their stores were the most educated, affluent food consumers in the country, and they expected to consistently be wowed by what was out there. At the other end of the spectrum, wearing branded polo shirts and crisp pleated slacks, were buyers from national supermarket chains and big-box retailers like Wegmans, Costco, and Walmart. As mainstream tastes grew more complex and sophisticated over the past several decades these stores had begun offering more variety in their grocery shelves with specialty foods. Although wealthy gourmands do shop at Costco and Walmart, their average buyer at their checkout counters tends to pick up on food trends much later in the cycle. That's why sea salt caramels will first appear in a small specialty market like BKLYN Larder years before you can buy them in a big tub at Costco. In the years that trend takes to trickle down, it will move from online and farmer's market sales to a selection of regional specialty food stores, then smaller chains until the trend is poised to enter the final stage before reaching the mass market: Whole Foods.

The Austin, Texas–based premium grocery chain is the key bridge between the niche market of independent specialty food producers and big-box grocery. Its importance in the evolutionary cycle of food trends is hard to exaggerate. Whole Foods works with small companies, helping them scale their business to supply larger markets while also providing the type of exposure that's impossible to buy. If you can get your product in Whole Foods, you're now on the ground floor of mainstream taste. If you can't crack Whole Foods, your trend is likely dead in the water. "The holy grail of this show is Whole Foods," said Hernandez as we walked around, tasting more olive oils. "So many of these food producers specifically create a product made for Whole Foods." Independent stores, like BKLYN Larder, won't even carry a product if it's already in Whole Foods—it has already become too mainstream for both the shop's discerning owners and their customers. Whole Foods divides its stores into eleven geographic regions (Northwest, NYC metro area, Pacific Northwest, etc.), and each of those regions purchase their products independently. This allows stores to source produce, meat, and fish locally, keeping with the company's sustainable ethos, but also it lets Whole Foods test out products one market at a time—as happened with Mamma Chia's drinks—allowing them to slowly build up a supply chain while also seeing how customers react. For the producers at the Fancy Food Show, the appearance at their booth of someone bearing a Whole Foods identity badge is a moment pregnant with promise. At the Fancy Food Show a dozen or so buyers from the different regions were walking the floor at all times, and though they were free to pick up any accounts they liked, they were under the watchful eye of the company's head global cheese and specialty product buyer, Cathy Strange, likely the most powerful tastemaker at the Fancy Food Show.

Strange met me the second morning of the show next to the entrance to the large basement exhibit hall. She is tall, broad shouldered, and was dressed in a billowy lavender shirt, worn jeans, and running shoes (she wears a different pair each day of the show). Strange has the strong hands and wide dimpled smile of a dairy farmer, which made sense, as she is basically the queen of American cheese. A native of North Carolina, Strange was selling wine for a local Durham, North Carolina, specialty market in 1991 when Whole Foods acquired it. She quickly moved through the company's ranks, first regionally and then nationally, eventually becoming the buyer in charge of cheese around the world, picked for her keen ability to recognize international food trends before they broke. Over the years she has headed up the American Cheese Society, made nearly every different type of cheese herself, and toured hundreds of dairies from Wisconsin to the Italian countryside, searching for the next cheese, chocolate, olive, or other specialty food trend that will resonate with Whole Foods customers. When Strange makes a pick, a trend begins its move into the big time, and her choices resonate so deeply in the industry that they not only shape the way other retailers buy food but also the way food is made, packaged, and sold around the world. As Anna Wintour is to clothing and Harvey Weinstein is to film, Strange is to gouda.

As Strange and I walked down the aisles of the show, heads began turning. Some people stared and turned their voices to hushed whispers while others shamelessly leaped over their tables, thrusting forth a handshake, a sample, or a business card at Strange. The attention was relentless. "When I'm at this show, it's like being J-Lo," Strange joked as she waved and thanked people and said hello without ever breaking stride or stopping longer than a beat. It was like watching a seasoned politician work a rope line at a campaign event—she was a pro. "I'm looking for colors," Strange said as I struggled to keep up, "how something's merchandised, what's hot, and how it would work with Whole Foods. Just flashes of it." Walking down an aisle, Strange would glance right, then left as she moved along, like a driver scanning the stores on either side of the street without ever stopping her car. "The way I tackle this is divide and conquer. I go row by row, see something, pull a card, write a note, or take a picture." Strange was constantly holding up her phone, shooting short videos with a small camera, and writing down notes on paper. "I'll look at a booth for half a second and make a snap decision. When something doesn't catch my eye I'm through there like a north wind." Like Hernandez and other independents, Strange wanted that undiscovered gem—the next trend before anyone even realized it—and she wanted it all to herself. Whole Foods signed producers up to an exclusivity contract for a period of time so that their food would only be available in their stores and not at other major grocers. "If Safeway has it, forget it," she said.

We charged through half the show in an hour, tasting smoked blue cheese from Oregon's Rogue Creamery, a creamy bouche from Vermont Butter and Cheese Creamery, incredibly delicate sauerkraut from the Champagne region, the dapper Spaniard Figueroa's mini-torta sheep's milk cheese, buttery Lucque olives from Languedoc, France, and a rosemary-infused honey from the quirky little Thistle Dew Farm in West Virginia. At one point Strange was flagged down and corralled for a second by someone she knew at Atalanta, a large importer that had set up next to the Peruvian pavilion. "Cathy! Cathy!" he said, grabbing her arm and pulling her over, "I want to show you something." In his hand he held a tiny red pepper, shaped like a teardrop and no bigger than an almond. It was called a Sweety Drop, and the company was the exclusive importer of this new pepper, which had been recently discovered in Peru's jungles. Strange was intrigued. She snapped some photos of the Sweety Drop, took a video of the importer talking about its attributes, jotted a few notes, and finally popped one in her mouth. "I like it," she said, after three or four bites. "It has a great taste. It's that sweet and spicy that Americans like. Visually it's very appealing." Strange then started asking questions: Did anyone else carry it? Was there distribution already? Packaging? Marketing? As the importer answered, Strange held her chin and nodded. "Okay," she said, "let's get some samples and packaging. Send them for fall to representatives from all eleven regions." The Atalanta folks could barely hide their joy and began pulling out other products for Strange to try, but she was already on the move, bound to sniff out the next trend.

"At the end of the day I want the Whole Foods customer to walk away remembering the product," Strange said when I asked her what the end goal was. "Food is sensory. It's a visual thing. You'll remember the smell when you bite down on that pepper just there, you'll remember the flavors as they linger in the mouth." At our last stop together, she encountered a beeswax cheese from Spain that was creamy, sweet, and mellow. "Do you feel that?" Strange asked, cracking the round of cheese open like a crusty bread, handing me half, and inhaling deeply. "The texture! And the floral notes! These are the gems you look for!"

∽

After Strange and I parted ways I headed upstairs to a brightly lit room where the sofi nominees were being judged. Any retailer or journalist attending the show was free to cast their votes, and when I entered, samples of all the nominated products were spread out along three chest-height tables that spanned the length of the room. Half a dozen catering staff dressed in cheap rental tuxedos circled around the entries, serving samples that required more care, such as bowls of Hard Times chili and Elena's Mediterranean Stew (nominees in the Soup, Stew Bean, or Chili category), or just making sure the judges didn't double dip. Overseeing all of it was Louise Kramer, the Specialty Food Association's wonderful communications director, who explained how the process began months before.

The Specialty Food Association is a membership-only organization, and brands need to be approved by a committee in order to be accepted. This isn't quite like joining a secret society, but it helps maintain a certain level of quality and keeps large conglomerates from dominating the trade. Each spring the Specialty Food Association sends out a call for submissions in the various categories. Each company is allowed to submit up to eight products, and for the 2012 summer show the association received over 2,500 entries from 113 companies that sent samples to the association's New York office, which is equipped with test kitchens. The samples are then prepared for the nominating panel, a group made up of nine different judges that rotates each year and includes a mixture of tastemakers:

independent specialty retail shop owners, buyers for national super-markets, executives from restaurant groups, and food journalists. Over eight full days the judges sit and evaluate all the entries. Each entry is judged on packaging, suggested retail price, ingredients, merchandisability, and, most importantly, taste—basically what a store's buyer would look at when assessing whether to carry a product. The judges then submit their scores and are asked to pick the top ten results in each category, lists they then debate and discuss with other judges. The data is tabulated, and the nominees are notified.

Over the first two days of the show the judging room is open to those who are eligible and interested enough to vote on products (that year close to three hundred votes were counted). The voting process itself can be a little random because you are eating as you would at the show, going from cheeses to chocolates, to salad dressings then cookies, and on to dehydrated basil crystals (which taste like pesto candy) in the span of several seconds—the taste buds simply don't know how to process it all. I walked a stretch of the judging room with Esther Psarakis, who owns the store Taste of Crete in New Jersey. When we came to the Classic category the nominees were a blue cheese chevre, aged Italian balsamic vinegar, another blue cheese, chocolate chip cookies, and ginger peach tea. "It's an odd mix," said Psarakis as she stood over what looked like the contents of a ravaged hotel gift basket. "How do you pick between these? It's impossible to be objective."

The randomness of this process must be chilling to a couple like Louisa Conrad and Lucas Farrell, the Vermont goat farmers with so much riding on the fate of their caramels. But with tastemakers like Cathy Strange and Ari Weinzweig whizzing past their booths at light speed, the sofi awards are the only competition that feels truly democratic. To know that their caramels are as likely to compete on the judge's palate with a rustic sourdough loaf as a Moroccan mint tisane and that all three may have been consumed in the space of ninety seconds has to be paralyzing. Yet it is inherent in the nature of the Fancy Food Show: The trends that look inevitable in hindsight are in fact the result of a chaotic, unpredictable environment, like complex life evolving from some bubbling prehistoric pool. How can you expect success in the food business when such important moments are inherently uncontrollable?

Even so, winners do jump out from the fray. Curtis Vreeland, a writer with *Candy Industry Magazine* who had just gone through the nominees, was particularly enthusiastic about the Big Picture Farms caramels. "The sofis help me see amongst the flotsam and jetsam who we don't want to forget. I'll use this as an indicator," Vreeland said, holding up the nomination sheet, which listed the booth number of each nominee. As for Big Picture Farms, he predicted that a win tonight would "catapult them to prime time."

A sofi win can change a food company's fortunes, but it's a fickle reward. Some products can see a doubling or tripling in orders, entry into new markets, and distributions by national chain, whereas others see no effect at all or, worse, get so overwhelmed by demand they can't meet that it forces their business to shut down. Still, the award obviously confers enough of a halo effect that goes beyond the statue's $125 value. Specialty Food Association folks love to tell the story about the great sofi heist of 1999, which actually involved an Italian pesto maker, possibly drunk, who came up after the awards and complained that he never received his gold statue. After he got back to his hotel, officials realized he hadn't even been nominated for an award, and he was tracked down the next day and threatened with expulsion from the Specialty Food Association if he didn't relinquish the sofi, which he wisely did.

The reality was that in a massive space packed with potential products and nascent food trends, the list of sofi nominations provided beleaguered buyers with a curated cheat sheet. "When we walk through this show, a sofi is an eye-catching thing for a buyer," said Kim Kristopher, senior channel director of specialty retail with KeHE, the largest supermarket wholesale distributor on the continent as well as a member of the sofi judging panel that year. "Something had to be intriguing for them to even be nominated, which is why the nominees are kind of a must-have list. You hit all those big items to make sure you see those items validated by leaders in the industry." KeHE represented mainstream grocery chains like

Supervalu, and for them, having the seal of approval from a sofi win or even nomination made picking up a specialty food and committing to a trend far less risky. "It highlights demand for that segment," Kristopher told me as her army of buyers surrounded her in KeHE's pavilion. "When a goat cheese product wins, it says, 'Hey, goat cheese won. So let's look at that segment.'" A few years ago sofis were won by chipotle-flavored chocolates and sea salt caramels, both of which have since become mainstream grocery items.

∽

On the night of the award ceremony, as the nominees walked down the red carpet to the audience's applause, a mime in a skintight silver bodysuit, dressed as a sofi award, poked around the crowd. After a rambling keynote speech by noted chef José Andrés that included anecdotes about serving Iberico ham in the Spanish navy and a screed during which he called inflexible locavores the "Spanish Inquisition of the fancy food industry" and also its "Taliban," the gold sofis were handed out. What was incredible was how emotional the evening quickly became. The mushroom frat boys from Back to the Roots pumped their fists and bounded around stage while Majid Mahjoub, a humble Tunisian farmer who won for his exquisite hand-rolled couscous, dedicated the award to his country's citizens and villagers who had ignited the Arab Spring just a year before. More than a few winners became visibly choked up when they took to the microphone, including a San Francisco sorbet company's founder who practically bawled his eyes out on stage.

When the nominees were announced in the confection category Farrell and Conrad were sitting together, their hands clenched. When their name was announced as the winners they seemed stunned for a second, then rose to embrace. "Our goats are going to be really excited about this," Conrad said, holding the award aloft like the Superbowl trophy when she took to the podium. "They find all shiny objects irresistible."

"It's just nice to come down from the mountain and be surrounded by nongoats," Farrell said, bringing a laugh from the crowd.

Tomorrow their booth would be swarmed with buyers and interested well-wishers, ranging from regional Whole Foods representatives to the editor of Oprah's magazine and even their state's senator, Patrick Leahy. Over the coming months sales at Big Picture Farms would quadruple, with a dozen new accounts arriving in the following weeks and more than fifty following up by the end of the year, including the upscale bakery chain Le Pain Quotidien. Their caramels would be featured in the *New York Times* and a number of other publications, and the clothing chain Anthropologie would place an order for a 180,000 caramels to sell at all their stores over the holidays, which would make Big Picture Farms a profitable company several years before Farrell and Conrad had projected. They would buy their farm, better milking and wrapping equipment, and, crucially, more goats. Their products would reach thousands more mouths, and their success would inspire others to begin making goat's milk caramels, perhaps even jump-starting a new mini-economy of goat's milk caramels that were once an isolated experiment on a small Vermont farm and then, just a few years later, could be found on the shelves of every supermarket in the country.

But that night, as they sat back down at their table, none of that had happened yet. Instead, Conrad sat there with her gold sofi award, beaming from ear to ear as she snapped photographs of it with her phone, pausing between shots to look admiringly at pictures of her goats.

6

DATA

THE TRENDWATCHERS

Six months after the sofi awards I was in San Francisco for the Winter Fancy Food Show, the West Coast version of the summer trade fair, which tends to be a bit smaller and more focused on companies from the region. I was also recovering from the flu, which had hit me like a ton of bricks three days before, and I spent the show drinking as many samples of green tea as I could while alternating bites of food and cough drops. On the show's last afternoon I headed into a dimly lit conference room and took a seat at the end of a long table, surrounded by ten women, plus myself, Louise Kramer, and Ron Tanner, the VP of communications for the Specialty Food Association. Tanner set down a cardboard box on the table and began pulling out half a dozen bottles of open wine, samples from the show that, everyone agreed, shouldn't go to waste. The television chef, cookbook author, and all-around culinary legend Sara Moulton began pouring the wines into little paper coffee cups.

"What about you, David?" she asked.

"I'm trying to get over the flu," I coughed from the other end of the table, where I'd distanced myself from the nearest person by a good eight feet.

"Okay, then," Moulton said. "I'll just pour you some rosé. Nothing's better for the flu than rosé."

Tanner thanked everyone for participating in this trends panel, which happens at the end of every show. The goal was to tap seasoned food trend spotters' observations in order to pull together a succinct summary of the top food trends that emerged from the show, and these would be condensed into a press release and sent out to the media the next day. Suzie Timm, a manicured Phoenix-area food events consultant who blogged at girlmeetsfork.com, kicked off with her thoughts. She saw a trend called "blue cheese redux," with blue cheeses appearing in unexpected places, like a blue cheese seasoning powder, and a "cha-cha-chai," with the Indian spiced tea blend being used to flavor maraschino cherries and biscotti shortbread. "I brought an Indian friend with me, and she approved of all the chai products," Timm said with great confidence.

Stephanie Stevitti, a culinary journalist who had authored a book about macaroni and cheese and contributed regularly to National Public Radio, noticed a lot of small Italian-style cakes, several boozy jams (including a pepper spread with Irish whiskey), and chipotle-flavored products everywhere. "I saw more coconut than anything else, and Indian," Moulton said, adding a loud snore for effect, as she named dozens of Indian food products she'd seen at the show. "Some trends seem to go on and on and on. Yeah, just a lot of Indian." Joanne Weir, a Bay Area chef and cookbook author, found a few gluten-free foods that were now edible, compared to the sawdust of years past, and noticed a lot of chia products edging out flax seeds as well as single-origin oils in a variety of herbal flavors. Nancy Hopkins, the food editor at *Better Homes and Gardens* was caught by vinegar-pickled fruits (like white balsamic–pickled pineapple), grass-fed milk, and organic Greek frozen yogurt, which she predicted would be a "game changer."

Then the floor turned to Kara Nielsen, who had been reviewing pages and pages of handwritten notes, and hundreds of photos she'd taken over the past few days. Nielsen's presence commanded everyone's attention. At this point she worked nearby at the Center for Culinary Development, a corporate food think tank that provided innovative product solutions to the food business (she would later move to Iconoculture, a consumer trends company). Her title was trendologist, and she knew more about food trends than anyone in the room and, likely, the country. "I'm also excited about blue cheese," Nielsen said, noting powdered blue cheese in a bagged popcorn and blue cheese–flavored Dijon mustard. Veggies were appearing in new places, including teas, ice pops, and even as part of pressed fruit snacks. "I'm seeing South American beyond just Peruvian," Nielsen added, with Argentinean chimichurri-flavored marinades and products jumping out this year, though Peru's aji amarillo pepper had still been growing in stature, an observation that would have brought great joy to Ricardo Zarate. "Pistachios have totally popped, and the Pistachio Council has done a great job. It's not just a snack anymore." Chia seed was also spreading out, appearing in pastas, candy bars, and new drinks.

After everyone had gone around the table, Kramer recapped their observations and then read the list of trends that had come out of last year's Winter Fancy Food Show, including Pickling 2.0, Gluten-Free Grows Up, Coconut Cracks, and Ancient Grains. Everyone realized much of what they'd been discussing was a rehash of the year before, and the room let out a collective groan. "There's no trends!" Stevitti said with mock horror. "Oh god!" Moulton echoed, to laughter. Tanner then began to shape a unified message. "I heard a lot today about herby drinks, like vegetable teas," he said. "We could say 'Drink Your Vegetables.'"

"We could call it Botanical Beverages," Timm suggested, to everyone's approval. At the end of the hour the group had a list of the five top trends from the show: Oil Nouveau, Blue Cheese Redux, So Many Seeds, Top Banana, and Botanical Beverages. These went into a press release, each with three examples of products that had appeared at the show, and the next day the story had already been picked up by *USA Today* and the *New York Times* in addition to other news sites, blogs, and food industry websites, some of which published their own trend lists from the show based on their correspondents' observations.

This short exercise was a rare public view into the world of food trend predictions and forecasting, a small, highly influential subset of the food industry that has grown alongside the prominence of food trends. Increasingly, trend forecasting is becoming a crucial activity for food companies, as the explosion of food culture has not only stimulated the interest of consumers but also accelerated the rate at which it changes. Whereas independent restaurant chefs and small food companies can quickly release products based on their own taste and instinct, the large, publicly traded corporations who operate restaurant chains and manufacture potato chips are much slower-moving creatures. Ricardo Zarate can have an idea at lunch, and it will be on Picca's menu by dinner. Lucas Farrell and Louisa Conrad can cook up a batch of coffee caramels on a Monday, tweak the recipe over the course of the week, and start selling them to customers by Friday. But for companies like Pepsico or Denny's, the innovation cycle takes years.

Ideas are brainstormed, prototyped, kitchen tested, debated within dozens of boardrooms, tested in select markets, subjected to refinements and focus groups, prepared for a launch, advertised to the public, and slowly rolled out store by store, state by state, and country by country. The time line from the initial idea for a food to a consumer's first bite can be months in the quickest moving companies and years for the largest ones, with the whole process costing many millions of dollars. Furthermore, the product development teams and executives in these companies often aren't on the cutting edge of culinary tastes. Most big food companies are located far from trendy culinary centers in New York, Paris, or Tokyo. More often they are found in suburban office parks in the American Midwest. Though the executives in these companies are skilled in data analysis, marketing skills, and business development, most in the mainstream food world do not know their buffalo milk mozzarella from their fior de latte. I have a cousin who works for a large processed food company in Canada and is in charge of their Chinese food brand's marketing. She has never once tasted the food she sells because she happens to keep kosher, but she is extremely good at her job, and the truth is that being a gourmand is not part of her work requirement.

Those in the mainstream food industry tend to find out about food trends at the same time as the rest of us—when it's already too late. This creates a problem because these same companies need to take advantage of the potential sales and interest food trends can generate, and the sooner they can release products that tap into those trends, the better. If they wait to find out about the trends by themselves, their products will hit the market years after the trend has already passed, like a fashion label debuting a line of bell bottom jeans in 1982. Large food companies are driven by a need to innovate and stay current, but paradoxically, the scale of their development process and its costs tend to make them extremely risk averse. On the one hand, they want to be cutting edge, but on the other, they need to stay safe enough that they won't squander millions of dollars on what turns out to be a quickly passing fad. They don't jump into food trends lightly.

This is where food trend forecasting comes in. Each holiday season, as the year ends, food trend predictions seem to rain down on the food media from the heavens like Christmas carols in the shape of top-ten articles and online slide shows telling us that 2015 will be the year for udon soup and pig's feet or other dishes making the rounds at various hot spots. Written by journalists, bloggers, and hospitality consultants, these are almost exclusively based on firsthand observations (i.e., "I went here and I ate this"), culled from the most widely documented chef's creations. In a time when any interested eater can travel to the most talked about restaurants, read local blogs, and buy the best-selling cookbooks, putting together an educated amateur's roundup of the trends that culinary tastemakers are talking about is a fun, reasonably accurate reflection of what is happening in the world of food today. Some of those ideas may eventually end up as frozen entrees or soda flavors in your shopping cart, but most won't.

Real trend forecasting happens behind the scenes, in detailed reports and presentations that the public rarely sees. It is a discipline that combines culinary obsession and food knowledge with economics, data aggregation, sociology, and anthropological field research. This is the intelligence wing of the food industry, its field agents and quants gathering info about what we are eating and what we'd like to be eating, and then pulling trends from that data. For the companies in the food industry, from the publicly traded behemoths like Dole to medium-sized firms such as POM, the forecasters are the equivalent of their CIA and Wall Street analysts, armed with twenty-page reports on the long-term viability of chia seeds as a food additive. They are the ones who shepherd food trends from the niche world of foodies to the mass market consumer.

 ∞

Many in the field credit the modern business of trend forecasting to a woman named Faith Popcorn. Born in New York to the less delicious name of Faith Plotkin, Popcorn initially worked as a creative director in Madison Avenue advertising firms but noticed that what her clients really needed was someone to tell them where the market was moving in the future. In 1974 she opened her own strategic marketing company called Faith Popcorn's BrainReserve, which quickly became a success despite sounding like a snack food for chess players. Popcorn gathered data by interviewing people from around the world, reading widely about culture in different languages, and collecting standard consumer research surveys. She organized these into seventeen overarching behavioral trends that were present in society, including cocooning (the need to protect yourself from the outside world), down-aging (Baby Boomers find comfort in pursuits and products from their youth), and small indulgences (stressed-out consumers treat themselves in moderate ways). Popcorn characterized the specific foods that came out of these greater trends as "fads." In the case of cupcakes, for instance, down-aging baby boomers sought small indulgences that reminded them of their youth. "None of those foods were the trend," Popcorn told me. "They were manifestations of the trend."

Popcorn is a masterful self-promoter and unashamedly boastful. She claims a 95 percent success rate in predicting trends, and though the robotic hugging booths and food replacement nutrition pills she forecast years back have yet to emerge (they eventually will, she believes), her firm has identified several key food trends ahead of time. Cocooning was Popcorn's first big theory in the late 1970s, based around a growing fear of the polluted environment and safety in urban areas as well as the hangover effect of the late-night disco era, when people basically curled up in bed the next day nursing physical and emotional hangovers. In moments like these people gravitated toward comforting foods, available at home but without the need for preparation, and Popcorn forecast this would give rise to ready-to-eat meals, which became one of the fastest growing segments of the supermarket business. Cocooning's safety driver led the way to Popcorn's recommendation to Coca-Cola in 1981 that they needed to get into bottled water, which has since proven to be one of their most profitable divisions. Currently Popcorn believes that the trend "99 lives," in which one has too much to do and too little time, causing a sort of schizophrenia, would lead to the rise of "clean energy" foods that will deliver sustained boosts of energy without the adverse health effects of caffeine, sugar, or products like Red Bull. "I think the future of food tells you how society's going to be shaped," Popcorn said. "Is it going to be a healthy society, a single society? If you want to understand a household, go and look through their garbage. That's what we're doing. We are analyzing future garbage."

Since Popcorn's start, the business of food trend forecasting has grown increasingly sophisticated, and the field falls into a number of different categories, separated by their goals and methodology. The most straightforward are the data-driven market research shops, which use publicly available sales figures, consumer surveys, and their own quantitative research to identify trends and advise their clients on how to best capitalize on them. These include companies such as Chicago's Technomic, whose foodservice research is headed up by Darren Tristano, a native of the city who met me in Toronto one winter day dressed in a Bears baseball hat and sweatshirt. Tristano's focus is the restaurant world, which includes everything from regional sandwich chains to catering companies like Sodexo that operate cafeterias and household names like McDonald's. Technomic's research covers nearly twenty markets around the world, and Tristano, who has a background in accounting, is constantly mining data to track food trends and divine where they are heading. "It's easier to define what a trend isn't," Tristano said as we sat down for a coffee in a hip new restaurant where he commented on how the Edison-style filament lightbulbs they used were now starting to pop up in upscale fast casual chains (such as Chipotle or Panera Bread) around the United States. "A trend is an area where there's growth and use. . . . You have to start with a food [or] flavor's life cycle," he said. "There's a ground zero for it, where you can see where it is happening."

The core of Tristano's methodology lies in the company's menu-tracking database, which monitors over two thousand menus and LTOs (a.k.a., limited time offers or "specials," to you and me). The database covers a wide range of the dining world, from independent fine dining restaurants in major cities like Chicago and Miami to pizza chains in Calgary, providing a representative sample of what the market is eating right now. That data is backed up with consumer research and sales figures to provide an accurate look at what food is being ordered and what isn't. Then Tristano and his team hit the road and complement their data with hundreds of field visits a year. Although being a restaurant tester sounds like a dream job, it's an incredibly arduous task. "Every experience at a restaurant is a laboratory experiment," said Tristano. "I'm ruined. I can't go out and have a meal without thinking about what's around me." In a typical visit Tristano will look at a concept's service format, decor, ambiance, price point, music, menu, service quality, presentation, taste, and many more factors. "We get really deep into the specific concept to see if it hits on a list of winning restaurant attributes. Within a study I'll go to sixty restaurants, dine at twenty-five, and you've got to go through with that meal whether it's a winner or not." Some days he'll check out twenty small chains, back to back to back.

For Tristano, trends can emerge out of several different areas. There are global-flavor trends, like chipotle peppers or harissa hot sauce that start in specialized markets and immigrant communities and then organically grow into the mainstream appetite over the course of decades. Forward thinking restaurant brands, such as the Cheesecake Factory, will send scouts around the world to look for dishes and flavors that they can eventually adapt and sell back in North America. There are supplier-originated trends, backed by branding campaigns, like the POM-driven pomegranate craze, and the recent upswing in avocado use, pushed by the Avocado Board, which has helped chains such as Subway develop a popular avocado sub for their menu. Fine dining trends continue to hold sway and trickle down from chefs to the mainstream market, though Tristano also acknowledges that the cycle is happening faster today, with chef-driven trends emerging quicker and dying sooner. Then there are the trends that come out of left field. One of Tristano's favorite examples came around 2010 from a San Francisco McDonald's, which was drawing a large crowd at 10:35 in the morning, when the restaurant switched over from their breakfast menu to the lunch menu. At that time there were still leftover breakfast sandwiches, and customers began ordering an Egg McMuffin along with a McDouble hamburger, combining the two of them to create a frankenburger McBrunch mashup that doesn't appear on any menus, but online the chain's fans have nicknamed it the Mc10:35, and discerning McDonald's fans coast to coast are now ordering it. One day soon it will probably migrate to the official menu.

"I'm much more interested in what's happening on menus at McDonald's, Applebee's, and Cheesecake Factory, because that's where real people eat," said Nancy Kruse, a former colleague of Tristano's who now tracks trends for *Nation's Restaurant News*, the magazine of the National Restaurant Association. "It's not the super-rarified high-end Alain Ducasse in New York or the down-and-dirty mom-and-pop stuff. It may bubble up or trickle down from the independents, but until it starts appearing on chain menus, especially early adopters like California Pizza Kitchen or Cheesecake Factory, it's hard for me to call it a trend." Like Technomic, Kruse relies heavily on menu data from the industry, and she does not consider herself a futurist or trend predictor. She has been successful in calling some trends, but she fell short with others she believed were around the corner, such as the mainstream crossover of Indian food in America. Predicting trends is hardly an exact science, and it is getting trickier. Twenty years ago the path that trends followed from the niche to the mainstream flowed down vertically, from high-end kitchens to restaurant chains and eventually to supermarket products. Today trends are flying in from all directions, emerging from sideways influences, bottom-up taste-makers, and landing without warning from way out beyond the periphery. "I could say I take a look at all these factors and lay out an algorithm," said Kruse, "but yes, to me, what it frequently comes down to is gut instinct. It's very risky to set yourself up as the sort of last word on what's going to be happening on menus because there's so much room for surprise. The best any of us can do is take a commonsense approach, one would hope rooted by history in experience with trends, and then have some expectations. I can't point you to one single reliable tool. We're like Wall Street analysts with less data and money."

Several food companies produce their own trend predictions that they either use as internal research or as a sales and marketing tool. One of the most high-profile is put out each year by McCormick, the Baltimore corporation that is the largest spice dealer in the world. In 2000, led by a recently appointed executive chef named Kevan Vetter, McCormick put together its first Flavor Forecast. The idea was to leverage the company's advanced product knowledge, both from what McCormick's divisions were working on and also what they were observing in the food world, and then use that knowledge to drive demand into new product categories by making their customers, particularly in the food industry, think about the possibilities around these trending flavors. Vetter's team solicited information and opinions from across the company and emerged with the prediction that bold flavors would rule in the coming years. This was distilled down into a top-ten list of flavors, which included cinnamon, cumin, dill, and fennel as hot flavors to watch. "What was big was using sweet spices in main dishes, and savory spices in desserts," Vetter told me, in an interview a few years back. "[We were] supporting trends with flavors we felt make sense."

The Flavor Forecast became a tremendous hit with McCormick's clients, and it grew from there. Each spring Vetter assembles his internal team, which includes members from McCormick's kitchens, their sensory science group, marketing and customer research, and an outside panel of culinary influencers and tastemakers ranging from well-known chefs and bakers to food bloggers and cocktail mixologists. Similar reports in Europe and China are prepared with local chefs, with the flavors reflecting the tastes of those markets. The whole process begins five to six months before the report is released, with the team brainstorming flavor ideas on a big white board at McCormick headquarters. Along with input on culinary trends, economic indicators factor into the list. One year a statistical increase in sales of ball jars, which are used for home preserving, was interpreted as a sign that America was ready for more exposure to pickling spices. Hundreds of possible flavor combinations are suggested and then whittled down over the course of a week to twenty or so final contenders.

Because of its association with Thanksgiving, pumpkin spice mix entered the 2010 holiday forecast early on. The team quickly thought beyond pie, breaking down the ingredients of the mix (cinnamon, ginger, nutmeg, allspice) to reveal flavors that often appear in Latin American and Caribbean dishes, such as jerk chicken. Often those same dishes require coconut milk, inspiring a potential pairing. Next, Vetter's team headed to the test kitchen to develop and test recipes based on pumpkin pie spices and coconut. In order to be successful, a forecasted flavor needs to be versatile. It has to hit multiple places along the food chain, working within at least three categories, such as a savory main, snack food, and a cocktail. Pumpkin pie spice and coconut milk–rubbed short ribs, pumpkin-spiced coconut fudge, and a pumpkin whoopee pie with coconut cream filling were just three of the dozen or so recipes Vetter tested for that one flavor prediction. After recipe testing, Vetter's team reconvenes to discuss what worked, what flopped, and which flavors will have the best impact with consumers, before settling on the final ten flavor combinations. The marketing department starts writing up the report, coordinating with McCormick product development to begin work on new industrial or consumer products that the flavor pairings may inspire, including the jars of McCormick spices you can buy at the supermarket. A few years ago, an entire line of toasted spices came out of one Flavor Forecast and have been one of the company's better-selling products in recent years.

The Flavor Forecast is released to the public at year's end, and over the next few months Vetter and the McCormick marketing team present its results to over a hundred major customers while the company's distributors give hundreds more presentations to smaller clients. Each talk is tailored to the customer, so one to TGI Friday's will be quite different from one at Nabisco. Sample foods are always provided, like cayenne and tart cherry brownies (2009), to suggest how McCormick's customers might integrate these new pairings in their particular products. "Within a matter of a couple of months [of the report's release] we'll get orders," said Alan Wilson, chairman, president, and CEO of McCormick & Company. "We'll turn [a pairing] into specific products quickly on an industrial standpoint. . . . A chipotle idea becomes a sandwich sauce for a quick-service restaurant, a frozen dinner for another customer, and an ingredient for another customer." In many ways the McCormick Flavor Forecast is a self-fulfilling prophecy. If they call something a trend and then use that prediction to sell those flavors up and down the food chain, it's like Goldman Sachs putting a buy rating on a stock they're promoting and then profiting when the stock's price inevitably goes up in reaction to that rating.

When food companies don't have their own trend forecasting units—and most don't—they often turn to two firms based around San Francisco who specialize in forecasting and responding to trends: CCD Innovations, where Kara Nielsen worked when I met her, and Mattson. A few mornings after the trend session at the Fancy Food Show I met Nielsen at CCD's downtown offices near the city's waterfront. A formally trained pastry chef, Nielsen found the CCD job on Craigslist a decade back and has since become one of the better-known trend experts in the business. Food trends, according to her, represented the evolving needs of people around eating, including economic needs, health needs, social needs, and political needs. A greater societal trend, such as green living, will emerge—that is, "I need to be better for the earth." It will exert pressure and change our value as consumers ("I need to eat local").

As the value changes, our needs change—"I need local food"—and an opportunity arises to serve that change: "My company needs to sell local food." Nielsen's job is to identify trends at various points of their development, a process she classifies into five stages, and then write reports on those trends, a task she does over a dozen times a year. Then she will work with food companies to understand the opportunities associated with those trends and help CCD's product development team create a packaged food product or menu item that brings that trend to their client's target market.

CCD's trend reports can focus on flavors, such as heat and spice, which may involve smoke-infused drinks found at cutting-edge cocktail bars at stage one of their development and something like Buffalo hot sauce–flavored ketchup at a stage five, when it is at its most accessible in the mass market. Nielsen remarked that I'd even factored into one of the company's trend reports, pulling up the company's sixty-eight-page 2010 sandwich report, which cited the reinvented Jewish deli as a stage-two sandwich trend. I read through, astonished, as the report quoted extensively from my book on the subject along with several articles I had written. A surge of pride shot through me—that I had played a role in turning the nascent artisan Jewish deli scene into a mainstream food trend—but it also unnerved me a little to know that my work had been used, without my knowledge, to sell the corporate food world on appropriating the handmade pastrami I loved so dearly.

Nielsen draws a clear distinction between trends, which are slower-paced evolutions with deep cultural roots, and fads, which are superficial manifestations of those trends. A fad is something like the Paleo diet, which first came into fashion in 1975 for its focus on an abundance of raw protein, but a trend is the astronomical growth of Greek yogurt, which drew one of its strengths from the rising interest in high-protein foods but also had a number of other factors going for it. When Nielsen first wrote about Greek yogurt in 2007, she talked about its American arrival via Greek grocery stores in New York and its rapid adoption through tastemaking retailers like Trader Joe's and Gristedes. "It was pushing a lot of buttons," recalled Neilsen, "it was natural, pure, wholesome, strained, simple,

and old world." Other factors she identified in Greek yogurt's imminent rise was its combination of high-protein, low-fat, and cultured
probiotics, which were all in line with diet trends globally. Greek
yogurt also benefited from a rising appreciation of tart dairy flavors, thanks to the popular Korean-style frozen yogurt chains, such
as Pinkberry and Menchie's, which were spreading from the West
Coast across North America. And it was a continuation of a much
longer lasting yogurt trend, which had begun in the 1970s with sour
yogurts, evolved into the chunky FroYo of the 1980s, and hit Nielsen's stage five in the 1990s when companies like Dannon and Yo-
plait added tons of flavorings and sugar to yogurt, to the point at
which it lost its healthy image. Greek yogurt was a reset, a return to
Yogurt 101, and now the cycle was ramping up again.

I asked Nielsen where Greek yogurt was today on its evolutionary journey as a trend, and she handed me a Greek yogurt–flavored
snack bar from the conference table, which was piled with products. "This is what stage five of a trend looks like," she said, pointing out several other Greek yogurt–flavored products, which were
now flooding the market. "There is a Greek yogurt flavor of Honey
Bunches of Oats cereal. It has thirty-seven ounces of fat in each cup.
Are there any probiotics in Honey Bunches of Oats?" she asked,
rhetorically. "Greek Yogurt has become a health halo. What's left
once it's in Honey Bunches of Oats?"

This line between trends like Greek yogurt and fads like the Paleo diet can be perilously thin. In fact, the evangelists for most any
fad are probably hard at work trying to convince you that it is, instead, a trend. The best advice I can offer is Supreme Court Justice
Potter Stewart's famous line about what constitutes pornography: "I
know it when I see it."

One of CCD's main competitors is Mattson, located about forty
minutes south, across the Bay from Silicon Valley. Peter Mattson
founded his eponymous company shortly after Faith Popcorn hung
out her shingle, though he focused exclusively on food. Mattson's
first food trend forecast came out in 1979, and it predicted the
rise of Mexican food, convenience cooking (one-pan dinners), and
bake–in-bag technology. At the time consumer-packaged goods

companies were growing into massive, unwieldy bureaucracies, and they were becoming increasingly insulated from the reality on the street. "Corporations are terrible at identifying trends," Mattson told me. "The food industry moves at the most glacial speed, and it's a risk-averse industry."

Though Mattson is best known as a prototype shop and science-heavy kitchen laboratory, credited with developing POM Wonderful and the Starbucks Frappuccino among other hit products, its work in trend predictions lies at the core of this, and the company has a staff of individuals who aid in putting together the forecasts that drive those innovations. "We don't want to hire anybody unless they're obsessed with food," Mattson told me when I asked what made a great food trend forecaster. "It's not a life-sustaining thing . . . you need to have an irrational obsession with food. Those are the kind of people who'll go where others won't go." These individuals need to be creative, intellectual, and able to substantiate and rationalize hypotheses about potential trends, the core of all food trend forecasting.

One of the best in the company is Barb Stuckey, a fit, fast-talking woman with a background in food science who first gained experience at Kraft, Chili's, and Whole Foods and has been developing foods at Mattson for well over a decade. Stuckey is an expert on the physiology of taste and wrote a fascinating book several years back simply called *Taste*, which is the best explanation I have ever read on how our body responds when we eat something. The day before I met Nielsen I drove up through the pouring rain to meet Stuckey for lunch at French Blue, a lovely whitewashed restaurant in the Napa Valley. "We see our role as translating trends," she told me after ordering a kale salad. "We are putting ideas in front of consumers that are both appropriate and challenging. We're here to test that line." When a company comes to Mattson with a need—"We want a drink for the urban market" or "we need a new sandwich that'll appeal to teenagers"—Stuckey will compile the market research and begin looking into related trends in that space. Five times a month she will organize on-the-ground eating tours for her clients so they can experience those trends "the way they're meant to be experienced." Recently, she led clients on a barbecue-eating tour of Austin, Texas, and a food truck tour in Portland, Oregon. One restaurant chain spent eight hours in Los Angeles on a breakneck ethnic food tour that covered nearly every neighborhood and culture of the vast city in order to experience tastes as diverse as prepared foods in a Japanese supermarket, tamales in a Mexican community-funded restaurant, and, to my delight, pastrami in a Jewish delicatessen. Each of these tours are carefully planned by Stuckey and her team of scouts, who hit the ground up to two months ahead of time to curate the essential trend safari. The Mattson company also puts on an annual trend lunch for all their clients, an eight-course meal that's a sit-down version of a national trend tour, where clients might be served something like a hot drink brewed from coffee leaves, instead of beans, to cite a recent example.

"It's never a straight line between a trend and what ends up in the market," Stuckey said, admiring the kale salad when it finally arrived and then using it to illustrate her point. "There's so many twists and turns along the way. The value, though, is that someday your restaurant will just *have* to have a kale salad. You need to have it in the pipeline for when that day comes." The kale salad, in her opinion, was the twenty-first century's Caesar salad, an international staple that began in the 1920s in a Tijuana hotel and snowballed into the most popular salad trend the world has ever known. "Slowly but surely, the kale salad will make its way to TGI Friday's menu, then McDonald's, Kraft, and, eventually, as a Doritos flavor."

After lunch I followed Stuckey to the nearby campus of the Culinary Institute of America at Greystone, which is an imposing former stone winery that is built like a castle. Inside, as young student chefs in towering white toques scurried up and down the large staircases, several dozen executives from across the food industry gathered around wine, appetizers, and several jugs of what was labeled "Mexican Lime with Chia Seed Water"—basically a chia fresca. The group covered a wide swath of the food industry: from Dow Agro Sciences and the Soybean, Mushroom, and Peanut Boards;

doctors from the Cleveland Clinic and professors from Harvard Business School; to representatives from Butterball, Dunkin Donuts, Chobani Yogurt, Wonderful Brands (the company behind POM), and McDonald's corporate dietician. They'd all gathered here for the opening session of the Worlds of Healthy Flavors retreat, put on by the Culinary Institute of America and Harvard University with a focus on how to make American food healthier. Everyone filed into an auditorium with steep stadium-style seating and a huge demonstration kitchen for a stage. After an introductory presentation by Dr. Eric Rimm of the Harvard School of Public Health, who warned of the dangers posed by diet trends, superfoods, and gluten-free celebrities, the host introduced Suzy Badaracco, one of the most interesting trend forecasters working today.

Badaracco, who has curly reddish-brown hair and speaks incredibly quickly, is a bit of an enigma in the food world. From the time she was nineteen until her midtwenties Badaracco worked for the Orange County Sheriff's Department as a forensic photographer and criminalist, covering hundreds of crime scenes, where she profiled criminals based on the available evidence. She is trained in military-grade intelligence and chaos theory with an expertise in pattern recognition, and she employs the same methodology developed by the US Marines, FBI, and Scotland Yard to predict military strikes, terrorist attacks, and murder sprees. If you married the quirky lab genius from *CSI* with the gastronomic curiosity of Anthony Bourdain, you'd get Suzy Badaracco. "I went from tracking serial killers to cereal bars," she joked to the room as she began her presentation.

After she burned out on blood-spatter recognition, Badaracco went to culinary school and worked in the research end of the food business for companies such as Nestlé, Mintel, the US Department of Agriculture, and the Japanese food and flavor conglomerate Aginomoto, who put her to work in their global think tank, tracking trends. When she left Aginomoto she felt like a "giraffe in a petting zoo" who didn't fit anywhere, so she founded her own firm, called Culinary Tides, which, along with six colleagues who work remotely around the United States and Japan, she runs out of her home in Oregon. "What we do is make sense of the chaos," Badaracco told me.

The information available today that relates to food trends is vast, often contradictory, and largely inaccurate. What Badaracco does at Culinary Tides is aggregate data from thousands of different points, including the industry reports produced by firms like Technomic as well as nearly every published article, government trade report, relevant scientific health study, and seemingly unrelated statistics, like the destinations Americans are buying plane tickets to. All of this adds up to more than fourteen hundred reports a month, which are then fed into a database that analyzes roughly two hundred units of data for each client every month, and this is then used to build an eighteen-month predictive window into the future, tailored to each client's needs. "Maybe they'll be focusing on a particular thing," said Badaracco, "then we can go and pull out micropatterns. We cross-analyze all of those areas. We deal with white space—things that don't exist. Chaos theory. And we prove it will exist by massive amounts of quantitative data." Badaracco had no interest in the type of firsthand observations that other forecasters used. She didn't take her clients on taste tours, suggest new products for them to make, or even get excited about a particular food she might happen upon at a restaurant. "In chaos you don't want to do your own field work. It's a dangerous practice. What you're seeing is food trucks in a single city. That's useless. It tells you nothing about the national trend and where it's going. We have to understand on a much larger scale of what something's doing." The idea is to get out so far head of the trends that they're not even trends yet. "If you can Google a trend, you've completely missed the trend," she said. "At that point you're not forecasting—you're just tracking."

Badaracco's presentation to the crowd at the Culinary Institute focused on long-term flavor trends. It was a rapid, whirlwind flood of data, organized into slides jammed end to end with text, charts, and basic diagrams along with the metaphorical buzzwords she uses to define the different stages of a trend's evolution. There are blips, which are noteworthy data points jumping out from the chaos, and shadows, which are pretrend events or precursors to a trend. Trends have births, and those can be strong births (a break-out, like Greek yogurt), stillbirths, and orphaned births, which is when a trend doesn't have strong parents to champion it. Yes, food trends have parents, and like children, they need support and nour-ishment or else they'll fail to thrive. They also need advocates and allies. Just as a trend is born, a trend can morph (whole wheat bread to multigrain bread to single-grain bread to ancient-grain bread), crash (the Atkins Diet becomes discredited), redirect (lactose-free moves from the mainstream back to a niche), and be killed by an adversary (GMO foods go from salvation to pariah, thanks to polit-ical opposition from the organic movement). Trends also have their own personality. Badaracco described the Greek yogurt trend as "the guy who comes to the party that just everybody likes, everyone chats with, he'll freshen your drink, pat your kids on the head." He's sweet, he's savory, he's breakfast, lunch, dinner, and dessert . . . all of which means that Greek yogurt isn't going anywhere soon as a trend."

She pulled up a slide on trend births and began talking about where consumers were today, comparing one month's American consumer confidence survey to another, which showed, based on her analysis, that recession signals were ebbing at this point in early 2013. "We are moving slowly, kicking and screaming into a recov-ery phase," Badaracco predicted before clicking on to the next slide, which focused on health trends. Seasonal and local-sourcing trends were all about control issues, Badaracco explained with great pas-sion, which are born during recessions as a way to control what food you bring into houses. "I want it," she said, holding an imag-inary organic apple in one hand, and then, turning her attention to the imaginary cheaper apple in the other, "I don't want to pay for it!" Conversely, foraging in the woods for mushrooms, a trend gaining favor with high-end chefs, was recovery behavior, because recovery brings out discovery instincts, and foraging is the ultimate discovery activity. "Because it can kill you," Badaracco said, noting that the fine line between a delicious morel and a poison fungus was something diners were happy to walk when wallets were flush, but they reverted to sure comforts like hamburgers when things felt rocky. Anything extreme on the palate—new flavors, textures, experiences—was recovery behavior, not recessionary.

This all led to Badaracco's slide on flavors, which she described in a variety of categories, each with its own personality. Cage-dancers (seasonings) were wild and included the Peruvian herb huacatay (another indication of Zarate's growing influence), Nordic flavors, flowers, ashes, flavored heat, and geranium leaf. Sensuals (fruit/veg) had white strawberries, kimchi, and finger limes; tree-huggers (dairy) would be Lebanese yogurt and paneer; bipolars (protein) had goat and lamb bellies, blood, skin, fin-to-tail seafood eating, and something called "lethal"; interpreters (grains) included not just chia but also faro, grits, and black rice (a Glenn Roberts hat trick); and type-A (beverage) featured barrel-aged cocktails, Vietnamese coffee, and sipping vinegars. Globally, American soul food, regional Mexican, and Peru were already rock stars, but Badaracco predicted, based on travel statistics, that North Africa, Nepal, Laos, and somehow even the Arctic were rising stars to watch. All of this was projected in a sprawling jumble of monochromatic text, with no photos or illustrations, that contained sentences like *Cocktails, craft beer, wine $ ↑, desserts ↑, insect eating = recovery behavior.* The whole presentation was undeniably fascinating but also a bit like stepping into a math class you quickly realize you are vastly unprepared for. The room at the Culinary Institute was full of astonished faces, partly in awe and partly in shock, as Badaracco kept on blazing through her talk.

What Badaracco, Stuckey, Nielsen, Tristano, and others in the trend forecasting business all agree on is that food trends are evolving quicker, with less of a predictable trajectory, and a more rapid evolution from the fringes into the mainstream. More uncertain trends make the need for their predictions even greater, and many people have jumped into the business in recent years, adding their own food trend forecasts to those already out there. Peter Mattson estimated that there were now thousands of people offering up some form of food trend forecasting, though only a hundred or so were actually good at what they did. "You want a trend?" asked Michael Whiteman, the restaurant consultant who has been publicly sharing his previously private trend reports since 2008. "More predictions!"

The future may be even more complicated, as the industry taps into the eyes and ears of amateur trendwatchers, whose passion for food and easy connectivity makes crowdsourcing new trends a possibility. In early 2013 the Spanish company Azti Tecnala, which has a food consulting and research business, launched an online initiative called the Food Mirror Game. Contestants from around the world entered a contest that involved three rounds of identifying different food trends where they lived. These were organized by eight overarching EATrends the company had created, including #foodtelling (food with a message), #slowcal (sustainable and responsible), and #eatertainment (fun on a fork). Over the course of four months over five hundred participants submitted photos, videos, and descriptions of new trends and products that they saw at restaurants, supermarkets, or at pop-ups and in food fairs. These participants were overwhelmingly women, who, for some reason, tend to dominate the food trend forecasting business, though I myself had entered and submitted several trends I'd come across during my research, including upscale Indian dosas, Sriracha-flavored products, and branded fruits (a trend I explore in the next chapter, about how an apple is marketed).

The Food Mirror Game's grand prize was an all-expense-paid trip to Bilbao, Spain, but the contest tapped into something deeper than the urge to travel. For every one of the hundreds of thousands of reviews posted on Yelp each day or the millions of cupcake photos shared on blogs and uploaded to social networks, there's a desire from these obsessive eaters to be recognized for their sense of taste. The Food Mirror Game indulged that, and in the process it built a global network of amateur trendhunters that the company could call on in the future. "We see the contestants like correspondents or antennas or food watchers," said Sonia Riesco, who headed up the project for Azti. "We could have one in Japan, one in the United States, one in South Africa, and so on." The idea for the contest actually came a few years earlier, when Azti would deploy their own staff around the world for months at a time to research trends. It was exhausting, logistically daunting, and terribly expensive. "Now, when we do a project with a company we have people all over the world who can look at the types of canned fish in the United States, for example. We'll have a network of people, so that if Nestlé wants to look at chocolates in some country, we can tap into that person so they can look at it." Imagine an ever-growing army of food trend scouts, motivated by the potential for some reward but also their passion for the newest item on the menu—not just the buttery embrace of a sweet cupcake or the feeling of well-being from eating chia but also the rush that comes from discovering something that you just know will be the next big taste and being the first to tell the world about that.

I never asked Badaracco and the other trend forecasters what they thought of crowdsourced competition, but I imagine they weren't too worried. "Neither love nor hate a trend," Badaracco advised the crowd when concluding her presentation. "Emotions will fog the trend's true pattern, and it will shift."

The weight of Badaracco's logic is hard to ignore. For all the hate snobby eaters and even well-published critics poured onto cupcakes, the cupcake economy continued to grow apace. But her data-driven approach also ignored something that another approach might capture: the importance of driven, food-loving people committed to making a trend happen and selling it to the public. You could see its value in the hands of Glenn Roberts or Ricardo Zarate. And, as it turned out, you could see it not far from my home in Canada.

7

MARKETING

SOMEDAY MY RED PRINCE WILL COME

Thornbury, Ontario, is a small, pretty town two hours north-west of Toronto, where the Beaver River flows into Georgian Bay, the giant backside of Lake Huron. The water in Georgian Bay is cold, clear, and remarkably clean, making it a coveted spot for weekend cottages and beachfront vacation homes. Just a few miles away from Thornbury are some of Ontario's best ski hills—a bit of an oxymoron, sadly—that drop down from the top of the Niagara Escarpment to the shore of the lake. My family has had a house five minutes outside Thornbury since I was a teenager, and we spend most weekends and holidays there.

In the summers my dad does a lot of bicycling and occasionally drags me out first thing on a Saturday morning to cycle thirty or forty miles with other baby boomers on their $9,000 carbon fiber stallions. A few years ago we left our house in the morning and rode up into the farmland beyond the vacation houses and golf courses along the shore. Within a few minutes the landscape opened up to rolling fields of canola, wheat, grazing sheep, and apple orchards. Thornbury is apple country and has been for well over a century. Lake air is held over the orchards by the heights of the nearby hills, creating a microclimate that's temperate and ideally suited for apple growing, with plenty of moisture and good frost protection.

Thick-trunked apple trees with drooping, snarled limbs are every-where, and you can't drive three minutes in the fall without coming across a stand selling bushels of apples or a bakery selling apple pies. There are apple vinegars and jams for sale at the supermar-ket and apple cider on tap in Thornbury's bars. On the back roads, giant trucks roll by carrying presliced and packaged apples for Walmart and McDonald's as well as tankers of apple juice destined for Tropicana.

Five minutes into the ride that day we rode past a farm that looked completely different from all the others. Instead of knotty old trees around high grasses, there were tight, precise rows of wires affixed to wooden posts. The trees were growing vertically through these, kept in place by the wires, the same way that high-end vine-yards grow their grapes. Along the fence were prominent signs aimed at drivers, so they'd know exactly what was there:

GLOBAL FRUIT
HOME OF THE RED PRINCE

What the heck was a Red Prince? The sign for Global Fruit had what looked like an apple in its logo, but I'd never seen apples growing like merlot grapes. Over the course of that summer I kept driving by the home of the Red Prince, each time watching as the trees grew more lush. They definitely seemed to be apples, though I'd never heard of the variety before. When fall came I finally saw them for sale at Foodland, the local grocery store. They looked like a cross between a Red Delicious and a McIntosh, with dark blood-red skin and a round body that fit perfectly in my palm. I bit in and was met with a sharp crunch, a firm flesh that was easy to eat, and a taste that started out tangy and mellowed into a lasting sweetness. It was a hell of an apple. Where had it been all my life?

Through the fall and winter of 2010 the Red Prince kept pop-ping up in front of me. I regularly saw the apples at grocery stores and fruit stands near Thornbury and Red Prince apple pies coming out of the oven at the local bakery. Down in Toronto the apples were even appearing in the produce section of big supermarkets like

Loblaws, the national grocery chain that frequently dictates mainstream Canadian food trends. There were even newspaper stories about the Red Prince. I'd never seen an apple—or really any produce item—arrive from obscurity and drop into the mainstream grocery world with such a presence. With a prepared product like Big Picture Farms' caramels, a culturally driven kitchen item like cupcakes, or a chef-driven flavor trend like Ricardo Zarate's, I understood the evolution from the tastemaker's mind to my mouth: they began with a niche audience, built up a demand, spread news of it organically, and eventually grew that into a mainstream trend. I also saw how it worked with packaged goods, like Dole's chia clusters, which were formulated, tested, refined, and targeted at a very specific market. Boatloads of money went into those efforts, and every aspect of those clusters, from their size to their color to the audible level of their crunch, had been taken into account with persistent market research and consultation so that they were targeted to the consumer's ideal taste before they even hit the shelves. That was why it took companies like Dole years to bring something like chia clusters to the market; they were constantly tweaking and refining the product so that its chance of success was basically assured. But how did you do that with something as imperfect and irregular as an apple or any other agricultural product? I had seen Glenn Roberts do something like this with ancient grains, but Roberts was an eccentric exception. He relied exclusively on a network of highly influential chefs to adopt Anson Mills products, and he knew that they would remain a niche product for the gourmet eater and cook, without ever making it into the mainstream.

What the Red Prince had me wondering was what it took to make an unknown food a recognizable trend with the general public, how you marketed an apple no one had ever heard of until consumers placed it in their grocery cart. I had heard about a similar thing being done with steak. In the 1990s, when beef prices were dropping, an organization called the Beef Innovations Group analyzed underused muscle groups and isolated more than a dozen new cuts that they then branded and marketed as new value-conscious steaks. These included the Delmonico steak, the Sierra Cut, and the Merlot steak (from the heel). Butchers and restaurants received this information and began requesting these cuts from their local meatpackers. Some actually succeeded as trends, like the Flat Iron steak, which quickly became the country's fifth-best-selling steak, whereas others, such as the Denver Cut, have yet to really capture the public's imagination. The Red Prince apple was something else: a nascent food trend hanging, as it were, right in front of my face, brought to life by the power of marketing.

～

Marius and Irma Botden are from Sambeek, a town in the south of the Netherlands, near the German border. Marius is the second generation of his family to work in the apple business. His father owned a nursery where he grew and sold fruit trees to other growers—but not the apples themselves. After marrying in the mid-1990s, Marius and Irma opened up their own smaller nursery and began experimenting with different breeds of fruit, especially apples. The European apple market was becoming increasingly competitive and innovative at the time, and growers were looking for new varieties and breeds of apples to sell to consumers and set themselves apart from the pack. The Botdens began experimenting with different apple trees, and one day a friend who was visiting brought them a new breed that they might be interested in. It had been discovered in 1994, at the Princen Brothers Orchard, close to the town of Weert. At a section in the orchard where both Jonathan and Golden Delicious apples were being grown, a single tree was producing bright red apples. It was an accidental crossing, an unwanted bastard child of the Jonathan and Golden Delicious that had created something better than its original parents. This is a needle-in-a-haystack event in the agriculture business. As I witnessed with Glenn Roberts's work at Anson Mills, most new plant breeds take decades of experimentation, with thousands of false starts and mistakes. The folks at Princen had a new, perfect apple dropped on them as though it were divine intervention. They named it the Red Prince.

(There is another Jonathan-Golden Delicious hybrid that is widely distributed, a red-green, round little fruit called, appropriately enough, the Jonagold. It is often used for baking, and its origins are as American as anything you might bake an apple into. But it is not bright red, and it has never been a trend. Perhaps there is a marketing lesson here.)

Red Prince apples are what the industry refers to as club apples because their intellectual property is protected with patents and trademarks, so only licensed growers are allowed to sell them. Most other apples, like McIntosh, are basically open-source apples: if you can get the seed, you can grow them. The Princen Brothers contracted the Botdens to grow Red Prince saplings for the Dutch market. They began selective breeding at a research station, making the Red Prince trees more resistant to disease and better at producing fruit commercially. Even before the trees bore fruit, Marius and Irma saw that there was tremendous demand for the Red Prince from growers, and they wanted a larger opportunity than the nursery could provide. "You always want to do something new and exciting," said Irma, who is slender, tanned, and wears her blonde hair short. The Red Prince was crisp yet sweet, had a bold color that drew the eye, and grew most often in the ideal size for large grocery stores like Walmart. It stored so well, you could release it months after harvest, in the winter, when your competitors would be out of apples; in fact, aging the apples in cold storage during that time actually improved their taste. "This was an apple with a long shelf life. It's good for baking and eating out of your hands," Irma said.

Land in the Netherlands was prohibitively expensive to purchase a new orchard, and the Botdens were less enthusiastic about relocating their four children to developing European apple growing markets like Poland. They had friends who had moved to Canada, and they liked the country when they visited, but when they looked into the apple business there they saw a few things that really interested them. Canada had an ideal apple growing climate, especially in Ontario, with an affordable guest-worker program (Jamaicans who were brought in to work the harvest) and decent land prices.

It was also ripe for innovation. After a decline of several decades Canadians were now eating more apples, but domestic production wasn't keeping up with demand. More than half the apples eaten in Canada were now imported, and the domestically grown varieties were comparably low in quality and innovation. Few farmers were growing branded, club apples like the Europeans or, increasingly, the Americans. "If you compared Canadian apples with the US, they weren't the greatest," Marius said when we all spoke in the company's small office, right off the orchard, one fall day. "Here you have a lot of big old trees, which looks nice, but the apples got smaller and smaller." If the Botdens could hit the ground with an exclusive, unique apple grown in a novel way, they could not only do well for themselves but also fundamentally shift the way the Canadian apple business worked.

New flavors in the apple world are a relatively recent phenomenon. Though there are tens of thousands of varieties in the world, the majority of North American supermarkets carried no more than a handful of different apples, chosen for their color, their durability in transport, and how they could sit on a shelf for a long time, but not necessarily for taste. Red Delicious, one of the first branded apples, which now has all the flavor and mouthfeel of a hand-me-down pillow, still accounts for 60 percent of the apples sold in America. That began to change in the past few decades with the introduction of branded varieties that sought to break out of the pack. From the mid-1970s onward, variety in the apple market increased dramatically, as new international breeds landed on American shores. The Australians brought the Granny Smith and Pink Lady; New Zealand introduced the Braeburn, Jazz, and Gala; and Japan flew over the Fuji. Recent entries have included the Kiku (a sweeter Fuji), the Junami (Swiss and very juicy), and, most recently, SweeTango from Minnesota, a state that also produced the Honeycrisp, possibly the biggest apple trend to hit North America since Red Delicious. Honeycrisp invigorated the apple business. Everything about it, from its pink and yellow speckled flesh to its zingy name and the earth-shattering crispness of it was an apple lover's dream. The

Honeycrisp made apples exciting again and really showed the potential for branded apples in the North American market.

"This is the future of apples," Irma said as she served me a slice of a deep-dish Red Prince apple crumble that she'd baked that morning: rich with cinnamon, a crunchy sugary topping, and the soft, sweet apples. "In Europe, all the produce is branded."

The Botdens acquired the exclusive rights to grow Red Prince apples in Canada as well as the apple's Canadian trademark. They moved to Thornbury in 2001 and bought an eighty-eight-acre orchard with thirty-year-old trees, then tore out those trees and replanted in 2003 with less than a third the density as before (to concentrate flavor), primarily in Red Prince but also some Honeycrisp and McIntosh for diversity. Marius used the vineyard-style cultivation method he had employed in Europe and even invented his own sprayer, which was better suited for the precise rows strung along wires. Fruit trees take four years to mature enough to bear fruit, and so they waited while the Red Prince came in, selling what they had from existing trees under the Global Fruit brand to pay their bills. Though they were allowed to sell Red Prince trees to other Canadian growers as part of their agreement with the Princen brothers, the Botdens kept the rights to themselves. "We didn't want someone to screw up the shape, size, and color," Irma said, noting that the American holder of the Red Prince rights, a grower in Washington state (the continental capital of apple growing) couldn't get them to grow right.

During this time, while the Red Prince lay in wait on the trees, Irma and Marius were busy planning for its ascension to the throne of the nation's produce department—essentially manufacturing a trend. To help them do this they turned to Virginia Zimm. A tall, gregarious woman bursting with energy, Zimm is the president of Faye Clack Communications, a produce marketing firm in Toronto that was founded by her mother in the 1970s. Faye Clack was a grade-school teacher who began working for the Ontario Apple Commission in education, then went to school at night, got a degree in public relations, and went on to dominate the male-dominated field of produce marketing in Ontario. Her nickname, a former buyer told me, was Faye Clack, Vegetable Flack. "People didn't know how to brand commodities," Zimm said, describing her mother's impact on the industry. "They'd say, 'Yeah, it's a pear.' Well, the past ten years the produce category really began branding, but I dare you to name a brand in the produce aisle." Faye Clack Communications specializes in taking fresh fruits and vegetables and making them into brands that customers ask for when they go shopping. "We understand fresh, seasonability, and perishability," Zimm said. "It's not like a can of soup that can sit for a month on a shelf. That apple has to sell in days. It has to move, so our campaign has to be supercharged, even if we don't have the budget of a packaged food manufacturer."

Produce marketing aims to create a story about the food it's trying to sell, because a story will stick with shoppers long enough for them to taste it—and taste is ultimately what wins. At its core is the attempt to alter the consumer's behavior so they think differently about an apple (or a bushel of kale) in a way they never did before. When it comes to apples, this is nothing new. The common expression, "An apple a day keeps the doctor away," was coined by J. T. Stinson, a Missouri apple horticulturist who was promoting apples at the 1904 World's Fair and went on to forever associate apples and health in the eyes of consumers. "The key thing with long-term change, and not just a [sales] bump in the next six months, is to affect behavioral change," said Terry O'Reilly, an author, radio host, and an expert on the history of advertising and marketing, who lives just south of Thornbury. "That's the toughest task to give someone in marketing. It takes time and patience and hard work." But when it succeeds, great food marketing can ignite trends that are difficult to extinguish. O'Reilly cites the coffee break, a previously unknown tradition that took root among Swedish immigrant housewives in Wisconsin but blossomed into a fixture of the North American workplace routine in the 1950s when coffee marketers, led by Maxwell House, popularized the ritual in advertisements to the point at which it became enshrined in union contracts and workplace culture to this day, vastly increased our coffee consumption, and made possible everything from Starbucks to Sanka.

If anyone excels at produce marketing today in the United States it is Frieda's, a specialty fruit and vegetable distributor based in Southern California. In the late 1950s Frieda Caplan, fresh out of UCLA and looking for a job, went to work for relatives in the wholesale produce market of Los Angeles. Like Faye Clack in Toronto, Caplan was the lone woman in the gruff, male-dominated market, and she stuck out like a sore thumb in the best way possible. "My mom was naturally a promoter and very friendly," said her daughter Karen Caplan, who is now the company's CEO. In those days farmers didn't put a lot of thought into marketing their produce. They would grow something on their land, then suddenly realize just before they picked it that they needed to figure out how to sell it. So the farmers would load up their trucks and drive down from the Central Valley to the Los Angeles produce market, where they would walk door to door with samples of their eggplant or strawberry, begging the distributors to sell what they were offering. If it was something new, the conservative buyers would basically brush them off. "All the old guys would say, 'I'm too busy selling lettuce and onions,'" said Karen. "'But if you walk down there to the end of the market, there's a woman named Frieda. She'll talk to anyone.'"

And talk Frieda did, lending an open ear to every farmer, importer, and dreamer who arrived at her door with boxes of strange-looking fruits and vegetables with unknown names and no presence whatsoever in the market. Her first success in 1960, back when she was still working for her cousins, were brown mushrooms. At the time North Americans bought white button mushrooms—clean, easy, white mushrooms, whole or sliced. Brown mushrooms, now that was something nobody wanted. They looked like dirt. Were they even safe to eat? Frieda took a chance and not only launched the brown mushroom into the mainstream of our food culture but also spawned a trend for eating a whole portfolio of mushrooms, from meaty portobellos to delicate shitakes, that continues to grow today. According to the USDA, national brown mushroom sales in 2012 were $212 million, up from just $168 million two years prior. Thank Frieda Caplan for that.

Two years later Frieda encountered the fruit that would launch her own business and put her on the map as an important taste-maker, especially where produce is concerned. A shopper at a Safeway supermarket in Salt Lake City had approached the store's produce manager with a request. He had just come back from a mission with the Mormon Church in New Zealand, where he had eaten a delicious fruit called a Chinese gooseberry. The fruit had originated in southern China, where it had been called by a variety of names, including the Gooseberry, Sunny Peach, Macaque Peach, Wonder Fruit, and, in a bit of decidedly un-Western branding, the Hairy Bush fruit. In the late 1930s it was introduced to New Zealand and cultivated with great success, at one point under the name Melonette, which is where the hungry missionary had encountered it. The produce manager had never heard of a Chinese gooseberry, but he promised to look into it and called his wholesale buyer at the market in Los Angeles to see whether he could track one down. The buyer walked around the market, asking about this strange, unknown fruit, and all the men there, busy with their onions and stacks of iceberg lettuce, pointed him in Frieda's direction. She said she'd never heard of one but would keep her eye out. A couple of weeks later a fruit broker appeared at her door with a Telex from ex-porters in New Zealand, inquiring whether anyone would be inter-ested in bringing a fruit called the Chinese gooseberry to America.

"It's all based on luck and destiny, our business," said Karen, retelling the story that was now a core part of the family legend. "Mom says, 'Oh my god . . . I'll take them all. I already have my first customer.' Remember that these things were brown, fuzzy, hard as a rock, and no one knows what they are. But my mother finds out they have a great shelf life. It takes her six months to sell 250 boxes. She sends all the profits back to New Zealand and sends them to the growers with specific instructions: work on its name." The name the growers came up with, based on the similarity between the Chinese gooseberry and the shape of New Zealand's small national bird, was the kiwi.

That was the beginning of the kiwi trend, though it would not reach critical mass for close to two decades. Before the kiwi came

into your house, before it was the go-to garnish on breakfast buffets and a punch line for jokes about 1980s nouvelle cuisine, the
kiwi was an unknown fruit in Frieda Caplan's warehouse that no
one even knew they didn't want. To sell kiwis, Frieda had to first
make them known and then make them desirable, and she did this
through a long campaign. "I call it gradually, then suddenly," says
Karen, borrowing Ernest Hemmingway's proverb on bankruptcy.
"It's the same thing that happens with cupcakes." First, she secured
a supply for the kiwis, helping growers perfect their yield and quality as well as contracting farmers to grow them the other half of the
year in California, so the demand would never be without a source.
Then, she began sampling kiwis. Frieda went to restaurants and had
them make French-style fruit tarts topped with sliced kiwis so she
could hand out pieces to prospective buyers and immediately show
its dazzling green color, bright taste, and potential uses. The kiwi
could be eaten cut up, diced into cocktails, sliced as a garnish, or
layered atop pastry. Each use represented different markets, from
grocery stores to bakeries and restaurant service contractors. Then
Frieda got the kiwi into the hands of food editors at newspapers and
magazines in the hope of generating press and some level of public awareness. The more people heard about kiwis, the more likely
they were to request them from their grocers, who would invariably
find Frieda and place an order. But it took time, and it wasn't until
the early 1980s, when tastemaking California chefs such as Wolfgang Puck and Alice Waters began integrating kiwis into desserts
and salads as garnishes, that the trend really took off. "You had a
chef featuring our product, and food writers wrote about it. It kinda
gradually then suddenly became a trend," Karen said for the second
time. "It's our eighteen-year success story."

Since that fateful encounter with kiwis Frieda's has introduced
over two hundred new fruits and vegetables to the American market and, in many cases, the Western world. Many of them are as
unfamiliar today as the day Frieda's acquired a sample. Ever heard
of kiwanos, oroblancos, or Buddha's hands? Me neither. But I can't
tell you how many times I have eaten passionfruit, sugar snap peas,
pink grapefruits, pine nuts, hothouse cucumbers, sweet onions, and

habanero chilies without realizing who made those trends possible. Karen told me that despite advances in agriculture, technology, and the food distribution business, the process of creating a produce trend is no different today from what it was when her mother brought in that first shipment of kiwis. First, they'll work with farmers to improve a fruit's or vegetable's flavor profile and shelf life, a process that takes several years, at the least. Once it's ideal, they'll sample it to customers and secure enough orders to justify a larger farming investment. With sales secured, Frieda's will go out and find more growers to cultivate the product so a consistent supply can be assured, because product shortages will stop a trend dead in its tracks. Then Frieda's will work to create more public demand to absorb the increased supply. They will reach out to the public through tastemakers like bloggers, food writers, celebrity chefs, influential restaurateurs, and even media personalities, such as Dr. Oz.

This is essentially the same process Faye Clack Communications uses with its own clients in Ontario, though their focus is on creating a brand rather than distribution, which other companies handle. Virginia Zimm's mission, like the folks at Frieda's, is to take an edible piece of nature and create a promise out of it, communicate that promise to the public, and then deliver on it with taste. A Honeycrisp is a perfect example of a branded fruit that delivers on its promise. It is a crisp apple that tastes sweet as honey, but without the name and the marketing behind it, it would just be one more apple in a pile at the supermarket. "If it's on the shelf and no one knows, they'll just walk on by," said Zimm.

On a cold morning in March I joined Zimm at the Ontario Food Terminal, a large, guarded complex of battered concrete parking lots, low-slung buildings, and loading docks just west of the city. Zimm and I had spoken before about produce branding, but I wanted to see how it played out on the floor of the wholesale market, which is the third-largest produce distribution center in North America, after Los Angeles and Chicago, and moves over five million tons of produce daily to customers in Toronto and surrounding communities. We walked around the U-shaped inner courtyard, where buyers backed graffiti-covered delivery trucks up to the docks belonging to each of the twenty-one "houses," which is what they call the different distributors that operate out of the terminal. Men in motorized loading carts stacked high with crates of fruits and vegetables zipped by in a constant stream, each dangling a lit cigarette out of their mouths, dodging each other by mere inches. On the loading docks everyone from uniformed logistics coordinators from national supermarket chains to elderly Chinese corner store owners with hand-drawn carts were filling their orders, to be shipped out and stocked in produce sections for shoppers to purchase.

Inside the windowed walls crates of pristine fruits and vegetables of every shape, color, and flavor were displayed in immaculate climate-controlled warehouses staffed by men in white butcher's coats and monogrammed T-shirts. There were skyscrapers of Valencia oranges, giant hills of russet potatoes, and crates of flawless figs lined up in precise formation like delicate purple soldiers. Zimm, much like her mother and Frieda Caplan back in the day, was still the only woman on the ground, but she knew all the men here and addressed them by their first name. At one house she grabbed a bag of red bird's eye chili peppers right from its crate, tore it open, and began eating the little red firecrackers like grapes. "These are my vice," she said, waving to the house's owner, who was suspended in an office above his warehouse. He saw her, acknowledged the peppers she had taken, and waved back nonplussed.

Inside another one of the houses Zimm stooped down to the floor and picked up a large artichoke with a purplish tinge to it from a box that said Ocean Mist. "This is probably the best artichoke in the world, which is interesting because it's not a native vegetable to California," where Ocean Mist artichokes, which dominate the North American artichoke market, are grown. Still, said Zimm, "no one in the grocery store will know this artichoke is Ocean Mist." It will just be an artichoke in a big anonymous pile, with a price per pound and the words *Product of USA*. Zimm wanted to approach Ocean Mist and propose a campaign that would bring their brand to life for consumers, increasing their value significantly. "If it were branded, this product [really, any product] would fetch a thirty to one hundred percent premium" at the cash register. Anything can be branded, Zimm said, even something as straightforward and commonplace as romaine lettuce, as she picked up a bag containing three Andy Boy romaine hearts, trimmed of their wilted outer leaves and sealed in a brightly labeled package with pink trim. I've bought Andy Boy–brand romaine hearts many times, despite knowing that it's nearly twice the price of a head of romaine lettuce, with no discernible difference in taste. But there's a value added in the packaging, said Zimm, picking up a loose head of Peter Rabbit romaine. "By the time this gets to the store, because it's not packaged, the leaves will wilt or tear, and they'll end up trimming and tossing away a lot of them."

The Gambles house was the market's largest distributor, a cavernous, windowless, refrigerated warehouse the size of a city block. Inside Zimm showed me an example of a branding campaign that had turned into a trend. She walked over to a box and picked up a Vidalia onion, the sweet, large, saucer-shaped onions from Vidalia, Georgia, that she had marketed in Canada for twelve years to the point at which Vidalias became so well known that there was no need to promote them further. In 1986 Georgia's state legislature had trademarked the Vidalia onion name, treating it like a European appellation for wine or cheese (e.g., Champagne is a sparkling wine only from the Champagne region), preventing others from co-opting their hard-earned brand and diluting it with a cheaper sweet onion that had a different flavor profile. The Vidalia Onion Committee, an umbrella organization of roughly a hundred Vidalia farmers who controlled the brand, engaged in various marketing exercises over the years to cement the onion's growing trend with customers. One of the most recent enlisted the services of animated green ogre Shrek (no shy lover of onions) to promote Vidalias to kids shopping in supermarkets with their parents. It may seem like an odd match between product and marketing strategy—we are accustomed to seeing cartoon characters associated with sugary, brightly colored cereals, not pungent vegetables—but the campaign caused Vidalia sales to shoot up by as much as 50 percent, according to the growers. That's the power of marketing on trends; it can even make stars out of ordinary onions.

As for Red Prince apples, Virginia Zimm had a running start—her product had a great name.

∽

Sometimes just a change in name is enough to nudge a trend forward in the commodity food world. A pear is a pear and a chicken is a chicken, but often farmers and distributors don't realize how much a bad name can be a roadblock to public acceptance. A name gives a food its identity and meaning. Before people taste it, smell it, or pick it up, they hear the name and make a quick calculation whether it sounds tasty or not. The world of produce marketing is filled with examples of this. When Canadian agricultural scientists developed a new strain of rapeseed in the 1970s that was ideal for a healthy cooking oil, they soon realized a name that immediately brought to mind sexual violence was a nonstarter in terms of marketing the new seed and its oil. So in 1978 a new name was adopted that mashed together the words *Canadian* and *oil*, canola, now the third most popular vegetable oil in the world.

Prunes had been a staple breakfast items for decades, but by the 1990s they had a major image problem. Because they were high in fiber, prunes had always been promoted as good for digestion, but as the generation that consumed them aged and the prune marketing campaign pushed the fiber angle ever more aggressively (to tap into the high-fiber diet trend), their reputation as a laxative robbed them of any appeal whatsoever. Prune juice was something my grandmother had a tiny glass of in the morning before she retired to the bathroom for half an hour. It was a product whose market share was dying along with its customers, as stagnant and immovable as the bowels it worked so hard to clear. So the California Prune Board enlisted the help of branding and marketing professionals, investing $10 million in a campaign to relaunch prunes as "dried plums," a more straightforward description that shifted the lowly prune's image in the mind of the consumer. "Research conducted in the U.S. showed that our target audience, women ages 25 to 54, responded more favorably to the name dried plums," notes the California

Dried Plum Board's website, alongside a photograph of US swimmer Natalie Coughlin, wet and smoldering like Cindy Crawford in a her bathing suit while promoting dried plums.

Perhaps the most striking story is that of the lowly Patagonian toothfish, a snarly species that swam in the cold waters of South America. So ugly that even the Chilean fisherman who accidentally caught the fish refused to eat it, the Patagonian toothfish (also called Cod of the Deep by fishermen) was an unknown, unwanted, and unmolested species up until 1977. That was the year that a young Los Angeles seafood importer named Lee Lantz took a trip to Chile to meet with suppliers and encountered a giant Patagonian toothfish as big as one hundred pounds, lying all but unnoticed on the deck of a boat in the Valparaiso Harbor. The fish piqued his curiosity, and when Lantz began asking questions he found that the Patagonian toothfish had the characteristics he was looking for: it was white-fleshed, meaty, relatively mild, and oily enough to withstand cooking heat. Not a fish that stood up on its own, but the perfect blank canvas for chefs who wanted to add their own flavor to a seafood entrée without the fish's taste fighting back. However, as author G. Bruce Knecht recounted in his 2006 book about the fish, *Hooked*, Americans wouldn't buy something called Patagonian toothfish (who wants to eat a tooth?) or Cod of the Deep (Americans aren't cod fans). "Lantz needed to create his own name, one that would spark some sort of favorable recognition in the American market," Knecht wrote. "'Sea bass' was an obvious choice. Although it is not a particularly meaningful term—it is included in the names of more than one hundred species—it has broad resonance among American seafood eaters." Lantz slapped *Chilean* at the front of *sea bass* to conjure up images of clean ocean waters and exotic locales (though, oddly, not the human rights violations going on at the time under the Chilean dictator Augusto Pinochet).

Though it took several years to catch on with the public, by the late 1990s Chilean sea bass was the darling fish of the seafood trade. Its price rose tenfold, to over $10 a pound, and I recall a time when you couldn't go to a wedding or catered event without finding it on your plate. The repositioning of Chilean sea bass was ultimately so successful that demand for the fish outstripped the relatively small population, and the species became overfished to the point at which it was driven to the brink of extinction. Illegal fishing, high seas chases with poachers, and restaurants banning its sale became the norm, and the trend Lantz launched with his name change proved so powerful that it hastened its own demise.

"If you sit down and are meeting a stranger for lunch, or a friend, and they lean over and say 'Lemme tell you a story,' you immediately lean in and listen," said David Placek, the founder of Lexicon Branding. "In very simple and easy-to-understand terms, that's what's in a name. It's the beginning of a story, the introduction to it." Placek understands the transformational power of names better than most. Since he founded Lexicon in 1982 outside San Francisco, the firm has been responsible for some of the most widely known brand names worldwide: Intel Pentium processors, Apple PowerBook computers, Blackberry phones, Subaru Outback and Forester cars, and many, many more. In the food world Lexicon coined Dasani water, Far Coast coffee, Nestlé Dibs ice cream treats, and even the clear alcoholic beverage Zima, which was a terrible idea for a boozy entry into the brief clear beverage trend that Crystal Pepsi initiated, but one with an unforgettable name.

Placek told me that naming food is the most challenging product category because, unlike a car or a computer chip, this is something you are ultimately ingesting into your body. "People are more cautious and looking for reference points to compare to something else. With the possible exception of candy bars and other sweets, you really have to make it food relevant and food acceptable," he said. "Calling a carrot Blue Sky would make people back away. It's a more conservative field and more challenging. Our canvas is not as wide as if we were naming a computer chip. With technology: the more unfamiliar I am with it, the more I might want to take a look at it. With food, the more unfamiliar you are, the more people are likely to back away from it. Naming a food product requires more caution and a framework that says, 'This has to go into people's mouths.'"

According to Placek's research, successful food names whip up an instantaneous expectation of how the food will taste by stimulating neural network associations in the brain—basically connecting the dots between memories, images, and sensations to create an idea of what that food will be like before you even see it. Lexicon recently worked with the agribusiness giant Monsanto, which had developed a hybrid seed for a very sweet honeydew melon that was more shelf stable than conventional honeydew melons. Through the company's naming process, which involves market research, consumer input, and several rounds of brainstorming sessions with Monsanto representatives, Lexicon emerged with the name Sweet Peak Honeydew. At one point a test group of consumers were brought in and given samples of the new melon. The new melon scored far better on taste when testers were told the name than when it was tasted incognito. "When we tested it with consumers, they said, 'On a hot summer day this tasted like a cold melon and perfectly sweet,' and they're taking that from just two words: Sweet Peak." This literal approach to the name has been used by Lexicon several times with Monsanto, including an onion that was meant to be eaten raw, called the Ever Mild. Others are more abstract, such as the company's Bellafina peppers, which are basically mini-bell peppers in vibrant colors. "We decided to be more positive and European and a little more poetic this time," said Placek. Names easily increase a produce item's value. Placek noted that Hawaiian cane sugar, which is a commodity that tastes the exact same, in every sense, as sugar from the Philippines, will command a 25 percent premium because customers simply perceive it as better tasting.

Food trends based around a great name tend to spawn imitators, broadening the trend from one product to a whole category of them. A perfect example is the rise since the 1980s of inexpensive, drinkable wines with quirky names. One of the pioneers in this was Barefoot wines out of California. This brand broke open the notion that wine had to be named after European castles. It was fun, it was something you could have at a picnic or a party or, yes, even drink barefoot on the beach. "All major wineries and wine groups jumped on this bandwagon and said, 'Wine is about fun and not quality, and we can sell tons of $10 wine,'" Placek said. Soon you had chocolate cake wines, cupcake wines, and wines named after every single species of cute animal, from dancing circus bears to naughty penguins, as though the wineries were transforming themselves into kids clothing boutiques. "What does 'Cherry on Top' do?" asked Placek. "It stimulates associations that aren't that close to wine. It's an inefficient name . . . imitation is suicide. You'll never be able to catch up."

When it came to the Red Prince, however, both the Botdens and Zimm agreed that they would keep the name intact. Zimm wasn't wild about every new apple's name. She felt the Jumami sounded too much like tsunami, but "we thought [Red Prince] worked," recalled Zimm as we visited a banana distributor in the food terminal, where she showed me some tiny papayas. "Prince also allowed us to suggest it as a premium product."

I asked David Placek to evaluate the effectiveness of the Red Prince name even though he hadn't had a chance to taste the apple itself. He believed it hit on the three key attributes of good names. First, it got his attention because of the way it sounded. Second, it held his attention because it conjured up an image of a prince and a color. And third, it led him to conclude that the name contained a new idea he should consider, which in this case was just how the Red Prince apple would taste. "When I hear Red Prince, my mind begins to imagine certain things about it." Placek said. "That affects taste. I bet Red Prince would be crisp, I see sort of a smaller, very symmetrical, good-looking apple. I think it's tight, not big, and I actually have an association that this would be a very good-tasting apple. I think it's a good name."

❦

With the Red Prince in hand, Zimm and her team set about creating a comprehensive identity for the apple that would resonate with the North American market. In many ways working with the Botdens was easier than many other produce clients launching a new fruit or vegetable. In cases like the Honeycrisp or SweeTango apples, the marketing effort was undertaken by cooperatives of growers who had bought into the license, sometimes as many as a hundred different farmers pooling their resources together. This can slow the decision-making process and steer people toward safe, compromised choices that may not resonate as strongly with the public. But the Botdens were insistent that they were launching the Red Prince on their own. They wanted to control the trees and the quality of the growth conditions and were prepared to foot the bill for Zimm's efforts. This was no small feat. At the end of the day they estimated spending over $2.5 million on marketing the Red Prince in Canada during those first crucial seasons, an astronomical investment for what is still a small family farm. But Zimm believed she had something special on her hands. "Apples are as old as the hills," she recalled as we finished our tour of the produce market. "The Red Prince, however, created a new product that was exciting."

She met with the Botdens over several days that year and took them through a series of exercises to flesh out just who the Red Prince was. She used an easel, sketch paper, markers, and a whiteboard, and she encouraged Irma and Marius to shout out words they thought worked with the apple: juicy, red, sweet, crisp, tart. Next, they yelled out who the target audience would be: wholesalers, shoppers, packers, distributors, buyers, consumers. The idea was to find out who would come into contact with the Red Prince and what they would want to hear. "What resonates with them?" asked Zimm. "If I told a wholesaler 'Red Prince is juicy and crisp,' he'd say, 'So, how can I sell it?' I'd tell him, 'It's a premium apple, and you can charge more for it—period.' Then I'd tell a retailer, 'You can make more in the apple category, but we'll support it with promotions to move it off the shelf.'" Then she worked on drafting factual proof points to back up the identity they were crafting. For instance, if Zimm said the Red Prince was good to bake in a pie, she could demonstrate through laboratory tests that the apple had a high sugar content and a firm cellular structure that could withstand heat.

Finally, Zimm conducted what she called her "creative silly brainstorming session," a sort of free-for-all, no-holds-barred jumble of words, images, and ideas designed to tease out the real Red Prince's personality once and for all. Although the Red Prince session had taken place years before I even met Zimm, she was conducting a similar exercise that afternoon at the Ontario Food Terminal, and after our tour we went upstairs to the spartan board-room of Gambles. Gambles was preparing to launch their own branded line of produce, called GoFresh, which would sell fruits and vegetables directly to consumers under the GoFresh label. Over the next five hours the company's key staff would sit with Zimm and figure out just what exactly the GoFresh brand would be.

"Stop me if you think this is really goofy," Zimm said as she opened up a marker and stood by an easel with a large sketchpad, "but there's a purpose in the end!" Then she drew the Mercedes emblem and asked everyone what people saw when they encountered that symbol.

"Luxury!" said Alanda Ferreira, who worked in sales and marketing.

"Yes," said Zimm, who drives a warhorse of an old Benz herself, "but that doesn't always happen. Luxury to the dealership means higher profit. Luxury to the consumer means status." She asked everyone to then shout out the word that they felt the Go-Fresh brand was about.

"Quality!"

"Consistency."

"Premium."

"Confidence."

"No waste."

"Expectation."

"Luxury!"

"I'm thinking luxury maybe isn't the right word," said Jeff Hughes, the company's president, though that spawned Zimm to suggest "premium," which led into "homegrown," which led Sean Balog, a young produce trader, to suggest the catch phrase "If it was any fresher, it would still be growing."

"Go fresh or go home!" Joseph Comella, the produce buyer at one of Gambles's larger supermarket clients, shouted triumphantly.

Zimm wrote down each and every suggestion, filling up sheets of paper and tearing them off just as quickly, and she then taped them around the walls of the room. "You need to stand for something," she said during a brief break in the wordplay. "You need to take the human condition into your brand. You can say all the fancy words you want, but at the end of the day if your brand doesn't resonate, the customer will walk on by." She then asked everyone in the room to think about the GoFresh brand in a more human sense. "If the brand was a person, who would they be? What kind of car would they drive? Where would they take vacation, or shop?" Everyone was given a sheet of paper and asked to write down a character sketch of GoFresh, then read them out loud. Ferreira's was the best in the bunch. She described her person, who was named Frieda Fresh, as a fashionable and trendy woman in her midthirties who drives a hybrid and is aware of new health trends but doesn't always follow them.

It was an important series of questions. A few years before, the growers of the milled carrots commonly referred to as baby carrots launched a $25 million rebranding campaign with a major advertising agency, which repositioned the little carrots as a young, healthy junk food. The vegetable's personality was picked as a rebellious teenager. The packaging went from pastoral scenes to skateboarding cartoon carrots and carrots doing extreme sports. It was the carrot as the energy drink! The rock-and-roll carrot!

For her work with the Red Prince, the existing name made matching the personality more straightforward. "What came out of that session with the Botdens was the idea of princely behavior," Zimm said. "The Red Prince is a gentleman. He has manners, he is polished. He lives in a grand house, drives a nice car, and he likes the nice things in life, but he's also kind to others. In short, a real prince of a guy." Zimm then crafted the marketing campaign around this image. Borrowing from the Red Prince's successful 2007 launch in Germany, she hired a handsome actor dressed as a prince in a red suit with gold brocades and a collar and sash embossed with the apple's new logo—an apple unpeeled like a corkscrew, because Irma was adamant on not using an apple with a crown, as the Europeans had done. The prince would appear at grocery stores across Toronto, handing out apple slices and performing princely acts, such as opening doors, kneeling down to kiss hands, and generally being a mensch. It was part of the apple's splashy launch in the winter of 2010.

One day Zimm unleashed the Red Prince's court into the vast interconnected underground mall that links Toronto's downtown office towers. Twenty-one young men wearing black suits with red ties, silk kerchiefs, and bowler hats handed out Red Prince apples in individually wrapped golden mesh bags, which were piled on silver platters. Members of the media were sent elaborate boxes that opened to reveal a Red Prince apple on a red silk pillow. The Red Prince had its own Facebook page and a Twitter account (@RedPrinceApple) with nearly a thousand followers that Irma and Marius constantly updated with photos from the orchard. Thanks to these stunts, the apple generated tremendous press across Canada, with articles in newspapers, business magazines, and food blogs heralding the arrival of what some were calling the next Honeycrisp. The campaign put the Red Prince on the map for the first time in North America, and the Botdens began collecting buyers: Kroger supermarkets in the United States and Loblaws in Canada, Walmart in both countries, and scores of independents—around two thousand stores in all. The groundwork was laid for the Red Prince to become the next great trend in apples.

The Red Prince continued its slow but steady growth through 2011 and 2012, but that winter, shortly after the previous year's apples went to the market, disaster struck. After a cold and snowy February, March brought with it an unprecedented heat wave that lasted close to two weeks, with temperatures rising into the seventies. I was up in Thornbury during one of those weekends. On Saturday morning I went skiing on the rapidly melting hill in a sweatshirt, then came back to the house and walked my dog on the beach in shorts as ice floated in the bay. Climate change had hit hard, causing the buds on the apple trees to blossom two months early. Unfortunately, it was still winter, and when freezing temperatures returned a few weeks later most of the apple buds died. By the time of that fall's harvest, the Botdens were only able to salvage a small portion of their Red Prince crop, and these apples were so small and damaged that they were either sliced and packaged generically or crushed into juice. The season's work was a total wash, and any momentum the Red Prince campaign had gathered toward a trend was now derailed.

"It's March," Zimm said as we sat in the market in 2013, "and we should be going crazy on the Red Prince, but they don't have any apples. That's agriculture. There's nothing you can do. Mother nature can be a real bitch."

The Red Prince's setback was a reminder that agricultural food trends, whether Red Prince apples or Anson Mills China Black rice, are tenuous, long-term projects. Growers, distributors, and produce marketers may want to hook onto trends in the culinary world, but it takes years, if not decades to perfect a plant's breeding, establish a secure and diversified supply network, and have the distribution in place to guarantee it a spot in the market. If a factory making M&Ms burns down, it's likely that the supply of the candy will be only temporarily affected, as setting up a new production line is simply a matter of money. But if a crop is wiped out by weather, disease, or bad genetics, its recovery takes years. Karen Caplan at Frieda's told me about a product called kale sprouts that shot for a trend before it was mature enough. Both the vegetable kale and brussels sprouts had been trending with chefs and home cooks in the past few years, thanks to dishes that paired them with bacon as well as kale's long, sturdy shelf life and its spot as a darling of urban farmer's markets. Then an American grower had found a seed in Europe that combined the two vegetables into a single plant. He paid tens of thousands of dollars for the seed, and when some distributors got wind of it, they began spreading the news on social media, sending samples to select chefs and driving up demand among foodies. In early 2013 popular recipe blogger Dorothy Reinhold called kale sprouts "the newest, coolest green veggie to hit the produce section since that kooky looking Romanesco showed up and made us all wish we spent more time studying fractals." But there was a problem: the grower had been so busy increasing supply to meet hot demand that they hadn't had the chance to breed the vegetables sufficiently to survive long-distance transport. "By the time they got to the warehouse, the plants had turned yellow," said

Caplan. "Kale sprouts had this huge spike and enormous drop off. They're not going to be mainstream for a very, very long time, even though brussels sprouts and kale are both still trending. The grower has to perfect mother nature."

The reality, said Caplan, was that produce trends still grow gradually, over the course of ten or more years, only arriving with a marketing push once they are ready. Frieda counseled her company's clients to grow slowly, establishing a sturdy supply and good breeding, allowing trends to emerge organically. In 2012 the company launched a campaign to introduce the Stokes purple sweet potato, which was a sweet potato that was purple in color. To the public's eye it appeared out of nowhere, but Caplan noted that its success was a convergence of several different trends, from the growing interest in colored vegetables to a Vitamin A health trend to the rising popularity of sweet potato French fries in North American chain restaurants. "We show up with purple sweet potatoes a year ago, and it looks like we're on trend," said Caplan. "But we did a tremendous amount of research to realize that this would be an easier product to introduce than any before."

Back in Thornbury, the Botdens weren't too worried. I visited them again in the summer of 2013, and things were looking up. A long, cold winter followed by a wet spring and hot summer was doing great things for the crop. Irma took me into the orchard and showed me the Red Prince apples growing in little clusters on the trees. Each was the size of a plum at this point, but they would soon grow as big as a fist before their September harvest. The family had planted more acres of Red Prince trees, and despite missing the market the previous year, demand for the apples had somehow increased from major Canadian supermarkets like Loblaws. "I still love the brand," Irma said, holding an apple in her hand. "It looks fresh and new and strong and bold." A decade after planting the first Red Prince trees in North America, she predicted this would be the first year that the apple would finally deliver them a profit.

PART III

WHY FOOD TRENDS MATTER

8

ETHNIC FOODS

AS AMERICAN AS CHICKEN TIKKA MASALA

In the large cafeteria of Hurley Medical Center, a trauma hospital in the battered, boarded-up downtown of Flint, Michigan, Dr. Rao Mushtaq, a pediatric resident from Pakistan, walked up to the steam trays at the Café Spice kiosk, took a spoon, and flicked two grains of rice pulao into his mouth. He chewed for thirty seconds, walked around to the vegetarian side of the counter, and repeated the taste test with another batch. After careful deliberation and a dramatic shake of his head, Dr. Mushtaq filled his plate with a pool of mint chutney, took two warm naan breads, and joined a table with his colleagues—other doctors from India, Pakistan, Bangladesh, and Nepal—who had all been eating curries, biriyanis, and other Indian staples from the Café Spice kiosk every single day for lunch and dinner since it had opened here in 2011.

"We were eating a lot of mac 'n' cheese before," groaned Dr. Mushtaq.

"My first year here, my cholesterol shot up dangerously high," echoed Dr. Vishwas Vaniqwala, an Indian-born pediatrician. "Honestly, I used to skip lunches because I was sick of eating salads and sandwiches and chips."

The South Asian doctors who made up the vast majority of residents at Hurley eventually demanded more familiar food from Steve

Dunn, the cafeteria's executive chef, who works for the national catering company Sodexo. Dunn had never even tasted Indian food,
but he consulted online recipes and made samosas, saag paneer, and
chickpea masala from scratch one day. The food sold out in minutes. "I couldn't do it every day," Dunn said, despite the doctors'
enthusiastic response. "I mean, it takes a hell of a lot of time and
knowledge. You've gotta know the keys and tricks to Indian cooking. It took my staff three weeks to learn how to make basmati rice
because they were used to Uncle Ben's. You've got to soak it, rinse
it, add butter and spices, and cook it in a certain way."

Instead, Dunn turned to Café Spice, America's largest Indian
foodservice company, which had recently launched a branded partnership with Sodexo and received their turnkey solution. Each
month he orders palettes of premade, frozen Indian dishes that his
staff simply thaws, heats, and serves in a kiosk designed and in-
stalled by Café Spice. Dunn took me back into the hospital's massive kitchen, where one of his young cooks, Chris Espinoza, was
loading up a steam oven with frozen containers of chicken tikka
masala, saag paneer, and bhindi masala. "I tried it once," Espinoza
admitted as he switched out the frozen food for freshly heated containers of the same dishes and poured them into serving trays, "but
I'm not into the spicy stuff. I like what I like."

So far the bulk of the customers at the Café Spice kiosk, which
was next to stations that served sandwiches, burgers, meatloaf and
mashed potatoes, pizzas, and salads, had been the South Asian doctors, but Dunn had noticed a growing interest in the Indian food
from other hospital staff, and the food was only available at two
other places in Flint. At lunch Dunn introduced me to Tracy Da-
viek, a nurse who had never tasted Indian food until Café Spice
opened in the hospital. "I tried it on the first day when they were
giving out samples," she said, dipping a piece of naan bread into a
steaming mound of bhindi okra masala, a tomato-based okra stew.
"I love to eat it. My favorite is the chicken . . . " she turned to Dunn,
"you know, the one in the red sauce . . . "

"Chicken tikka masala," Dunn said, noting the company's
most popular dish of roast chicken pieces in a creamy curry.

"Yeah, that stuff and the dish with the garbanzo beans and the mango smoothies . . . "

"Lassi," said Dunn.

Just then, another nurse came up to Dunn and looked at his plate of chicken vindaloo and biriyani. "Hey Steve," she said, "I want a taste of that tomorrow. I don't know what it is, but I want to see if I like it."

∽

When you've just read the fifth article in one week about the benefit of chia seeds and the lines down the block for the new burger truck make it impossible to get to your car, it's hard to see just why we should give a damn about food trends at all. Caught up in the seasonal fashion cycle of flavor fads, we tend to miss the subtle shift under the surface that food trends are exerting. But if you think back to what you ate ten, twenty, or even thirty years ago, their effect is apparent and is glorious. It is hard to believe that there was a time, well into my teenage years, when I had never tasted pad Thai, sushi, or ceviche. These days appetizer platters are filled with garlicky hummus and fluffy pita, golden tortilla chips and spicy salsa verde. But as recently as fifteen years ago they were nothing but cut veggies and ranch dressing or round crackers with a chewy, low-flavor cheese. Remember salad without the rich coating of extra-virgin olive oil? It seems remote today, but even a generation back we lived in a land of meat-and-potato eaters who feared garlic as we now fear trans fats. We liked our bread white, our vegetables overcooked, and our food bland. We ate at steakhouses, taverns, and pubs, and we only strayed out of that model in baby steps, with Americanized Chinese food that involved plates of grenadine-smothered chicken balls and checkered tablecloth Italian restaurants that boiled down that glorious nation's cuisine to leaden lasagna and pepperoni pizzas.

Contrast that with today, when chipotle hot sauce and miso paste are as common in restaurant kitchens as ketchup and mustard, and even the smallest towns have somewhere serving pad

Thai. One of the big reasons why food trends matter is that they have the power to pick up one culture's cuisine and push it above the fray of cheap, marginalized ethnic foods to the point at which it becomes part of our everyday diet. Once, these global foods were exclusively confined to their urban immigrant neighborhoods, but as food trends have grown more pervasive in recent decades, bold global tastes are penetrating parts of the continent that were once the uncontested territory of meat and potatoes. Not only did these ethnic food trends shape what was on our plates; they have also slowly changed what was in our minds about the cultures behind these foods. They broke down barriers of language and race and made the exotic every day, the foreign familiar. Ethnic food trends can open up minds. Taste something you like, and suddenly you find yourself wanting to discover more about that culture's cuisine. The more sriracha hot sauce you eat, the more curious you become about Southeast Asian cooking. With each visit to a Vietnamese, Thai, or Cambodian restaurant, you try new dishes, new flavors, and new foods. You begin to wonder what those countries are actually like. Are they nice? Are they safe? Is the food even better than here? Next thing you know you're squatting on the sidewalk in Ho Chi Minh City, enjoying an incredible sandwich procured with no knowledge of Vietnamese but the words "banh mi."

The United States and Canada (and, more recently, Western Europe) are nations of immigrants, and each successive wave of new arrivals brought the seeds of food trends, whether it was Germans in the nineteenth century and the rise of hot dogs and hamburgers or the more recent influx of South Koreans and the current fever around kimchi. Cultural forces have played a role in feeding these trends, whether through travel, music and movies, or even a country's exposure through the news. The sushi boom rode the wave of Japanese interest that peaked in the 1980s, spurred by novels like *Shogun*, Nintendo video games in every household, and the country's seemingly unstoppable corporate culture. These food trends were also driven by key tastemakers from these cultures, often immigrants, who not only brought their food to our shores but also figured out how to translate it for a mainstream North American audience. Before we were ready to embrace raw fish in the 1980s there was entrepreneur Rocky Aoki in the 1960s, who opened his chain of Benihana teppanyaki steakhouses in the United States, with their cooktop theater tables and chefs with samurai knife comedy skills, paving the way for Japanese culinary inclusion with rivers of teriyaki sauce.

The road from an unknown ethnic cuisine to a widespread food trend isn't assured. Some cultures fare better than others, and others struggle, despite the right mix of immigration statistics and cultural cues. The Polish and Irish communities in Chicago are much larger than the city's Thai population, yet you'll find many more restaurants serving pad Thai than you will featuring pierogies and soda bread. Similarly, Somali-style samosas, though a central part of the large community in Minneapolis, haven't become a Minnesota staple in the same way that Swedish meatballs have in that Midwestern state. So what are the elements that make an international cuisine go mainstream in North America? One of the most instructive and surprising examples is Indian food. With its large immigrant community in America and its rich, bold traditional flavors, Indian cuisine should have been every bit the staple that Chinese has become. Yet for decades its fortune has confounded chefs, trend forecasters, and industry predictors, who have said, with great confidence, that *this* year will definitely be the year Indian food breaks out of the curry house and into your kitchen.

In her fascinating history of Indian food's journey to the West, *Curry: A Tale of Cooks and Conquerors*, Lizzie Collingham reveals that what we know today as Indian food, from chai to curry, is in fact an international hodgepodge of influences and cuisines, pulled together on the Indian subcontinent through a collision of colonial rulers, politically aligned kingdoms, and fate. Anglo-Indian hybrid dishes, like mulligatawny soup, were the first pan-Indian foods, bridging the distinct regions and cultures of the vast empire, presenting a spearhead into the West. In Britain the Indian food trend arrived with returning colonial officials who had served in India, and it quickly grew in the decades following World War II, as immigration from Britain's former colonies brought Indians and other

South Asians to the United Kingdom in great numbers. By the 1960s "going for a curry" was as familiar to Brits as Chinese food was for North Americans. Canada, with its links to the commonwealth, experienced similar Indian immigration on a much smaller scale from the early twentieth century, especially in Vancouver.

In the United States Indian food's first beachhead was New York City. A handful of restaurants appeared there in the 1920s, catering to spice traders, seamen, and students from India, often run by men who had little experience in the kitchen. These weren't places Americans frequented, and the few articles that mentioned these restaurants did so briefly, warning readers off the powerful smells found in their walls. Some writers called curry "barbaric" or portrayed it as exotic, and not in an appealing way. Owing to restrictive immigration policies on Indians and other Asians, the Indian community in New York remained tiny for most of the first half of the twentieth century, and though several curry houses held on in Midtown Manhattan, popular references to Indian food were few and fleeting. That began to change slightly in the mid-1950s, in the decade after India's independence.

Dharum Jit Singh, a Sikh living in New York, published the first cookbook aimed at an American audience about his homeland's food. "Pinned down on what specific dishes might open up new culinary avenues to American home cooks, Mr. Singh suggested that they look into the various ways Indians prepare rice," the *New York Times* wrote in an article on Singh in 1955, a year before his *Classic Cooking from India* was published. Despite a favorable write-up when the book came out, including recipes for pakoras and rose petal shrimp pellao, Singh's ultimate impact was minimal. But in the 1960s things began to pick up. More open immigration policies brought a new wave of Indians to America. These were educated, middle-class individuals, including doctors, engineers, and graduate students who established roots around universities in New York, Boston, Berkeley, California, and other cities, and they began building proper expatriate communities. India began exerting its own cultural currency, which shaped the country's international image. Prime Minister Jawaharlal Nehru gained fashion in progressive political circles for his modern socialist vision of a New India as well as the distinctive high-collared jacket he wore, while Ravi Shankar and the Beatles popularized the hippie discovery of India's spirituality, from meditation to yoga.

Into this came Sushil Malhotra, the godfather of Indian food in America, who was born in Bombay and moved to New York in 1966 to study engineering at City College. He worked at Shell Oil and American Electric Power after graduating, but in 1970 he and his father, a naval engineer, opened a spice trading shop in the city called Foods of India, supplying New York's curry houses with spices, chutneys, and papadums while at night he pursued his MBA at New York University. "There was and is no professionalism to these places," Sushil said, referring to the majority of Indian restaurants in North America, from his lavishly decorated living room an hour north of Manhattan along the Hudson River. The midcentury colonial house, with its formally dressed butler, hand-carved jade elephants, and long settee piled with silken pillows, was the perfect metaphor for his mission to bridge Indian and American tastes over the past four decades. Describing the majority of neighborhood Indian restaurants in America, restaurants that tend to serve identical menus of British-influenced North Indian dishes, often from a buffet and surrounded by the same faux Taj Mahal and sitar-heavy décor, the passionate Sushil nearly knocked over his chai tea several times.

Many of these restaurants had been opened by Bangladeshis who were fleeing conflict and poverty back home. They were often called "ship jumpers" because many arrived as seafaring crew and then claimed refugee status once they landed. In New York strips of garishly colored curry houses emerged on sixth street in the East Village, further uptown in the neighborhood labeled Curry Hill, and out in Jackson Heights, Queens. On the West Coast Indian food coalesced around Berkeley, California, and the adjacent city of Oakland. In Toronto Gerrard Street became a teeming, colorful bazaar with many Punjabis. Though the owners of these restaurants frequently lacked prior kitchen experience, they succeeded in establishing a foothold for Indian restaurants in American cities, but not without a downside. "The mom-and-pop curry shop has been a barrier to the acceptance of Indian cuisine in America," said Josaim Barath, a professor of hospitality management at North Texas University who has written on the subject of Indian restaurants. "You run into a slew of problems with management, including cleanliness of the restrooms, and they find it difficult to understand the concept of standardization and consistency. They are outside the field, and I admire them for their entrepreneurship spirit, but while they open the doors to Indian cuisine, often it's a bad experience."

Sushil Malhotra was even less sympathetic. "They bastardized the food," he said dismissively. "Students loved it, but there was a fairly good chance you'd get a runny stomach."

One day I made a pilgrimage to Curry Hill (a three-block strip whose name is a play on the neighborhood that surrounds it, Murray Hill) to have lunch with Krishendu Ray, a professor of food studies at New York University and the country's preeminent expert on ethnic food's place in North American society, especially the food from his native India. We met at Curry in a Hurry, one of the pioneers of fast food–style Indian restaurants in the country, which Sushil Malhotra had been involved in opening. With its tattered takeout section up front and the shabby 1970s dining room above, it was filled mainly with South Asians eating classics like daal lentils and saag paneer spinach with plastic cutlery. Nearby was a table of grizzled backpackers who looked like they just stepped off the Appalachian Trail. "Chicken tikka?" one of them asked out loud. "Is that hot?" Ray explained that North Americans had two distinct ways of looking at food trends brought from other cultures: foreign and ethnic. Foreign was refined, upmarket, and expensive. Ethnic was exotic, downmarket, and cheap. French and Japanese were foreign. Chinese, Mexican, and Indian were ethnic. With ethnic, "people start to complain if a meal costs more than $10," Ray said, using buttery bits of naan bread to scoop up the fragrant daal in his bowl. "If you enter from up high, you can move low," he said, pointing out how sushi had gone from an expensive rarity to something you could now buy in your supermarket for a few bucks. "If you move from low to high, however, it's much more difficult." Indian food had been stuck in the ethnic category for decades, consigning it to the fringes, as far as food trends go.

Motivated to undo this, Sushil Malhotra opened Akbar in 1976, a fine dining restaurant on Park Avenue that would showcase the untapped potential of Indian cooking. But the public still associated Indian cooking with cheap eats, and the restaurant struggled. In 1984 he tried something different further uptown with Dawat, offering a more regionally focused take on India's varied cuisines. He brought in food celebrity Madhur Jaffrey to help design the menu and head up the kitchen. A beautiful actress originally from Delhi, Jaffrey had gotten into cooking when she was performing in London and continued to cook in New York, where, eventually, Craig Claiborne, the influential *New York Times* food critic and journalist, profiled her as he enthusiastically embraced global foods. Although Claiborne's story was more focused on the stylish novelty of Jaffrey being an actress who could cook, in 1973 it led to Jaffrey publishing *An Introduction to Indian Cooking*, an instantly classic cookbook that established her as the Julia Child of Indian food, demystifying it and bringing it to the West.

"My job was to introduce real authentic Indian food, and that's what I tried to do at Dawat, to great resistance initially," Jaffrey said. Customers expected certain dishes that they knew from cheap curry houses, like spicy chicken vindaloo and saag paneer, and both Jaffrey and Malhotra had to struggle to keep things authentic and regionally varied. "Several things were happening at the same time," said Jaffrey. "Cookbooks were coming out, and we used to sell them in the restaurant. I had cooking shows on TV. It was this combination of things. Dawat was only in this part of this world. It began to change all over in America. Sushil was one of the first to present authentic Indian food in the US."

Despite Jaffrey's own success and the role Dawat and similar high-end restaurants played in trying to elevate the cuisine in New York and other cosmopolitan cities, Indian food never fully blossomed as a North American trend. Each year the food industry forecasters would call for its imminent crowning—"1987 will be the year of Indian food!"—and each time they would be proven wrong. Neighborhood curry houses grew and spread out, but their appeal beyond a core of South Asians and adventurous eaters never materialized. Fear was a big reason for this. Indian food was perceived as dirty, heavy, and a recipe for gastrointestinal trouble. I never ate Indian food as a kid because my family was too afraid of it, and the first time I tried it, as an eighteen-year-old backpacker in London, I chewed each bite like it was a live grenade. It took years for me to shed this fear, but not without learning why it existed in the first place. I have indeed gotten sick numerous times from Indian restaurants in Canada and the United States, ranging from food comas induced by ghee (the clarified butter bad Indian food is drenched in) to marathon bathroom sessions. Friends who ventured to India fared much worse. Their stories of the country's culture and beauty were always laced with the punch line about horrendous stomach ailments, and more than a few were hospitalized with E. coli and other parasites, some suffering permanent damage. Indian food can often be overwhelmingly spicy, so much so that a chicken vindaloo is almost impossible to eat without shedding tears and drinking gallons of cool yogurt lassis. To some people this is an attraction, but to the majority of North American eaters, raised on a fairly bland European palate, it's enough to prevent them from coming in the door.

Tariq Hameed knows this all too well. As one of the most famous Indian restaurateurs in New York—he owns Shaheen Sweets, in Queens—he has struggled for forty years with the North American fear of spice. When he first opened a Manhattan outpost in Curry Hill in the 1970s he toned down the spice significantly, and still American diners complained. "Oh, I don't like the spicy," they would say with wrinkled noses when he tried to coax them in from the sidewalk. "Too spicy." As in the UK, which saw a nativist anti-curry backlash back in the 1970s and similarly to the early fearful reception of Chinese food in America, Indian food was derided as spicy, stinky, and gross. "Our windows were broken every single day," recalled Hameed of the first years in business. "Kids used to throw firecrackers inside the restaurant."

∽

The turning point for Indian food's fortunes in America came in the early 1990s. Sukhi Singh was an Indian Air Force officer's wife who had operated various food businesses while she followed her husband to postings around India and the world. She had run ice cream trucks, hamburger stands, and thrown dosa parties on bases, but when her husband left the military and the family immigrated to Oakland, California, in the late 1980s, she found herself working at a small sandwich shop her husband had purchased in an office building. Because her time was spent working at the deli and raising her kids, Singh didn't have the same time to prepare her curries each night from scratch, toasting and grinding the spices and simmering her sauces for hours. She worried that her kids would be totally lost to pizza and other American foods, so she began making condensed curry pastes, which she kept in the fridge. Now she could toss a spoonful in with vegetables, water, and other ingredients to make a quick dinner for the family. On Wednesdays she sold some Indian meals at the deli, and when customers asked about the recipes, she offered hand-packed jars of her sauces for sale. After the devastating 1988 earthquake forced them to close the sandwich shop, her husband switched to the dry cleaning business, and Singh decided, at forty-five years of age, to try selling her sauces full time. "We were already at rock bottom," her daughter, Sanjog Sikand, said. "It couldn't get much worse."

Under the name brand Sukhi's, the Singh family began knocking on the doors of specialty shops and farmers markets in nearby Berkeley, where many Indian graduate students lived around the University of California campus. Sanjog and her brother Dalbir would arrive after school to pack up bottles of the sauces their mother had made until one in the morning. Then, on weekends, the family would split up, each member taking a different grocery store or farmer's market in the Bay Area, where they would man a demonstration booth and try to entice shoppers to taste their product. "We were one of the first selling a branded ethnic product," said Dalbir, who began hawking Sukhi's sauces at farmers markets when he was twelve years old. More than half the people would turn away when they found out the product was Indian food, without even giving it a taste. "People would literally spit it out in front of me," Sanjog said.

Then came the Internet—not the contemporary web of ideas and commerce that has propelled ethnic food brands through social media but rather the technology that transformed Silicon Valley in the 1990s and ushered in an immigrant wave of Indian engineers and computer scientists who powered much of this innovation. America's Indian-born population ballooned from 450,000 in 1990 to over 1.6 million in 2008, making them the third-largest immigrant group in the country after Mexicans and Filipinos. In areas such as Silicon Valley and San Jose, Indians and other South Asians became a significant minority community in a relatively short period of time. While this was happening Sukhi Singh was doing her best to grow her fledgling business, adding cooked meals to her repertoire of sauces. "Life was tough for us then," Mrs. Singh, who was dressed in a sari, told me one morning in the company's drab office in the industrial suburb of Hayward, across the bay from Silicon Valley. "It was a big decision if we were going to spend three hundred dollars."

But in 1995 she got a call that would change her life. Marriott Catering was servicing the cafeteria at Hewlett Packard, and the woman in charge wanted to know whether there was a way she could rent a tandoor oven because the company was losing business with all the Indian workers who refused to eat the company's American cafeteria food. Singh somehow talked her way into a contract as Hewlett Packard's Indian food service manager and began selling food to the tech giants in the Valley, including IBM, Dell, Oracle, Cisco, and Intel, all of whom were struggling to keep Indian-born engineers happy at lunchtime. The funny thing was that even when these companies all regularly featured Singh's Indian lunch specials, the most enthusiastic customers weren't Indian expats. "They thought they'd get all the Indian brown baggers to eat lunch," Singh said, "but they weren't getting that. The Indians were saving money for back home, and they brought last night's leftovers. The clientele mostly ended up being Americans."

Though her catering to dot-com business fell away when the web bubble burst at the end of the decade, Sukhi's had already built its core as a business, so it simply expanded horizontally. Sukhi's Gourmet Indian Foods began selling frozen meals to Costco, catering educational institutions from kindergartens to graduate schools, and supplying frozen samosas and hot curries for buffets to Whole

Foods stores, first along the Pacific Coast and then in other regions. Though Sukhi's has targeted a mainstream customer, the company is careful to stay close to its ethnic base. "A lot of [Indian] grad students go to middle-of-nowhere universities in Ohio, and their taste in food spreads out to the surrounding population really well," Dalbir said, noting how it is impossible for others to ignore their cuisine. "If someone's eating Indian food in your office, you can smell it ten cubicles down."

Around the same time that Sukhi's gained traction, Sushil Malhotra had his own important decision to make. Dawat was a critical and financial success, but he wanted it to reach a greater audience, to emulate what was happening in the UK, where curry had outpaced fish and chips as a national food. In 1998 his solution was the first Café Spice, located near New York University. It was revolutionary in its design and simplicity: a modern Indian bistro, positioned between the familiar curry houses and the upscale experience of Dawat. The food was served thali style, with a partitioned plate that featured a selection of curry, rice, daal (curried lentils), and naan bread for a set price. A year later the company opened a Café Spice Express, a takeout counter in the renovated food hall of Grand Central Station, spearheaded by Sushil's son, Sameer, who now runs the company's day-to-day operations. Most of the food was made on site, including naan bread baked in a gas-fired tandoor oven, but Sameer quickly saw the potential to scale up production and put these takeout kiosks in places where Indian restaurants had never ventured. Outlets like Hurley Medical in Flint were the result of that, as the Malhotras brought Café Spice curries into supermarkets, hospitals, colleges, and corporate cafeterias across the nation. Today there are Café Spice kiosks on the campuses of MIT and NYU, USAA military insurance, and the New York headquarters of Goldman Sachs, Morgan Stanley, and Bank of America. The company's food is sold without the brand name in another four hundred cafeterias and on the Indian hot bars and grab-n-go meals at hundreds of Whole Foods stores nationwide. In 2011 alone Café Spice's business grew 40 percent, to some $20 million in sales. Malhotra's Café Spice is the chief rival to Sukhi Singh's company, competing for the same accounts and customers—the East Coast Hindu Biggie Smalls to Singh's West Coast Sikh Tupac.

Café Spice's food is prepared in a fifty thousand–square foot industrial kitchen in New Windsor, New York, just up the Hudson River from West Point, about an hour north of Manhattan. Inside over a hundred workers (almost all Latinos) fold samosas using empanada dough, fry potato pakoras, grind spices, and stir giant vats of curry. "At the end of the day I'm not making a batch for the University of Massachusetts, one for Goldman Sachs, and one for Whole Foods," said Sameer as we walked through the kitchen. "It's all the same three hundred–pound batch, and the Indian grad student at Georgia Tech is getting the same spice level as someone in Tulsa."

Spice is a delicate issue when it comes to Indian food. It's the main reason Americans will or will not try it, and criticism is unavoidable. "If I don't spice it enough," said Sushil Malhotra, "some guy who's been to India will call me up and say 'You fucking bastard, this isn't a vindaloo!' If you say it's a vindaloo, it better damn well be hot." So rather than mute the spice level on all its dishes, Café Spice's menu features a range of dishes with different heat levels. Within the range of the company's four main simmering sauces, 90 percent of diners can find a spice that suits them. For those who want to make their own adjustments, the company launched a chutney bar at its outlets, featuring a variety of condiments (including a sriracha-spiked tomato chutney) so diners can add more heat if they wish. The curries and sauces made for Café Spice are also ghee-free. This gives the food a longer shelf life, lower cost, meets the low-fat requirements of Whole Foods, and opens up more sales to vegetarians and vegans, a key demographic for Indian food sales. It's one of several adjustments the Malhotras have had to make in order to broaden the food's appeal and to streamline production. Whereas traditional Indian restaurants bake naan breads and roast meats in cylindrical tandoor ovens, the skill required is too difficult to teach the plant's workers and nearly impossible to scale at multiple retail locations. Instead, frozen naan is imported from Toronto, and the chicken tikka, the key component in the company's most popular dish, chicken tikka masala, or CTM, is baked in a convection oven rather than roasted in a tandoor.

Lately the company's chefs have begun experimenting with less-traditional fare, such as a line of pressed naan sandwiches, that they sell at Whole Foods and on college campuses. "It's catered to the global palate," said Sameer Malhotra's wife, Payal, who works in the business as well. She described the naan sandwich as Café Spice's entry-level item, something that curious curry virgins might be willing to try. "To the consumer it's just another flatbread sandwich with a different filling. People eat it and then say, 'This sandwich had chicken tikka in it, and I like that, so what else is comparable?'" While taste testing several new flavors of the sandwiches one morning, including crumbled paneer with Monterey jack cheese, potato with turmeric, and chicken tikka, Payal picked a chunk of green chili out of the paneer sandwich and made a note to have the plant workers dice the chilies into smaller pieces. "If someone bites into that, they might be put off our food for a while," Payal said, shaking her head.

༄

The Malhotras also own Junoon, a lavish, multimillion-dollar, Michelin-starred fine dining restaurant in the flatiron district of Manhattan, the jewel in their curry empire's crown. With two hundred seats, hand-carved latticed screens of imported khaddapa stone, a gleaming open kitchen, rolling wine carts driven by stewards, and a dedicated spice grinding room, it illustrates Sushil and Sameer's multipronged approach to propel Indian food into a viable mainstream trend. Café Spice's cafeteria food can convert multitudes and masses one meal at a time, but the prestige and exposure a place like Junoon can generate through reviews, articles, and word of mouth from well-connected, wealthy tastemakers has the same multiplier effect that Ricardo Zarate's success has generated for Peruvian ingredients. Although Café Spice customers at Hurley Medical will likely never get to taste tequila with muddled tandoori pineapple or monkfish tikka with a mango and mustard chutney, those flavors may eventually trickle down through other chefs, trend forecasters, and supermarket products, thus becoming less foreign and more familiar to Americans. This is the chef-driven approach, and though Sushil Malhotra has tried it time and again since the 1970s, no Indian restaurateur or chef in America has yet succeeded at elevating their cuisine into a trend.

To be fair, there are several successful, highly praised Indian chefs and restaurants around the continent. In Vancouver Vikram Vij is one of the most respected Indian chefs working globally today, and he runs two of that city's arguably hottest restaurants. In Los Angeles the Indian-style gastropub Badmash (which means "naughty" in Hindi) opened to great fanfare in 2013, and San Francisco's DOSA is consistently packed, serving updated South Indian crepes in a space that feels like a nightclub. The one Indian chef who has achieved celebrity status in North America is Floyd Cardoz, who lives in New York. A native of Bombay, Cardoz quit a master's degree in biochemistry to enter hospitality school with the prestigious Taj Group. He trained in global cuisines, including French, Italian, and classical Indian, but he drew his biggest inspiration from his family, who came from the province of Goa, which has strong Portuguese roots. In 1988 Cardoz moved to New York and cooked at the type of cookie-cutter Indian restaurant that made one pot of curry in the morning and spread it out over all their dishes. "These owners were farmers and truck drivers in India," Cardoz recalled when we spoke at his restaurant North End Grill, an American brasserie in the financial district. "The cuisine was like a game of broken telephone, until these restaurants got diluted down to what they were."

At the time there were several fine dining Indian restaurants in the city, including Akbar, Bombay Palace, and Raga, though each was a model of traditional service and dishes, with little distinction in the kitchen. Replace their copper serving pots with cheap dishware, and they were no different from the curry houses, right down to the old sitars hanging on their walls. Cardoz wanted to do something different. He ended up in the kitchen of Lespinasse, an innovative French restaurant whose chef at the time was interested in global flavors and let Cardoz integrate Indian influences into several dishes. He made a duck curry; lamb with eggplant caviar, cumin, and ginger; and a dish of soft shell crabs breaded in a cream of wheat crust like he had known back in Goa. All of it was very restrained and understated, but it helped establish Cardoz's reputation among chefs and diners in the city and caught the attention of the powerful restaurateur Danny Meyer, who approached him to open an Indian restaurant. "I was twenty-seven at that point, and I didn't want to do just another Indian restaurant," Cardoz recalled. "I convinced Danny we had to do something different. I knew there'd be pushback at another upscale Indian place. People had preconceived notions: it was too spicy, too dark, they won't understand it, etcetera. But India had to be more than chicken tikka masala and saag paneer. There were various different flavors from around India that never got used and local produce you could use."

Starting with a local, seasonal approach to ingredients and a restrained flavor profile, Cardoz and Meyer build the foundation for what would become Tabla, which, in 1998, opened to great reviews. Cardoz took some of his favorite dishes from back home and deconstructed them for a more Westernized dining experience. He fried skate in a semolina crust, then served it with a Goan curry and tamarind paste, but with the heat turned down so the contrast of sour, bitter, sweet, and spiced flavors was more pronounced. He braised, steamed, and glazed oxtail so it was candied on the outside, resulting in this tender, unctuous piece of meat when you bit in. The biggest hit was the crab cake, an American spin on the fresh crab dishes he'd grown up with in Goa, served with a tamarind chutney. "After we did that you saw crab cakes in Indian restaurants all over town," Cardoz said. Every dish was plated individually rather than served in the family style (as was traditional in Indian cooking), and Cardoz refused substitutions and special requests. "I wanted to showcase the food in the best possible way," he said, "so you had no choice but to enjoy it."

In its first year of business a large percentage of Tabla's clientele were curious Indians and Indian Americans who often resisted what Cardoz was doing. "How dare you!" they told Cardoz. "Where's my free papadum? My buffet? The chicken tikka masala?" Nevertheless, the restaurant was a success, both critically and financially. Then 9/11 happened. "We got hammered," Cardoz said, noting how Tabla's drop in business had more to it than the citywide recession that hit other New York restaurants following the attack. "People associated [Tabla] with the Middle East. People didn't want to eat ethnic or Indian food at that time. All the other restaurants in the Union Square Hospitality Group [Meyer's company] were doing fine, but we saw a sixty percent decline in business from before nine-eleven." Tabla took a full two years to return to its previous pace, but it never recovered the energy or buzz that it had when it first opened. Though Tabla remained profitable until 2010, the size of the large restaurant and the cost associated with running it led Meyer to close Tabla down at the end of that year—his first failure in an otherwise perfect streak of opening restaurants. Cardoz went on to win *Top Chef Masters* a year later and opened North End Grill, also with Meyer, shortly after that.

"I think high-cost Indian food will almost never be accepted," Cardoz said with a sigh when asked about his thoughts on Tabla's impact. "The hard part is there are still so many people afraid of those flavors. It's halfway where it needs to go." Cardoz now felt that a big-name chef, such as himself, couldn't pave the pathway to locking in Indian cuisine as a trend; it had to be something targeted at the average American. "The day it'll become popular is the day you have a fast food concept. It needs to be more mainstream so people can hang their hat on it." It needed to have presentation that was clean and fresh in a format that was easy to relate to and eat by hand, Cardoz said, adding that it needed names that don't require explanation and translation—do you know the difference between aloo gobi, rogan josh, and chaat papri?—at a price point that was accessible. In other words, Indian food needed its Chipotle.

∾

To North American diners Chipotle Mexican Grill is a place to get delicious, fresh burritos and other quick Mexican foods, but to aspiring restaurant tastemakers looking to turn a global cuisine into a widely accepted trend and profitable business model, it is nothing short of the holy grail. Founded in Denver, Colorado, in 1993 by chef Steve Ells, Chipotle's concept was based on the idea that fresh, quality Mexican food, similar to what Ells had eaten in San Francisco, could be served in a standardized, highly replicable quick-service format without turning to the processed glop that was found at Taco Bell. Instead of premade meals waiting under a heat lamp, assembled from outsourced products, Chipotle offered a selection of freshly cooked proteins, toppings, and entrée formats that could be combined to make any variation of burrito, taco, or salad on an efficient assembly line. The chain's success, with over a billion dollars in annual sales at more than fourteen hundred stores (serving 750,000 customers each day), did more to bring fresh Mexican flavors, such as chipotle peppers and chopped cilantro, into the American mainstream than the great Tex-Mex chips-and-salsa boom of the 1980s and 1990s.

Two major trends emerged from Chipotle. First, it helped Mexican food spread to far more places, both in North America and abroad. In London, England, Mexican food previously had a limited presence. "Taco Bell had tried and failed in the UK," said my friend Ben Fordham, who operates the London quick-service Mexican chain Benito's. What was typically found in the city were small chains like Chiquitos. "It was the worst Tex-Mex stuff; coated in cheese and tasteless," Fordham said. "That became what was known as Mexican food. All were places called Amigos or Desperados and had walls littered with sombreros and donkeys." In the early 2000s, when Fordham was in law school, he spent a year on exchange at the University of Texas, in Austin, where he fell in love with both his future wife and Mexican food, especially Chipotle. Years later, after a miserable stint practicing law at one of the top firms in London, he struck out to open Benito's and brought Chipotle-style quick-service Mexican to the United Kingdom. Several other entrepreneurs were launching similar concepts at the time, and a Mexican food trend hit London like the blitz. "The boom of Mexican food is incredible. It's all the food trade has talked about," Fordham said. "It's gone from not being on the radar to a central part of what they'll put on the high street." One of the reasons Fordham credits for Mexican's success in the United Kingdom is the cuisine's similarity with aspects of Indian food, which is firmly wedged into the mainstream of British eating culture. Both cuisines share a diverse spiciness, a mix of textures—stewed and grilled and fried, all together on one plate—and a colorful palate, all of which is why American entrepreneurs betting on Indian food believe they can ride the coattails of the Mexican boom stateside to great success.

The larger trend that Chipotle spawned was its business model, the quick-service restaurant, or QSR, which essentially took over the 1950s fast food model McDonald's established. Less processed and more streamlined than typical fast food models, QSR provided a template to modernize and mass market any global cuisine. There are QSR concepts for nearly every single culture food now on the market, from Vietnamese (Shop House, a prototype devised by Chipotle), to Middle Eastern (Roti, in DC), Chinese buns (Wow Bow, in Chicago), and Philippine-style burgers (Jollibee, in California). Each of these is essentially a Chipotle with different food. "Chipotle has become a verb," Sanjog Sikand, of Sukhi's, said, adding that the winning format for Indian food in America is still up for grabs. A number of concepts are already trying to stake a claim as the Indian Chipotle, including the Kati Roll Company, with three New York locations serving Indian-style roti wraps. In Chipotle's hometown of Denver, Amar Singh, a former financier from Delhi, with no relation to the Singhs from California, launched Bombay Bowl in 2007 with the idea to deconstruct Indian food so it would appear healthier and fresher. Meals are served in bowls—sort of like a hot salad—on divided plates, or in burrito-style wraps. "Consumers say, 'It looks fresh, it looks healthy,' when we show a photo of the bowl in presentations," Singh said. "But I've yet to see someone say, 'It looks Indian,' which is key. Traditionally you won't have a bowl with rice, meat, and vegetables in it. We've changed the way you look, eat, taste, and perceive Indian food." So far there is only one location, but Singh hopes to start franchising new Bombay Bowls this year.

So far the most successful Indian quick-service restaurant concept is Amaya, based in my hometown Toronto and run by Hemant Bhagwani, who has opened, operated, and often closed nearly every single type of Indian restaurant over the past two decades, first in Dubai and Sydney and most prominently in Toronto. Bhagwani, who has the laid-back demeanor and slick fashion sense of a professional cricket player, made his name in Toronto when, in 2007, he opened Amaya: The Indian Room. It was a modern Indian bistro that broke the mold of the city's numerous Indian buffet-heavy restaurants (South Asians are one of Toronto's largest ethnic groups) by pairing modernized curries and dishes with fine wines, all at a reasonable price point. The Indian Room became so popular that Bhagwani soon opened up a second restaurant, Bread Bar, on the same block to handle the overflow from the Indian Room, but he was surprised when the Bread Bar's takeout business dwarfed what they were doing in the restaurant each night. People wanted high-quality Indian food, but they wanted it quickly, Bhagwani realized. So he launched the concept of Amaya Express, which was primarily takeout and delivery focused, and it began rolling out different locations across the city.

"When I started Amaya in 2007 I just wanted to make a bit of money and survive," Bhagwani told me from behind the wheel of his Mercedes with its vanity AMAYA license plate as we drove to several of the chain's dozen-odd locations one day. "Then I opened two more, then one more, then wrote a new business plan. In five years we'll need one hundred Amaya Expresses in the city. That's my benchmark," he said, adding, "I want to have everybody."

At its core Amaya's food isn't revolutionary. The chain serves traditional North Indian fare made from scratch at each location, with higher-quality ingredients and far less ghee, and in settings that are modern and design conscious. "Even in food courts we serve from pots, not steam tables," stressed Bhagwani, who has stood at other restaurants with a stopwatch to time how long a typical order takes. "What you're eating here is the same recipe, sauces, and ingredients as Indian Room and Bread Bar," Bhagwani said as we sat over a Styrofoam container of chicken tikka masala and spiced lamb from Inde by Amaya, one of his company's concepts, which is located in an office building's food court in downtown Toronto.

Bhagwani was quick to point out that Indian food contains certain inherent challenges that make it difficult to scale across a large chain. First, there is the problem of consistency. Indian cuisine isn't hemmed in by strictly defined recipes. It's a pinch of turmeric here and a dash of nutmeg there, all of which makes controlling twenty different chefs spread across a city a logistical nightmare. Second, the mainstays of popular Indian cooking in the West are largely curries and stewed dishes, foods that require eating with cutlery and discourage dining on the go—just try to eat a gooey dish of butter chicken in your car. Finally, Indian dishes are not exactly the most visually appealing sights. Compared with a brightly layered sandwich, a pot of chicken tikka masala just looks like a wet orange mess. Curry is essentially stew, and no one has ever built a mass-market restaurant empire on stew. Stew isn't sexy. Stew is actually the polar opposite of sexy.

To counter this, Bhagwani has dabbled in cross-cultural culinary experimentation. Over the years he has put a number of items on Amaya's menus that bridge the divide between Indian flavors and Western formats. There have been chaat tacos covered in spiced chickpeas and chutney, korma chili hot dogs (called a Slumdog), cheeseburger samosas, butter chicken–topped pizzas, and poutine. Although all of these are based in some sort of traditional dish or flavor profile, they're as much an exercise in marketing as they are in culinary achievement. "It's still Indian food," Bhagwani said, noting that these types of modern fusion dishes are what you will find if you eat in Mumbai or Delhi today. "I can either call it naan bread or a taco." Others have gone this route as well. In Baltimore, Naumann Hameed, nephew of the pioneering Queens restaurateur Tariq Hameed, took things one step further with his concept Krazy Kebab, which mixes Pakistani-style kebabs and curries with burritos, made from fresh naan wraps, and nachos. "I'm serving traditional food in a nontraditional fashion," Hameed says. "It makes so much sense. Changing the way you serve something can attract a vast majority of people."

Over time Bhagwani hopes that diners will come to embrace Indian food as it is. This is what happened with Benito's in London. Initially Fordham decided to describe the carnitas burritos as "braised pork" because he feared the Spanish word may have placed a barrier in front of British customers unfamiliar with Mexican food. Now that the Mexican trend has been established across London, Fordham describes the pork burrito as "our version of carnitas" on Benito's latest menu because the British public is now familiar enough with the cuisine that they are ready to accept it.

Whether that majority is prepared to embrace Indian food as the next great North American food trend is another question, however. For that to happen it will need to move beyond curries and naan sandwiches to the point at which Doritos is selling masala-flavored tortilla chips and Burger King features a spicy chutney Whopper. That reality seems distant now, but these things can gather steam very quickly. In a video posted in 2011 on the blog of the Private Label Manufacturers Association, Brad Edmondson, a demographics consultant, laid out why Indian food will be the next big hit for the American market. "Ethnic food is successful when immigration combines with international travel and restaurants to create a buzz loud enough for food manufacturers to hear," Edmondson said, holding up a plate of samosas. "The number of people from India in the US shot up nearly seventy percent just in the last decade and is now well over two-point-eight million. If Indian Americans keep growing at this rate, they will soon surpass Chinese Americans to become the biggest Asian group in the country."

Indian-born Americans, along with their American born children, are today working beside many more Americans than they were just a decade ago. They go to school with other Americans, play on their baseball teams, treat them in hospitals, and marry into their families. Americans laugh at the jokes of Indian American comedy stars like Aziz Ansari and Mindy Kaling, make the novels of Jhumpa Lahiri and Salman Rushdie best sellers, and watch food celebrity Padma Lakshmi judge contestants like Floyd Cardoz on *Top Chef Masters*. Indian accents, faces, and foods are appearing in lunchrooms and living rooms, and this creeping social exposure has directly affected America's acceptance of Indian culture and, in turn, their food. Both Sameer Malhotra and Hemant Bhagwani cited the film *Slumdog Millionaire* as the most significant tipping point for the industry they have ever encountered. For Bhagwani, the night that film won an Academy Award for best picture was Amaya's busiest night ever for takeout orders, inciting a demand that led to his decision to pivot from fine dining to a quick-service format. He uses the terms "before *Slumdog*" and "after *Slumdog*" to mark the eras both in his own business and in the public's perception of Indian food. All of this happened during a decade when India rose from abject poverty to become a symbol of emerging market power and economic sophistication, a place to be envied rather than pitied.

The market may finally have begun reflecting these changes. According to research provided by the Mintel Group, 13 percent of American consumers surveyed in 2010 prepared Indian meals in their homes at least once a month. In the past decade the number of Indian restaurants in the United States has increased 30 percent according to numbers compiled by the NPD Group, whereas a 2011 Technomic survey found that 46 percent of Americans would likely order menu items with typical Indian flavors and ingredients. Still, it is decidedly an uphill climb. In a 2013 National Restaurant Association survey of chefs, curries ranked all the way down at number 161 as a hot food trend, surpassed even by foam/froth/air, the molecular gastronomy fad that was the food world's equivalent of snap bracelets. Indian food, which had previously appeared as a category, didn't even make the list.

"I haven't seen our efforts being all that fruitful," said Madhur Jaffrey of the four decades she has been evangelizing about Indian food to Americans. "I've watched it over the years, and I keep saying, 'Next year will be the year for Indian foods!' Look at supermarkets. There's very little of Indian food. True, on the campuses it is changing. You do see it in the big cities and in Whole Foods, but if you go to the ordinary supermarket and to the ethnic section, you'll see Thai, Japanese, and Mexican, but very little Indian."

The Malhotra clan, however, keeps pressing on, opening up new fronts to bring Indian food to Americans, wherever they are.

In the fall of 2012 they unveiled the latest evolution of the Café Spice empire: the Dosateria. Set in the middle of a Whole Foods store in New York's posh Tribeca neighborhood, the Dosateria was the Malhotra's own Chipotle-style entrant into the race, with a distinctly Southern Indian spin. Dosas are large crepes made from a fermented batter of rice and lentils that are then filled with a variety of toppings. In the center of the large kiosk, cooks ladled out dosa batter onto large round cooktops, rotating and flipping them with long spatulas until their fragrant smell filled the air and the dough puffed up crisp and golden. The dosas were available in signature combinations with names like Bollywood Chicken and Good Korma, and the meals were fully customizable in the QSR tradition as either dosas, uttapams (thicker breads, served open faced), frankies (a grilled roti flatbread), or rice bowls. Customers picked their format, selected a chutney, and then added additional toppings for an extra charge. They could also select a fresh yogurt lassi, in flavors ranging from traditional (cucumber with mint or mango) to imaginative (salt with cumin or chile with avocado). I had a small asparagus uttapam, filled with freshly chopped asparagus, cooked in a spicy sambal sauce, and an amazing shrimp dosa, with a tangy batter crisp as an army bed sheet and plump shrimp nestled in with a heap of caramelized onions that had been stewed in coconut milk.

Dosateria was managed by Sandhya Malhotra, Sushil's youngest daughter, who had recently left the large accounting firm Deloitte to enter the family business. She told me that in Whole Foods the Dosateria had taken the space of the Japanese food station, which had previously cooked tempura, udon soups, and rice bowls and was now reduced to a small sushi counter at the Dosateria's rear. The seats surrounding the dosa cooks were full during the lunch rush with nearby workers from the financial district. Initially, Sandhya said, more than a third of customers were Indian or other South Asians, but that was decreasing daily as word got out, and even the Indians ordered the Bollywood Chicken dosa more than any other item. This was surprising because its combination of chicken kofta kebab, avocado, roasted onions, jack cheese, and a wasabi-avocado chutney was a serious departure from tradition.

"This gives us portability," Sameer Malhotra said with a smile, showing up to check on how his sister was doing during the lunch rush. Dosas, while traditionally torn and dipped into small bowls of soup, could be folded into cones and eaten on the run, in true American fashion. Café Spice now had a foothold into proper fast food, a way to eat curry and chutney in a car, and although this may not matter to New Yorkers, it would be crucial when expanding into the rest of America, where life was lived behind the dashboard. I asked Sameer why the family chose dosas, and he swept his hand at the men pouring and flipping batter in front of us. "Action! Action!" he said, beaming. "We want to have dosas being cooked in windows. That's what's always been missing from our stuff." This first Dosateria was a spearhead, an experiment. Sushil Malhotra told his children not to worry whether it made money—it was all about a proof of concept. If it worked here, expansion was next, both within Whole Foods and on its own as a chain, which could one day even go public on the stock market. Whole Foods was already discussing what other stores this could work in. Would it fly in Texas? Or Seattle? There was even talk of Dosaterias replacing the underperforming panini bars in other Whole Foods locations because, as Sameer put it, "paninis just don't sell anymore."

It was funny, in a way. Twenty years ago, if you had to pick the hot trends shaping North American tastes, paninis and Japanese food would be near the top. Back then you couldn't swing a pot of chai without hitting a place selling hot-pressed Italian sandwiches or cheap California rolls. They were ubiquitous, and they ushered in a profound change in the way we not only ate but also how we viewed the world. Japan went from being the most exotic foreign culture to something of an everyday comfort, and Italy went from grandma's meatballs to a vroom-vroom Vespa with a panini neatly tucked in the basket. Soon we discovered more foods from there: ramen and izakayas from Japan, Neapolitan pizza and prosciutto from Italy. It seemed poetic in a way that Indian food was now taking over the Japanese and Italian stations in the nation's most prestigious and trendsetting grocery chain—their time had come. They had paved the way, the public had embraced those trends, but now that public was hungry for something else, and Indian food was rising to the challenge, at least in this one store.

It made me recall something Sushil Malhotra said a year before, when we were speaking in his ornate living room. I had asked about all he had done to try to make Indian food a central fixture in America, all his successes and the experiments over half a century, and what they had ultimately accomplished. Making Indian food matter was important for him, as it was for Sukhi Singh, Hemant Bhagwani, Floyd Cardoz, and many others like them, whether it was through fine dining, quick-service takeout concepts, or even food trucks. But with each Indian food entrepreneur I spoke with, I could tell their motivation to keep at it went beyond their hopes for financial reward; they wanted to take things further, to make their company influential enough and get their food into enough mouths that Indian food would finally break through a certain cultural barrier and gain the widespread acceptance that it still lacked compared to other global cuisines. These entrepreneurs were driven by pride: pride in their names, their businesses, and, most importantly, their culture, which they loved dearly and wanted everyone else to love as well. Making Indian food a vibrant trend was the only way to do that, and this is why it mattered so much to each of them. "It's there," Sushil Malhotra said, a look of gold lust in his eyes, as he held his thumb and index finger just an inch apart to indicate how close that moment was. "It's there!"

9

FOOD POLITICS

THE TACO TRUCK MARCH
ON WASHINGTON

I t was a quarter past nine on a Wednesday morning, and Patrick Rathborne's Jeep had already circled DC's Farragut Square three times as he rounded the corner for a fourth loop. "It's like musical chairs here," said Rathborne, who is tall and slender, with a shaved head. "You can't be the first to park because it's illegal before 9:30, but you can't be the last either." He talked a mile a minute as he kept one eye on the road and another on the eighteen highly coveted metered parking spots that ring the picturesque square. Located just three short blocks away from the White House, Farragut Square is surrounded by blocks of prime office space filled with employees from government agencies, law firms, lobbies, and unions. If you are in the business of selling lunch, Farragut Square is the most valuable real estate in the nation's capital. Rathborne owns the Big Cheese DC food truck, which specializes in gourmet grilled cheese sandwiches, so lunch is definitely his business. But before he so much as unwraps the gruyere or switches on the griddle, he first needs to secure a parking spot. This was exactly why every other food truck operator, their employees, siblings, cousins, and even paid parking spot holders—who can be hired on Craigslist for $200—were circling the square like buzzards that very same moment.

205

"Farragut is a first-tier spot," Rathborne said, entering his fifth and, he hoped, final pass around the square at 9:20. "On a beautiful day like this we'll do as much business as we possibly can." Second-tier spots, like one near the rather isolated State Department, are easier to park in but draw far less foot traffic. "When I started back in 2010 there were fifteen trucks in the city. You could leave your kitchen at 11:00 a.m. and still get a prime spot for 11:30. Now, with more than 150 trucks, you have to get out here and play musical chairs until parking enforcement leaves." With that, Rathborne jerked the Jeep into a spot in the middle of the block on the park's west side. "I might just wait here and take the $100 fine today," he said, looking around. "Officer Freeman is the one to watch out for. If the food trucks are the Road Runner, she's Wile E. Coyote." Rathborne got out and stood by the meter, scanning the sidewalk in either direction for Officer Freeman or, possibly, a falling anvil. He nodded to a Middle Eastern–looking taxi driver and a conservatively dressed Korean man, whose cars were parked in the adjacent spots, waiting by their meters. "These guys are saving spots too," Rathborne said. "The taxi in front of me is probably waiting for his brother to arrive with an Afghan kebab truck."

At the stroke of 9:30 the parking meter sprang to life with a click. Rathborne and others all around the square pumped handfuls of quarters into their meters, then hopped into other circling cars or food trucks, which took them to the off-site kitchens where they would finish preparing lunch. Rathborne spotted a Vietnamese soup truck circling the square, honking its horn with the sad desperation of a calf separated from the herd, and he shook his head. "He might be out of luck already," he said as we bounded down the stairs of the DC Metro station to catch a train out to Alexandria, Virginia, where the Big Cheese shared a prep kitchen with the BBQ Bus and the Borinquen Lunch Box, which sold Puerto Rican food. There Rathborne checked on his employees, who were assembling and wrapping stacks of grilled cheese sandwiches in cellophane, and raced around, piling sandwiches, drinks, napkins, and other essentials onto a small cart. He kept up a steady patter with Tad Ruddell-Tabisola, the owner of the BBQ Bus, who was rubbing spices onto dozens of racks of ribs and sliding them into the smoker to cook overnight. The main topic of conversation, aside from smack talk about parking, was around "regs," or the city's proposed regulations, which the DC Food Truck Association was in the midst of a four-year battle to quash. Food truck owners were fearful that the new laws the mayor's office had tabled would take the food trend they had generated, a trend that created tremendous public joy, changed the nature of commerce in DC, and fed the families of the truck owners, and crush it under the weight of unnecessary and onerous fines and penalties. It would snuff out DC's food truck trend with the stroke of a pen. "One of the things about the new regs is that trucks need a licensed owner on trucks at all times," Rathborne explained to me as Ruddell-Tabisola nodded in agreement. "That's a five hundred–dollar license for two years, per person, and it's like saying that I can't have a restaurant open if my waiter doesn't have a license. Turnover in this business is high for employees. I can't afford to buy each new one a vending license at five hundred dollars a pop! In Arlington it's thirty to forty dollars."

Half an hour after he arrived at the kitchen, Rathborne's Big Cheese truck, with its smiling sandwich logo, was packed, gassed, and ready to go. With Rathborne at the wheel and me and his two young employees squeezed into the back, sitting atop coolers, the truck charged back toward DC, its kitchen-backseat banging and clanging loudly all the way. "Hold on tight!" Rathborne bellowed over the loud engine. "We'll go through yellow lights, because this thing don't stop!" We arrived, slightly shaken, at his Jeep, still parked in its spot, at 11:24. One of the employees jumped out to move the car to a nearby parking lot, and Rathborne gave two friendly honks to the drivers of the Kohinoor Dhaka Indian and Yellow Vendor trucks, now parked on either side of his spot. They maneuvered a few crucial inches so Rathborne could wedge the Big Cheese truck into its spot. Rathborne turned off the engine and stepped outside just as the parking meter ticked to red. He fed it more quarters, then helped his other employee open the large service window. They turned on the generator and the grill, powered up two iPads as an ordering system, and hung a rack of potato chips off the side of the truck. Rathborne took one last look, then sent out a message to the Big Cheese's 8,950 Twitter followers at 11:39, telling them where the truck was parked. Within seconds a line began forming, due more to the fact that it was lunchtime than to warp-speed social media, and the first order of the day, a Thrilled Cheese (chipotle cheddar, jalapeño, and guacamole on sourdough) hit the grill. Then, remembering one last thing, Rathborne placed a sign in the truck's window that every truck around Farragut Square had also prominently displayed. It featured a map of the city's core, with most streets and squares blocked out in red to show where food trucks would be prohibited from parking in just over a month if the DC city council adopted the current regulations the mayor's office proposed. On the bottom, in big bold letters, was their twenty-first-century call to arms: #saveDCfoodtrucks.

❧

Biting into a greasy, crunchy, altogether delicious gourmet grilled cheese sandwich, politics are probably the last thing that enters your mind. After all, food is one subject that tends to cut across ideological and political divides. Republicans and Democrats love bacon just as much as hardcore communists and die-hard capitalists enjoy ice cream. Few of us would associate kale bought at the farmer's market with a particular cause or their morning latte with a stance on global trade policy because we rarely realize how much food trends matter as an impetus for political power and change. But matter they do, because food trends have the ability to change laws and behaviors by the sheer nature of their popularity, shaping everything from economics to social policy well beyond the plate.

In many instances a food trend's political influence is straightforward and overt. The rising popularity of organic foods, locally produced foods, and ethically raised animals are all significant food trends that grew from political ideals but later became intertwined with taste and flavor trends. They began in places like Northern California and bourgeois hippie restaurants like Chez Panisse, but eventually they spread out across the food world's tastemakers. Where importing the finest ingredients from around the world was once the chief point of pride among the finest restaurants, today the best kitchens in the world, from Denmark's NOMA to Charleston's McCrady's, all try to outdo each other with seasonal, local, organic ingredients, sometimes from as nearby as the restaurant's own rooftop gardens. These are places where the chefs made their names by foraging in the dirt, taking seaweed and wild flowers and crap that nobody even took a second look at, and charging $20 a plate for it. It is a movement that has made farmers like Glenn Roberts stars in the culinary world, and it is now affecting chains as large as Chipotle, in which the company strives to serve vegetables that are local and organic and meats raised humanely without hormones. Although the political aspect of these trends remain at their very core—they are a yin to industrial food's yang—the diners and shoppers opting for these options today do so increasingly out of a sense of taste. Organic food and local food tastes better, the advocates say, and although this isn't really always the case, it is driving the industry's tremendous growth.

Trends like these can directly impact government policies. From the moment Michelle Obama entered the White House as First Lady, she vocally promoted local, sustainable food for families, communities, and, most significantly, schools. A lot of this has been chalked up to photo ops of Mrs. Obama in the White House garden or distributing apples to cute children, but over time her stance has had a significant impact. Hundreds of schools across the country have begun planting their own gardens, sourcing local food, and working with farmers to develop better lunches and cafeteria offerings. In 2012 the Department of Agriculture introduced a pilot program that offered grants to farmers and schools pairing up to provide healthy, local foods to children. Its funding was minimal, just $5 million, likely what the nation's schools spend each week on French fries, but its symbolism was significant. Mrs. Obama's evangelism for local food has signaled to policymakers, from school principals to town mayors and even national agencies, that the White House will view this issue favorably.

Food trends are powerful political forces because they draw together a diverse group of motivated consumers and tastemakers. In 2011 an investment group backed by a Boston hedge fund made an application to develop a massive aggregate quarry on thousands of acres of farmland the company had been quietly acquiring north of Toronto—just a ways down the road from Thornbury. Local farmers and weekend residents, including the celebrated chef Michael Stadtlander, who runs a gourmet farm restaurant nearby, formed a grassroots opposition campaign to what they dubbed the "Mega Quarry." They began spreading word through the chef and foodie community in Toronto that the quarry would greatly affect the food and water quality that provided the same local, seasonal food that went on their plates. "Stop the Mega Quarry" bumper stickers and T-shirts soon began appearing at the city's most coveted restaurants as well as on the Volvos and Audis parked outside. That fall Stadtlander organized an event in the community called Food Stock, which brought eighty chefs and thousands of food fans to a wet, rainy potato farm near where the quarry would be located for a day of eating, drinking, and advocacy. The farmers and the chefs had vastly less money than what the investors had wagered on the quarry, but in the end they leveraged the trend of local seasonal food by using the chefs and their sophisticated customers to turn a local land use issue into one about choice on the plate. The quarry's investors withdrew their application, and the land was sold to a consortium that promised to keep it for farming.

Other food trends exert political influence by their economic might. The rapid rise of espresso coffee culture in the 1990s was spearheaded by Starbucks, which quickly became the largest coffee shop chain in the world. As Starbucks grew and other coffee chains proliferated, the politics of the coffee business seeped into the conversation, largely focused around fair wages paid for coffee beans grown in producing countries. Under consumer pressure, in 2000 Starbucks began purchasing Fair Trade–certified beans and quickly grew into the largest Fair Trade coffee seller in the world. This gave the Fair Trade coffee movement greater visibility, and other competing chains and coffee retail brands adopted the standard in order to compete with Starbucks. Now, even mass retailers like Costco and 7-11 sell Fair Trade coffee. Starbucks has also leveraged its trendiness so as to lobby lawmakers to support free trade deals with countries such as Colombia, Peru, and South Korea. Their lobbying budget is small, less than a million dollars a year, but the company's influence is derived from its popularity. A green and white Starbucks coffee cup is a powerful symbol of American capitalism on a par with McDonald's' golden arches or a red can of Coke. The lawmakers, bureaucrats, and power brokers in DC and other capitals know that, as sure as their staffers know their morning order of a venti double skim latte, no sugar.

In the case of food trucks, a culinary trend has morphed into a political issue that is having profound effects on the way commerce is conducted in cities all over the world. Since Roy Choi launched his Kogi Korean BBQ truck in Los Angeles in late 2008, caravans of new food trucks have rolled out in cities and towns all over North America and, increasingly, other countries. Estimates of the number of food trucks in North America range anywhere from roughly ten thousand to over a hundred thousand. From the Swiss-style hot dogs at Swieners in San Diego to the pad Thai at the One of a Thai truck of Yellowknife, in Canada's Northwest Territories, the food truck revolution has covered thousands of miles in a short period of time and emerged into one of the most significant, fastest growing food trends of our time. Food trucks have rolled out with nearly every cuisine imaginable, capturing lunch diners by offering freshly cooked, often innovative food that is easily accessed at an affordable price point.

The politicization of the food truck trend happened almost immediately. In every city and town where trucks have established a presence they have been met with almost immediate opposition in the form of restrictive regulations, outdated bylaw enforcement, and lobbying campaigns from a collection of interests headed up by established restaurant owners and others who are threatened by the new business model food trucks present. In every case the nascent food trucks have banded together and formed coalitions and associations in order to fight for their very livelihood. They quickly learned the art of politics and leveraged the power of their food trend not only to safeguard their business but also to change the laws of commerce across the continent. And this should matter to all of us because food trucks not only increased our lunch options; they also fostered innovation in the food business in a way that allowed new economic models to emerge where there were none before. Before the food truck trend the idea of selling quality, innovative meals on the street was something people talked about when they came back from travels abroad, and those who wanted to start a new food business had to either open up a costly restaurant or keep on dreaming. The food trucks have changed this. Roy Choi's Kogi taco has upended the way food was sold in our cities and towns and the way young cooks and chefs brought their ideas to the public. More than their individual businesses, the food trucks were fighting to save this, while the opposition was trying to keep it from spreading further.

Washington, DC, was one of the fiercest battlegrounds in the food trucks wars and, because of the city's highly political nature, one of its most interesting. The first of the current generation of food trucks (alternatively called "gourmet," "hipster," or "Twitter" trucks) appeared in the city in early 2009 around the time of President Obama's inauguration. One of the pioneers was the Fojol Brothers, which sold a mix of Ethiopian and Indian street food out of a carnival caravan, complete with decorative turbans and waxed mustaches. Other trucks soon followed, as the city's lunch crowd rapidly embraced new options, which were often cheaper and better quality than the takeout lunch spots in the core of the city. In mid-2009 the DC city council set up a task force to look at amending the regulations governing who could sell food on the street. For decades street food in DC was limited to roving ice cream trucks and stationary hot dog carts, which served the same menu from fixed locations around the Washington mall and other tourist sites. The rules that governed them were over four decades old, and the market was as stagnant as the water the hot dogs steamed in. The food trucks provided a direct challenge to the regulatory status quo. They served all sorts of unexpected foods, from southern barbecue to Vietnamese soups, and though they changed locations each day, most parked for hours during lunchtime in one spot instead of the quick stops ice cream trucks typically made. The task force that city council had appointed was heavily skewed with restaurant owners and representatives of business improvement districts (BIDs), which are associations of landlords and business owners from a particular area. Only one food truck owner was invited to join the task force, and others who requested a seat were flat out told not to join because it wouldn't be a friendly environment.

In early 2010, as the number of trucks in DC grew to over a dozen, restaurants, through their trade group the Restaurant Association of Metropolitan Washington (RAMW), and a number of BIDs intensely lobbied the city council to halt food trucks' rapid expansion. They argued that food trucks took up valuable parking spaces, obstructed the sidewalks in front of restaurants with crowds, and encouraged litter to pile up nearby. Most importantly, the trucks were perceived to be pulling away paying customers from the established, taxpaying restaurants and food stores in these areas, and in the midst of a recession, no less. In the past the BIDs and the RAMW had directly supported several city councilors' election campaigns, and their relationships were longstanding, so it wasn't a total surprise when the DC city council proposed a moratorium on new licenses for food trucks later that year. The move would have slammed the brakes on DC's emerging food truck scene. When the food truck owners heard about the moratorium, they immediately called each other and raced down to the city council's offices.

"City council was going to drop emergency legislation, and everyone would have been out of business in a matter of months," recalled Che Ruddell-Tabisola, who co-owned the BBQ Bus with his husband, Tad. "We all ran down. Some guys wore dirty chef's coats and smelled like French fries. We were running up and down the stairs, and it was our first time lobbying, but we did it!" Through pure persuasion and a relentless last-minute effort, the food truck owners had banded together and finally got their voices heard. The city's moratorium was shelved, and the District of Columbia began a long and arduous debate over how to effectively regulate street food as well as street vending. The food trucks' first battle was won, but the war was just beginning. To continue the fight, DC's food trucks would need advice, organization, and allies to keep their trend alive. They got all three by way of California and a man named Matt Geller.

∽

In the politicization of the food truck trend, Matt Geller is the central figure who has linked disparate truck owners across the nation, organized their ranks into formidable forces, and taught them to fight for their rights. He is the Cesar Chavez of food trucks, and he lives to make sure that food trucks everywhere can sell their meals without undue restriction or constraint. Geller was no stranger to the food business. He managed restaurants in his twenties but later received a law degree from UCLA and had some experience in local politics. Just after Christmas 2009, Dominic Lau, a friend of his who owned the new Don Chau Taco truck in Los Angeles, called Geller with a problem. "'Matt, I don't know what to do,'" Geller recalled Lau telling him. "'My truck got shut down for three weeks because I didn't have access to a restroom for one night.' My immediate concern was that my friend is being harassed," Geller said. "I grew up in Venice, California, and I have a problem with authority. Don was getting harassed by other municipal forces—in any given day he would get harassed by the county health department or the LAPD, which is run by the city. What did I have to do to make sure my friend didn't get harassed? The food truck thing was just a passion project for him. He said, 'Matt, I don't know what to do. I just lost $25,000. I don't know what to do.' When I heard that, I thought *Hell no!*"

On January 4, 2010, Geller convened a meeting with seventeen of the city's gourmet food trucks in a vacant lot in Santa Monica, where he was planning on creating the city's first vending lot on private property. Every food truck owner there, whether it was Dosa, Barbies Q, Slice Truck, King Cone, Sweets Truck, Nom Nom, or Baby's Bad Ass Burgers, faced the same problems. Their trucks were getting towed and ticketed repeatedly—even seized—for violations that included being within a hundred feet of a restaurant or selling in one spot for longer than thirty minutes. Truck workers were routinely harassed by police, meter maids, and health department officials, with each citing different and often contradictory regulations. Geller looked up these laws and quickly realized that some of them were in violation of California's own constitution, whereas judges had actually struck down others over thirty years before. At that meeting the truck owners decided to form an association in order to pool their resources and speak with a common voice, led by Geller. They called themselves the Southern California Mobile Food Vendors Association (SCMFVA).

The SCMFVA launched their food truck lot the next day, with four trucks, tons of customers, and three TV stations coming to cover the event. Two days after that the city of Santa Monica showed up and shut down the lot for an apparent zoning violation, kicking off Geller's first battle. He quickly researched the applicable laws and saw there was no substance to the zoning claims. Then, in what would prove to be a core strategy of the food truck battles in years to come, Geller got all the trucks in the association to send out Twitter and Facebook messages to their followers, already numbering in the thousands, urging them to write the Santa Monica city council to rectify this injustice and posting the e-mail addresses of councilors. "Suddenly these five part-time councilors are getting hammered with e-mails," Geller said. "They were getting pissed. Santa Monica put us on the very next agenda meeting. In that meeting, two weeks later, they tasked their planning department to come up with a mechanism to allow street truck vending." The harassment stopped, and within a few months the planning department agreed to offer the food trucks temporary vending permits in the areas they wanted. However, they still enforced an old rule that vending could only happen for thirty minutes at a time in one spot, an impossible situation for a food truck needing to capture a steady lunch business. "It had no connection with public safety," Geller said. "We asked Santa Monica, 'Why's it there?' 'Because we said so,'" the city said. "But it contradicts California state vehicle code 22455, which allows the regulation of food trucks only for public safety." So Geller and the SCMFVA took Santa Monica to court, where the judge ruled in their favor and revoked the time limit. It would be the first legal victory of many for Geller and a precedent for how he would use the courts to fight for food trucks everywhere.

In the years since he founded the SCMFVA, the organization has grown to include over 130 trucks, each paying dues that fund

Geller's legal challenges to antitruck legislation across Southern California. He and his lawyers have filed over two dozen lawsuits against cities, towns, and counties and brought significant public pressure on lawmakers at every level of government. When a state representative proposed a law restricting food trucks from selling within fifteen hundred feet of any school in California, Geller went to Sacramento, had 180,000 Twitter followers send messages to the lawmaker who proposed the bill, and rallied the press until the legislation was scrapped. He is aggressive and unflinching in his advocacy—a bulldog for food trucks.

"I'm not going to make deals," Geller said. "I'm not going to get involved with sitting in a room with restaurant owners, splitting consumer dollars. Not going to do that. I'm going to take that hard line approach because the public's been so supportive. I don't look at lawsuits as aggressive. The only mechanism you have in that case is the court system. If a city says no, and we sue them and they back off, we'll still go in and help them write regulations. What I'm saying is that you [the city] doesn't have ultimate say."

Geller's goal is to establish a legislative standard for food trucks that takes care of the necessary health and safety requirements for serving food and operating trucks while also prohibiting regulations that exist purely to curb competition or impose some arbitrary aesthetic standard. "In a perfect world there's no associations," said Geller. "Trucks do what they want to do, cook food for their customers, and just run their business. Why would you want to form an association and spend another five to ten hours a month fighting for the right to do what you're doing? In an ideal world I'd be doing something else."

That seems unlikely, given the reality on the ground. In nearly every territory where food trucks have emerged, which is pretty much most cities on the continent, legislation has been tabled or selectively enforced that has curbed food trucks' ability to work. New York requires truck owners to have valid licenses and permits but has capped the number of permits it issues, as did New Orleans so that they are only available on the black market. Toronto has prohibited food trucks selling on its streets and, depending on the location, private property as well. Rochester only allowed food trucks to sell from two locations, selected by lottery, and Cincinnati restricted trucks from parking in certain areas of downtown. Trucks in some cities were required to rent space in stationary commissary kitchens, whereas other cities only let their trucks serve reheated food, with nothing being cooked fresh. Some districts have levied proximity restrictions, which prohibit food trucks from parking within a certain distance—anywhere from two hundred to one thousand feet—of a restaurant or any other business selling food. In cities like Chicago this has basically banished trucks from the city center, which is rife with restaurants. Chicago also instituted a GPS tracking system so it can monitor food trucks by satellite and automatically fine them if they stray outside that boundary. One article compared their use to the tracking bracelets people under house arrest wear, but an infraction of these rules would saddle Chicago food truck operators with a $2,000 fine, which, the same article noted, is more than the city issued for possessing certain drugs.

In other cities the inconsistency of existing laws and enforcement make legally operating a truck a Kafkaesque experience. When Dan Pennachietti opened his Italian sandwich truck Lil' Dan's Gourmet in Philadelphia in 2010, the process was a merry-go-round of approvals and agencies. "To the health department, to licensing and inspection, back to health, back to licensing, wait six weeks, wait for a stamp, wait thirty days," recalled Pennachietti with exasperation. "I spent three thousand dollars on permits and those things before I could get the truck on the street." Then he was given a prohibited street list, which was "pretty much any street that's profitable," and had to wait another year until a stationary vending spot opened up. After Lil' Dan's Gourmet opened, the health inspections began, and these were no more consistent. Once, he was fined for having a generator even though the licensing department had already approved its use on the truck's design.

In pretty much every one of these cities the regulations were proposed once officials, who restaurants lobbied, noticed the food truck trend gaining in popularity. When one or two trucks initially emerged they were ignored as an oddity, but once there was a substantial number, the crackdown began. When it did, the truck owners quickly realized that no matter how tasty their wood-fired pizzas or burritos, if they didn't challenge the legislation, they soon wouldn't be able to sell anything, and the tens of thousands of dollars they had invested in their new businesses would be lost. Whenever a city's food trucks found their livelihood threatened, which has occurred in every single city at one point or another, the truck owners have reached out for help, often to Matt Geller.

Geller frequently flies to cities around the country to help them set up and organize food truck associations. His travel is paid for by sponsors that include truck manufacturers like MobiMunch and the industry website Mobile Food News. In some cities the associations are informal gatherings of truck owners who meet regularly to discuss common problems, and in others they operate as a for-profit business. In San Francisco, which has relatively restrictive vending rules, a private company called Off the Grid formed in 2010 to create a safe space where trucks can sell their food without running afoul of the city's regulations. Off the Grid manages over twenty locations around the city where trucks can operate, from simple parking lots to regular summer festivals with bands, bars, bathrooms, and outdoor seating. "The difference between Matt Geller and myself is that I don't believe in lawsuits or food trucks at all cost," said the organization's founder, Matt Cohen, who I met one day in San Francisco at the Fort Mason Center, a federal park where Off the Grid regularly holds truck markets. Cohen also employed a professional state lobbyist and continued to advocate at San Francisco city hall on behalf of trucks, succeeding in the past few years by lowering the cost of a food truck license from $10,000 down to just $800.

In DC's case things came to a head in early 2011 when the city council began looking at other cities for regulatory models and focused on San Francisco. "Che [Ruddell-Tabisola] called me and said, 'Oh shit, DC is going the route of San Francisco,'" said Geller, who had been advising Ruddell-Tabisola and others from afar. "They'd have to pay to be anywhere—it'd be very restrictive." Geller flew out to Washington to help the truck owners there set up the DC Food Truck Association (DCFTA). One of the features that has defined the current trend in food trucks, especially in its early years, is the background of the truck operators. Whereas the previous generation of hot dog cart and food truck operators were most often recent immigrants, it is common to find former white-collar professionals operating the new fleet of food trucks, and most truck owners tend to be far more media and technology savvy than traditional food vendors or even restaurant owners. When it came to the DCFTA, the membership represented a crack squad of politically experienced individuals. Its first director, Kristi Cunningham Whitfield, who owns the Curbside Cupcake trucks, had a master's degree in economic development from MIT and worked in that field for a number of years. Che Ruddell-Tabisola, who was interim director and co-owned the BBQ Bus with his husband, Tad, had worked for gay civil rights organizations for years, with a focus on the marriage equality campaign. Doug Povich, another director, passed on a partnership at a big law firm, where he still practices business and regulatory law, to help run the DC location of his sister's Red Hook Lobster Pound truck empire, which is based in Brooklyn. Among its members the DCFTA had former economists from the International Monetary Fund, biochemists making cupcakes, and several veterans of political campaigns, including the pivotal 2008 Obama presidential contest.

Over the next year and a half the DCFTA lobbied city hall for favorable regulations, built public support through online outreach and live events, and did all they could to influence the new vending regulations that Mayor Vincent Gray's office had been working on since food trucks emerged on the scene. In October 2012 the mayor's office released its proposed regulations, and the food truck owners were aghast. If passed, trucks would be limited to selling only in Mobile Roadway Vending locations, in a select number of spots that would be assigned by some sort of undetermined lottery. Other trucks would be prohibited from parking within five hundred feet of these zones, and parking infractions from expired meters would rise from a $50 ticket to $2,000. Food trucks would be banned from selling anywhere where there was less than ten feet of unobstructed sidewalk.

Truck owners immediately cried foul, saying the regulations were little more than a capitulation to the demands of the powerful restaurant and real estate lobbies. The new laws would push the majority of trucks out of the central core of DC, where the bulk of the lunch business was. All the momentum, culinary innovation, and jobs they had created over the past three years would dry up and vanish along with the livelihoods these entrepreneurs had risked so much to establish. Several truck owners had already closed up shop or reduced the number of trucks they operated, anticipating what the proposed rules would do, and others were wary about the future. "I'm going to lose my business if the regulations go through," said Michael Habtemariam, the Ethiopian-born owner of DC Ballers, a business that already operated two falafel trucks. "I wouldn't put out my third truck if this passes," he said during a busy lunch in Farragut Square, where the lineup for his truck ran ten people deep. "Here, in Farragut, they'd only allow six trucks to park"—the actual numbers were yet undefined—"the other dozen trucks here will just go out of business." As many of DC's truck owners told me that week, if the mayor's proposed regulations passed, the entire food truck industry in DC would be legislated out of existence. A vote was set for some time in the spring of 2013, and the battle lines were drawn.

ꙮ

The Big Cheese, DC Ballers, and the other trucks at Farragut Square took off after the last lunch customer left, and I walked around the corner to the offices of the Restaurant Association of Metropolitan Washington, where I spoke with Kathy Hollinger, the organization's president. Hollinger came to the restaurant association midway through the battle over food trucks from the city's film and television development office. "It's been a pretty exhausting battle," she remarked. Hollinger wasn't entirely unsympathetic to food trucks. Though there were members of her association who operated restaurants as well as food trucks, such as chef José Andrés's Think Food Group, a vocal number of the association's seven hundred restaurant owners had nothing but ire for food trucks, and they looked to the RAMW to do something about it. These restaurants had experienced food truck customers obstructing their entrances, using their restrooms, and even eating their food truck meals on the restaurant's patio as though their tables were picnic benches. But the restaurant's biggest complaint came from the idea of unfair competition. Restaurants paid many more taxes and fees than food trucks did, and their businesses simply cost more to operate. "They should be held to a similar but scalable standard," Hollinger said of food trucks. "It's not fair for them to have the same regulations as restaurants, but currently they have *nothing*. They have zero. It gives the appearance that they are rogue in nature, and that's disturbing other businesses."

There was a tone of disappointment in Hollinger's voice about how the whole issue had devolved into a pitched battle, past the point at which compromise was possible. Prior to coming onboard the association, Hollinger had eaten at food trucks occasionally, though she had avoided them ever since. "I'd love for us to come together as food service providers," she told me with a sigh. "There are trends, and any trends that exist as foodservice providers, we should embrace as much as we can without compromising our core membership. . . . It's unfortunate that there's a disconnect between restaurants and food trucks. Doug [Povich, president of the DC Food Truck Association] and I realize we should be having communication and talking. A consensus would be terrific. I don't want to close the door and take the hard line against them." But at this late point in the game, with a council vote pending in the next two months, proposed rules on the table that had been in the works for several years, and several highly vocal restaurateurs leading the battle cry against food trucks, Hollinger also realized that the march to confrontation was inevitable.

After our chat I walked back across Farragut Square to Loeb's New York Deli, a family-owned Jewish delicatessen that I'd written about in my previous book and whose owners, Marlene Loeb and her brothers, Steve and David, I knew well. They had seen the food trucks in Farragut grow from a handful to two dozen over the previous two years, and they were as frustrated as any of the area's restaurants about it. "I almost feel like the city is in cahoots with them," Steve said. "They take up spaces and park in bus lanes!" To them it was a question of competition. Loeb's paid tens of thousands of dollars each month in rent, utilities, salaries, benefits, and insurance in order to keep running. And each day they looked out the door and saw food trucks paying their rent in handfuls of quarters, with minimal staff and overhead. They cut corners literally and figuratively, and they paid people to save them parking spots. "Just recently they had to start paying sales tax. That was a big woo hoo!" Marlene said sarcastically, slapping the table before giving me a rundown of the dozens of local, state, and federal taxes that Loeb's regularly paid. "I'm all for free enterprise. That's what this country has been built on, but it's got to be fair and regulated."

All over the continent restaurant associations and their allies were pushing back against food trucks with every means at their disposal. Their numbers were vastly greater than the food trucks—hundreds of restaurants in a typical city vs. a dozen or more trucks—they were better funded, and their political access was well established through restaurant associations and personal relationships with politicians, who were more likely to sit down for a steak at a favorite restaurant than line up for a grilled cheese sandwich and eat it standing up. "What we see is the classic battle between a new form of business model and incumbents," said Steve King, an economist with Emergent Research, a trend-forecasting firm in San Francisco that focused on the small-business sector. King had been researching the economics of food trucks across the country and saw how the fight unfolded at a larger level. "Because they can't fight back at a business-model level, the incumbents are fighting back at a political level. Food trucks snuck up on the restaurant industry. The food truck industry tends to win initial battles because consumers love them and the politicians like the idea of them because they bring vibrancy to neighborhoods. They've got some natural allies and were able to take advantage of that." In the long run, however, the restaurants and their allies can press the fight with more force. "Now it's the empire strikes back," King said. Still, he believed that the food trucks would ultimately prevail. "No industry has fought off a good business-model innovation through the political process. If you look at the battles going on, it's the classic industry in the back room, saying, 'You've got to protect me, I'm paying your taxes, I'm paying for your campaign' and in the front room you have voters saying, 'We want food trucks.' In the end the voters win, and innovation wins."

ᴑᴖ

The DC Food Truck Association's campaign operated on a five-track approach. At the top was the association's communication efforts, which involved crafting a steady stream of press releases and arranging interviews with local and national media, who were overwhelmingly sympathetic in their coverage. More important was the use of social media to spread the message, both to the public and lawmakers. Though the DCFTA's membership hovered around fifty trucks, its combined social media audience reached hundreds of thousands. This allowed them to speak with a unified voice and leverage the popularity of the food truck trend into political capital. Kathy Hollinger admitted to me that the voice of the food trucks had been significantly louder than the restaurants with both the public and politicians, precisely because of social media. What the food truck associations lacked in money and power they made up for in organization, communication, and sheer chutzpah.

The DCFTA engaged directly in formal lobbying efforts through a registered lobbyist, who took meetings with city councilors and bureaucrats, kept his ear to the ground at city hall, provided strategic political advice, and wrote policy documents and commentary on the proposed legislation, helping to prepare food truck owners, DCFTA executives, and their allies for the day they would testify in front of city councilors prior to the vote. There was some small-scale, crowd-sourced fund-raising, such as $5 donations, which paid for some of the association's expenses, as well as efforts at coalition building with local neighborhood groups and the food trucks' other potential allies. The association also organized a number of different field activities, which ranged from handing out #saveDCfoodtrucks stickers and flyers during busy lunches to collecting signatures for petitions. Sometimes the DCFTA would bring food trucks to underprivileged areas of the city that had few restaurants, setting up in abandoned lots or along blighted blocks, demonstrating to local politicians that food trucks served as vital proof of a neighborhood's commercial viability when the trucks inevitably drew crowds. In the weeks before the council's vote the DCFTA staged a Day Without Food Trucks, which deployed trucks at their usual spots across the city to hand out literature, petitions, and stickers but not serve any food so as to drive home their point that if the city passed the legislation, food trucks would be forced out of business. If you were one of the people who showed up that day, hungry for a half-rack of ribs from the BBQ Bus, only to be handed a flyer, your motivation to take action was as powerful as the rumbling in your belly.

Perhaps the biggest activity the association organized was food truck festivals, which assembled a large number of trucks (up to forty in some cases) on private lots during a Friday or Saturday, with live music, licensed bars, and carnival games. These events presented tremendous potential for political outreach because they drew the most devoted food truck fans and because the sheer size of the crowds provided a visually dramatic venue to show politicians, press, and other influencers the power of the food truck trend. Festivals are either organized by the DCFTA, such as their signature Curbside Cookoffs, or by private businesses, such as the Truckeroo series, which takes place in a giant lot called the Bullpen, which is ringed by converted shipping containers, outside the Washington Nationals baseball stadium. My last day in DC happened to coincide with the first Truckeroo of the season, so I headed down to the Bullpen to see how the DC Food Truck Association made their case to the public.

Right before the event I met up at a coffee shop with attorneys Bert Gall and Robert Frommer as well as political activist Christina Walsh, all of whom worked for the Institute for Justice, a nonprofit libertarian legal organization that was spearheading the court fight on behalf of food trucks across America. Though food trends are rarely clear-cut partisan political issues, the libertarian movement, which basically espouses an ideology of regulation-free commerce, had been a persistent advocate for consumer choice in the food arena, opposing such initiatives as New York City's proposed large soda ban and restrictions on salt. "As libertarians, our objection is to regulations that serve no public purpose," Gall said. "It's about food trucks having a *right* to earn a living." In general, the Institute for Justice, and Gall in particular, worked closely with Matt Geller and local food truck associations across the country, filing lawsuits in some cases and advising legally and politically in others. Walsh traveled frequently, forming disparate truck owners into associations, educating them about their rights, providing their members with media training and legislative support, and even bringing restaurants onboard, when possible.

Their initial victory was a suit against the city of El Paso, Texas, filed in 2010 on behalf of the city's food trucks, which were largely Mexican taco trucks at the time. The El Paso city council had passed a law slapping a one thousand–foot truck-free buffer zone around each restaurant, and also prohibited trucks from idling or stopping. "Those rules had nothing to do with health and safety," Gall said. "They were designed to benefit the restaurant association. If a regulation isn't designed for health and safety purposes and really just exists for economic protectionism, it can't withstand judicial review." The laws were tossed, and following the victory the Institute for Justice, which has represented other street vendors in the past— immigrants selling souvenirs, for example—began looking at food truck laws in other cities. They had since challenged laws in Atlanta, Chicago, and even smaller municipalities like Highlea, Florida (a Miami suburb), and advised local associations along the way in places like New Orleans and Pittsburgh. Washington, DC, was their hometown, and they were loath to see the nation's capital set a precedent for restrictive regulation that other cities would emulate.

"Food trucks are spreading," said Walsh. "They're still going into new towns and cities, especially small and midsized ones. As cities see other cities passing good laws, it will normalize. They'll realize that the sky doesn't fall when you see food trucks. We have a few years of hard fights and winning victories in small cities ahead of us. The more good laws that pass, the more it becomes morally unpopular to pass bad laws." Matt Geller said a similar thing, noting how the more wildly restrictive and unreasonable a city's proposed laws were, the easier they would be to defeat. In Geller's opinion DC's proposed regulations were among the most far reaching in the nation.

"The legislation will destroy the food truck industry here," Frommer said. "The only place where they can vend will be in stationary locations."

"Right now is a critical time," echoed Gall. "Food truck owners are trying to run a business twenty-four-seven, but they realize that if they don't spend significant time talking to the media and politicians, they won't have a business."

We all walked the few blocks to the Truckeroo event, which was gearing up for a lunch rush of defense contractors and military personnel from the nearby Navy Yard. The crowd was split between uniformed soldiers and men and women in khakis and golf shirts with ID badges that said foreboding things like "missile intercept group" and "chemical warfare." Twenty trucks had shown up to Truckeroo, and by noon lines as long as forty people were forming at some of the most popular trucks, including the BBQ Bus, the Maine Lobster Roll truck, TaKorean, and Goodies Frozen Custard, a blue-and-white retro VW van where men in bowties and bright shirts served malts, floats, and sundaes to the tune of classic Motown hits blaring from a speaker. A dozen volunteers from the DC Food Trucks Association and the Institute for Justice, dressed in "Truck Yeah! I Support DC Food Trucks" T-shirts, were handing out "I Stand with DC Food Trucks" stickers at each line, explaining the impending regulations to customers and collecting signatures for a petition to councilor Vincent Orange, who was in charge of the city's vending regulation committee.

"Have you heard about DC's food truck regulations?" Asher Huey, a political consultant with the American Federation of Teachers and one of the founders of the DCFTA, asked every single person waiting in line for the Curbside Cupcakes food truck. He held up a large copy of the association's widely circulated map depicting restricted zones and explained in as few words as possible the rules that would affect food truck customers the most. "Would you sign our petition and Tweet to councilor Vincent Orange to save food trucks?" Huey asked. Nine times out of ten people in line complied, waving him off only when they were trying to stuff a cupcake into their face. No one rebutted Huey's argument or stood up for more regulations. One woman ran up to him to sign the petition, calling the mayor "an idiot" for even proposing the regulations. Another said "that sucks" before sending a Tweet to councilor Orange on his phone.

"It's one of these issues that brings people of all political stripes together," Huey said as he moved on to the lineup for the Pepe truck, the mobile outlet of Spanish chef José Andrés's Think Food Group. As I ordered an asparagus and hand-carved Serrano ham sandwich with romesco sauce and a side of patatas bravas—which was amazing, by the way—Huey compared the struggle of food trucks vs. restaurants to David and Goliath. "We don't have the money or power of the restaurant association, but we have the public on our side and as activists. The past four times the city proposed regulations, the public flipped out. They take action when we ask them to."

It reflected something Matt Geller said when I spoke to him about the source of the food truck movement's political power. "A food truck organization isn't about large numbers," he told me. Instead, it was about the power of a popular food trend. The public had some sympathy for the economic plight of food truck owners and the opportunities their business model created, in everything from incubating new foods and concepts, to employing workers. But fundamentally they would fight for food trucks because they liked the food they bought there. "I say to politicians, 'Do you really want to be the guy that we point to and say, *that's the guy who is trying to restrict your access to reasonable food at good prices?*' People get pissed about their access to food. Everyone eats. It's visceral."

At a picnic bench in the middle of Truckeroo, Che Ruddell-Tabisola sat and talked strategy with Doug Povich. Ruddell-Tabisola had been meeting with several city councilors over the past weeks, facilitating visits with food trucks to demonstrate the economic opportunities they can create. This included their expansion into brick-and-mortar businesses such as Pleasant Pops, which began as a food truck selling gourmet Mexican-style ice pops in 2010. Two years later Pleasant Pops had opened a store in the popular Adams Morgan neighborhood and sold their products at various markets around the region. Ruddell-Tabisola hoped to torpedo the restaurants' core message that food trucks were killing their businesses. "The truth is you cannot show one single restaurant that closed because of food trucks," he said. "In fact, it's showing the exact opposite." When it comes down to it, most food truck operators eventually want to become brick-and-mortar restaurant owners. Food trucks may have lower overhead and startup costs than restaurants, but they are limited to one customer at a time and constrained by weather—their business is dead all winter or whenever it rains. Food trucks don't have seating, and they can't sell liquor, which makes up a majority of a restaurant's profits. For all the popularity, experimentation, and fun, owning a food truck is actually a pretty lousy business that is nearly impossible to scale. Owners enter the business in a truck to test out a concept, but if it works, they almost always convert that into one or more stationary restaurants.

And this seemed like the core point: The arrival of food trucks had enlivened a middling restaurant scene in many parts of DC and elsewhere. To regulate it out of existence was to choke off an innovation that people not only liked but were also willing to pay good money for. This was food trends at their best, awakening the culture and the food economy. (Even if they also, unfortunately, awakened some twee lunch concepts and awkward, pun-ny business names.)

"There's a huge opportunity missed when you talk about restaurants and trucks working together," Povich said. His sister's original Red Hook Lobster Pound truck had already spun off two successful seafood restaurants in Brooklyn and Long Island in addition to its lobster roll trucks in New York and DC. Across the continent the battle between food trucks and restaurants was slowly giving way to a convergence. Truck-to-restaurant expansions included El Naranjo in Austin, 5411 Empanadas in Chicago, Lardo in Portland, and Seattle's Marination Station, to name but a handful, including Roy Choi's Kogi BBQ Taco truck, which had grown into four trucks and three Choi-affiliated restaurants. On the flip side restaurants were moving into food trucks. In Toronto the charge to open the city up to food trucks was actually led by my friend Zane Caplansky, who saw a chance to promote and expand sales of his eponymous Jewish delicatessen by taking it mobile, something that other restaurants, including national chains like Taco Bell, Chick-fil-A, Applebee's, and Burger King—which launched forty trucks in 2012—were trying to take advantage of with trucks of their own. Even Steve and Marlene Loeb, the deli owners who had no love for the food trucks in Farragut Square, were considering a truck. They already had the kitchen space, and it could expand their business into areas where they could capture whole new populations of customers. "I mean, if you can't beat 'em, join 'em," Steve said with a shrug.

Already the National Restaurant Association, America's umbrella restaurant lobbying group, reported that nearly a quarter of its fast-casual members were interested in starting food trucks, and food trucks have been invited to the annual National Restaurant Association trade show for the past few years. "Most of your food truck owners will eventually become members of a restaurant association," said Richard Myrick, the Chicago-based editor and chief of the food truck industry news site Mobile Cuisine and author of the book Running a Food Truck for Dummies. Once that happens it will be far more difficult for those same associations to lead the opposition to food trucks in their respective cities. Food trucks associations will also see increased funding, as the companies profiting off of food trucks—from truck builders to food suppliers like Sysco to insurers like Progressive, which offers specific food truck owner policies—will back efforts to defend food trucks and the dollars they generate. That may still be several years away, but as the food truck trend moves from an urban novelty to a fixture of our everyday eating landscape, the will to fight against it will surely evaporate.

༄

On May 10, 2013, Washington, DC's Committee on Business, Consumer and Regulatory Affairs convened in council to take public comment on the proposed Vending Business Act of 2013. The session was chaired by councilor Vincent B. Orange, who presided that day over testimony from dozens of stakeholders, from food truck and restaurant owners to bureaucrats and academics.

"I'm looking for common ground here today," Orange said in his opening remarks, "to fashion something where we can all move forward." He was eager for compromise, and even though the vote was originally supposed to be a straight yay or nay on the proposed rules, the city was now willing to be flexible. "I'll tell you, I got ten thousand e-mails, and people love food trucks," councilor David Grosso said. He was ashamed that the city was so unfriendly to entrepreneurs and joked that he was trending on Twitter for the first time in his career. Councilor Jim Graham noted that the debate reminded him about the hubbub decades back over whether to allow sidewalk cafés in DC. "People were aghast about people sitting outside, eating food, breathing dust, and listening to cars," he said. "The irony of that reminds me that the vitality that comes with the food trucks also came with sidewalk cafés."

In her testimony Kathy Hollinger noted that in the seventy-page bill, which encompassed all street vending regulations for the city, fewer than five pages dealt with food trucks, and it would be irresponsible to discard the long-delayed legislation simply because the food trucks imagined it contained restrictions that in reality didn't exist. The claims of the food truck associations and their fears over an apocalypse were unfounded, overhyped, and false. "We strongly advocate sending it to council for approval," Hollinger said.

Then it was the DC Food Truck Association's turn. Stella*s Popkern truck owner, Kristina Kern, nearly came to tears talking about how her gourmet popcorn truck allowed her to provide for her daughter Stella and that if the legislation passed, she would likely lose her business and their home. Brian Farrell, who owned the Basil Thyme truck, called the proposed regulations "toxic" and "ill conceived" and noted how he had already closed down one of his three trucks in anticipation of the new rules. Che Ruddell-Tabisola and Doug Povich testified as well, as did Matt Geller, who told the councilors that "no other city in the United States requires food trucks to have ten feet of unobstructed sidewalk in order to vend. If adopted by city council, these proposed regulations would transform the District overnight from having one of the most vibrant food truck industries in the country to one of the worst."

The whole forum lasted nine and a half hours.

A month later DC City Council passed a revised set of emergency food truck regulations, which achieved the desired compromise councilor Orange had sought. The minimum required amount of unobstructed sidewalk space was reduced from ten feet to six, and the fine for expired parking meters dropped from $2,000 back to $50. Vending zones were still going to be implemented, but the truck-free buffer zone would now be limited to two hundred feet instead of the proposed five hundred feet. There would still be a lottery to determine spots, and some of the restrictions that the DC Food Truck Association had opposed would remain in the bill, but it was the kind of solution that left both trucks and restaurants equally unhappy, which, in its own way, was an ideal political solution.

Che Ruddell-Tabisola, who led the fight for close to three years, was relieved though still hesitant when I spoke with him a few weeks later. "We have to wait and see how it's actually implemented," he mentioned with a note of caution. "I'm optimistic, but I know there are no Waterloos in politics. I think there's a good reason why we're popular. If there wasn't a trend, we wouldn't have been successful."

He was right. By fighting for their existence the food trucks in DC and elsewhere have changed something far more than our mobile lunch options: they had secured new business models, affected the very social fabric of our cities, and changed the law of the land.

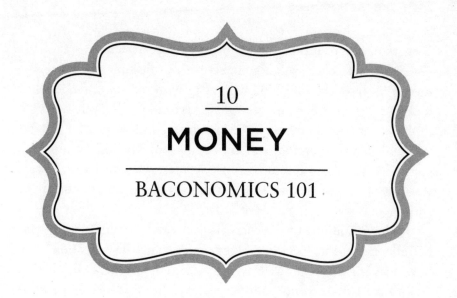

10

MONEY

BACONOMICS 101

When my taxi pulled up to the University of Illinois at Chicago Forum on the cold Saturday morning I flew in from DC, a crowd of several dozen people were already milling about outside, cradling coffees in their hands as they formed the start of a line. From a nearby tent the deli meat company Eckrich was handing out slices of five different delicatessen meats that had been infused with bacon. A banner proclaimed this "The Best Idea Ever," and they were scarcely able to open the packages quick enough for the hungry crowd that rushed to devour them. Inside the doors of the building several dozen volunteers were lined up behind long registration tables, ready to process the thousands who would soon arrive, ravenous and ramped up for greasy delights at the sold out event called Baconfest.

The sprawling twenty-two thousand–square foot floor of the Forum's event hall was abuzz with activity. Six long tables, each stretching the length of the room, had been taken over by eighty-two local restaurants and bars, beer and liquor companies, and other vendors. Another eighty waiters and bartenders, working for the catering company Sodexo, wandered like lost children in black shirts while chefs, cooks, bakers, and owners scrambled to get ready. Pallets of beer kegs were being pushed around to all corners of the room, as James Brown played over the sound system. Along the back wall a giant screen was flashing the Baconfest logo: Chicago's sky blue–and-white flag with red stars, rendered to look like a strip of bacon. Everywhere I looked people were carrying in trays, casseroles, Tupperware containers, and pulling huge hand carts piled with mountains of cooked bacon. Michael Griggs, one of the founders and organizers of Baconfest, now in its fifth year, was busy running around with a walkie-talkie, trying to corral the activity into some semblance of order.

"Hey," said one of the chefs from the restaurant Belly-Q, who literally stepped in front of Griggs's path to get his attention, "we have a fryer going. Can we leave the hot oil in or take it with us?"

"Take it with you," said Griggs over his shoulder as he blew past the chef and kept moving on to the next issue.

One by one the restaurants turned on their portable griddles and ovens, reheating their bacon creations, which ranged from simple candied strips of bacon to concoctions like bacon-spiked bloody Marys, bacon peanut butter macarons, bacon cupcakes, bacon pineapple donuts, bacon pizzas, bacon biscotti, chicken-fried bacon, bacon meatballs, and bacon cotton candy, to name just a few. Puffs of bacon vapor were visibly rising into the air, settling down a few minutes later as a fine mist of aerosolized bacon grease that clung to every possible surface. In the corner of the hall a chef from one of the restaurants walked up to a table run by Jones Dairy Farm, one of the few dedicated bacon producers attending Baconfest. They had hung a whole slab of bacon, several feet long, from a rack next to their table, while a glistening warm pork belly rested on a carving board, lit up by a heat lamp like a Broadway diva. "Look at how beautiful this is," said the chef, who was tapping his fingertips together rhythmically like Mr. Burns plotting something diabolical. "I'm like a moth to a flame. Or a fat guy to a slab of bacon."

At 11:30 the doors opened to 150 advanced guests. These VIPs had paid $200 each for tickets that allowed them to enter an hour earlier than the rest of the 1,500 Baconfest attendees (whose general admission tickets still cost $100 each). All of the event's three thousand–odd tickets, for both the lunch session and the dinner session (identical format, but with different restaurants) had sold out months before, in just forty-one minutes, and others had paid even more for scalpers' tickets. The VIPs quickly fanned out with their Baconfest program guides in hand, heading to the tables that most interested them. There were families in newly purchased Baconfest T-shirts (including one portraying the Blues Brothers as flying pigs), wealthy well-dressed couples, hardcore foodies with expensive DSLR cameras, and a lot of burly men in Chicago Blackhawks jerseys. I walked outside and looked at the general admission line, which now stretched all the way around the corner and down two full blocks. Inside Griggs gave the signal over his radio to unlock the doors, and when they were flung open a cheer went up from the line. One man shouted "BACON!" at the top of his lungs like a general leading the cavalry charge.

"Oh my god," a woman said as she came into the hall and saw its sheer scope.

"Where's the bacon?" asked another man in a panic, making a beeline to the nearest restaurant's table, where he encountered the Signature Room's smoked bacon bread pudding, with pork tenderloin stuffed with chorizo and wrapped in bacon and topped in bacon-braised red cabbage and a bacon ancho sauce. He ate it in a single bite, then packed away another.

Some people entered the room and bolted to a particular booth, while others just froze for a minute, drunk with excitement at the overwhelming sight of so much bacon. Two men stood at the entrance and slow clapped. Nearby a police officer turned to his partner and said, "If this crowd gets out of hand, we may have to use bacon spray instead of pepper spray."

Baconfest Chicago was a display of the bacon trend's culinary inspiration and scope, literally a giant buffet of every possible bacon dish that had wound its way into the American food chain over the past few years, from restaurant meals and sandwiches to drinks, desserts, and candies. If an economist wanted to examine the culture of a food trend, from the irrational exuberance of its core followers and what bacon represented in their lives to what the bacon trend said about the time and place we were living in, that economist could not choose a better place to start studying. I am no economist, but I am a journalist, and as much as I wanted to indulge in all the baconalia, I was here for the money. Of all the reasons food trends mattered, none was more important than their economic impact. Whether they were cultural or culinary in their origin, all the trends I had encountered—chia seeds, Red Prince apples, Indian cooking, food trucks—were ultimately motivated by commerce. What drove people to open one more cupcake bakery in cities filled with them wasn't their desire to unleash the perfect strawberry buttercream on the world—it was to make a buck. Food trends were products of capitalism, the edible manifestation of the free market deciding what was valuable to eat and what wasn't. The bacon trend, which began in the early 2000s and really hit its stride a decade later, was a powerful example of why food trends mattered economically. It took a food that was common but undervalued and raised its value significantly, affecting everything from farming practices to commodity trading while also generating economic opportunities worth billions, including jobs, investments, and tax revenues. In terms of a food trend having a financial impact, this one literally brought home the bacon.

෬

There is nothing new about bacon. Salted cured pork bellies have been eaten for thousands of years, particularly in Europe. It is relatively cheap and easy to produce. Pigs will eat anything and don't require much space, and you only need pigs, salt, and smoke to make bacon. Bacon travels well and can sit around unrefrigerated for long periods of time. Its high-fat content and dense flavor make it an ideal protein to use in cooking, even sparingly. A few cubes of cooked bacon can elevate the lowliest salad or plate of vegetables into something extraordinary. The experience of eating bacon is everything humans are designed to love: a crunchy, chewy, salty, smoky, fatty powerhouse of umami wallop. Nothing else comes close. Bacon's smell is unmistakable. It seeps through doors and wakes up roommates, and when cooked in a house, the scent will cling to the walls for weeks. It is a powerful meat.

In North America bacon has long been tied to breakfast. That's how I first encountered it, at Camp Walden, where despite the fact that most of the campers were Jewish and pork wasn't served in the dining hall, when we went out on camping trips in the wilderness bacon was a constant presence. Before we would enter the park with our canoes and packs the camp's school bus would stop at a supermarket in a nearby town so our counselors could go inside to buy the week's essentials. We'd wait impatiently in the bus, and when they emerged they would hoist the supersized packages of bacon into the air triumphantly as we chanted "Bacon! Bacon! Bacon!" peering out the windows at the prized pig. On that first morning, when the mist rose from those pristine lakes, before our tents were packed up and we pushed off our canoes, a glorious sizzle would spread through our campsite, as strips of precious pink bacon popped and danced in the camp's beaten skillets. We ate it with eggs, with pancakes, with French toast, and on the last morning, when nothing else was left, we just ate bacon on its own. Often the counselors would dare a camper to drink a shot of bacon grease. Someone always did.

The bacon business in America has been relatively predictable since the successful campaign of Edward Bernays and Beechnut to pair bacon and eggs at breakfast in the 1930s. Bacon consumption followed a steady, seasonal pattern. Throughout the year people ate a consistent amount of bacon for breakfast, with the bulk of bacon sales to restaurants destined for pancake houses and diners or hotels that served breakfast buffets. Then in the summer bacon consumption would rise significantly, in parallel with the availability of fresh tomatoes in supermarkets. During these months bacon branched out from a breakfast side into the anchor for club sandwiches, BLTs, and Cobb salads, then faded back to breakfast after Labor Day. There were geographic and cultural exceptions of course: most Jews and Muslims still didn't eat bacon, whereas places like the Deep South practically put it in every dish, but for the most part bacon eating in the United States and Canada was based on steady breakfasts through the year, with a summer pop. Pork belly prices reflected this, ramping up at the start of summer, when the first tomatoes were coming in, and then plunging in fall, when the last tomatoes were pulled from supermarket shelves. For the hog farmer with a bunch of bellies in his hands come October, things were grim.

This created a problem. Hog farmers couldn't easily breed more pigs for slaughter in the summer because the demand for other pork products (chops, sausages, hams) was steady year round. So what the farmers did was freeze their bellies in great quantities, stockpiling them for the spring, when they would sell them to smokehouses to make bacon, hopefully at a good price. Some savvy financial minds sensed opportunity in this latent demand, and in 1961 the first pork bellies futures contract was written up on the Chicago Mercantile Exchange, the world's premiere market for trading commodities. Now the farmer could enter a contract with a broker months before the summer and secure a guaranteed price for their bellies. The contract would specify the price per pound and the total pounds in the order, the specific cut of pork belly the buyer wanted, and which months the contract would be in effect. The farmer would deliver the frozen bellies to the broker as they were processed, and the broker stored them in a warehouse, often operated by a third party, until the time was right to sell them.

This was where things got interesting, because the broker who now had a contract for forty thousand pork bellies at 40 cents a pound went out and tried to sell off that contract for more money, making their profit on the spread as well as hedging their risk by opening up the contracts to outside investors. Pork belly prices rose and fell based on a number of factors, from the related cost of grains that pigs ate, like corn, to weather patterns in pork-producing states like Iowa, available space in the warehouses where bellies were stored, and the fluctuations of the market. The pork bellies futures market also acquired a reputation as the cavalier corner of the commodities exchange. It was highly speculative business, as you can imagine a loud pit full of men shouting multimillion-dollar bets on slabs of pig would be, and it was central to the lore of the commodities trade, captured perfectly in the classic Eddie Murphy comedy *Trading Places*. Because they were so widely traded and because the belly made up nearly 20 percent of the hog's weight, as went belly prices, so, too, went the price of the whole hog.

Throughout the 1970s pork belly prices—and the corresponding price of bacon—followed a relatively stable annual pattern. They

rose and fell with seasonal demand, largely in a range that was between 60 and 40 cents a pound. By the early years of the 1980s,
however, things got tough for bacon. The low-fat diet trend took off,
and when it was combined with a health scare over the nitrates frequently used to preserve meats, the corresponding demand for bacon rapidly dropped. "That was really the first food scare," recalled
the aptly named Joe Leathers, now a retired VP of the National Pork
Producers Council and a lifelong veteran of the pork industry. "I'll
bet you bacon sales fell off thirty-five to forty percent," Leathers
said. "I joined the National Pork Producers in 1985, and we were
struggling with bellies then. I was on a trade mission to sell bellies to
Poland and recall going to DC, and we just had freezers full of bellies. This was a government giveaway program to Poland. There was
such little demand that the US was literally giving away bellies. They
were cheap—I think about nineteen cents a pound." Another industry veteran called the belly "a drag on the carcass" at the time, a
marbled albatross that no one wanted because fat phobia was steer-
ing people away from bacon. Boneless, skinless chicken breasts were
the hot meat to watch. Sure, people still ate bacon with breakfast
and in club sandwiches, but the future was lean meats, and the pork
industry had to get on board or get trampled by the latest trend.

"Back in 1985 we were right in the start of 'lean lean lean lean
lean', and that was what we needed to be talking about—how lean
it was," said Robin Kline, a pork industry communications spe-
cialist in Des Moines, Iowa, the country's pig capital, who worked
for the Pork Producers Council for fifteen years. "Bacon was kinda
something we didn't want to think about." The solution was a
widely publicized marketing campaign to rebrand pork in the eyes
of consumers that launched in 1987. It was called Pork: The Other
White Meat, and it succeeded in shifting the consumption of pork
to leaner cuts, such as the loin, chops, or roasts, essentially piggy-
backing off the success of chicken. This trend continued throughout
the 1990s. Lean cuts of pork grew in sales, while bacon stayed at the
breakfast table, and pork belly prices largely wallowed in the mud.
"Pork took a real beating during that period of time," said Stephen
Gerike, director of food service marketing for the Pork Marketing

Board. "That's why we came out with the Other White Meat campaign . . . and the parts of the pig that were not white, middle meat, suffered from that period of time in the consciousness. Bacon was the big victim."

Ironically, the lean trend was also a turning point for bacon mongers. Fast food chains across America were conscious of the same trends that pork producers were, and they began introducing sandwiches and burgers that they could sell to fat-phobic diners. Grilled chicken breasts, turkey subs, and low-fat hamburgers, like the McDonald's McLean Deluxe, started appearing on menus of fast food chains across the world. At the same time fast food restaurants began cooking their burgers to well done, following a deadly outbreak of E. coli virus at a Jack in the Box in 1993, which was traced to undercooked beef. The result was lean meat, which began with less fat and moisture, being cooked to the point at which the sandwiches tasted so dry and flavorless that no amount of special sauce could salvage them. These chains didn't care about people's diets—they simply wanted to sell more food, and they needed something that would deliver a jolt of flavor to these cardboard specimens. They found it in bacon.

"There's no good reason to eat bacon," said Jim Sibarro, the retired CEO of Farmland Foods, a major pork slaughterhouse and meat packer in Kansas City. "It's two-thirds fat with a bit of lean. Bacon is high in calories . . . it's terrible for you. But it adds flavor. That's all it does. It adds flavor to sandwiches. Bacon is the greatest thing in the world because it adds that smoke, hickory, juiciness to a product. It's two-thirds fat!" By putting a slice of bacon on a very lean burger or a grilled chicken sandwich, you instantly improved its taste by leaps and bounds. Not only that, but restaurant chains could present bacon as an optional addition to a sandwich and then charge a handsome premium for it.

None of this happened by accident. In 1998, as warehouses of frozen pork bellies were languishing unwanted, the pork industry was compelled to take action. "The proposition was, why don't we go to the foodservice world and talk about putting bacon on burgers as a flavor enhancer?" Stephen Gerike said. The Pork Board's farming members funded research at Iowa State University on developing a circular bacon that could fit perfectly atop a hamburger, while Gerike and his colleagues reached out to the menu development departments of restaurant chains, offering to help them develop more bacon-centric sandwiches and entrées. "If you can focus on one big quick service restaurant, like McDonald's, Burger King, and Wendy's, everyone else will inherently follow," Gerike said. If one of them managed to create a successful bacon burger, the resulting increase in pork belly demand and prices would grow exponentially. The pork board launched a Bacon Makes It Better Campaign and subsidized the restaurants with funds for market testing, product development, and advertising around these products.

Adding bacon atop burgers had always been a dream for the fast food chains, but it was logistically difficult. Bacon was a tricky meat to cook. There was a fine line between undercooked chewy bacon and overcooked dry bacon, and walking that line required patience and skill. Bacon generated strong odors and smoke, demanding lots of ventilation, and the grease it produced as a by-product presented its own problems. Restaurants that cooked bacon required larger grease traps, services to remove that grease, more thorough kitchen cleaning, and greater safety training and insurance to deal with grease burns and fires. Bacon was wasteful: you could buy a pound of raw bacon, but by the time you cooked away that fat, you might end up with half that weight or even a third. In short, bacon was a bitch.

The solution that made the bacon trend possible was precooked bacon. By the turn of the twenty-first century, innovations in precooked bacon allowed restaurants to reheat consistently precooked slices of perfect bacon in the round shape of a burger or sandwich with almost no smoke, grease, or associated headache. The companies that made the precooked bacon, which included Miller Food Services, a division of ConAgra, and the pork giant Hormel, could sell the precooked product at a premium because the customer knew exactly how much they were getting—and how much they could charge diners—in terms of its final weight. A pound of precooked bacon, once reheated, was pretty close to a pound.

"All of a sudden you could use bacon on everything, and you didn't have to worry about cook time, yield loss, and grease traps, which is a huge deal," said Andrew Doria, a meat commodity trader at Midwest Premier Foods in Iowa. "Precooking bacon all of a sudden became something every pork producer had to do. Then there had to be thirty to forty percent of your bacon in precooked format or you'd be missing out."

"The increase in demand was initially driven by this idea that you could get bacon on any sandwich you wanted," said Doria's colleague, Steve Nichol. "Pretty soon, from a foodservice perspective, you were going out and saying, 'We've got bacon on all of our sandwiches,' and if you've got it and the next guy got it, it becomes a factor of quality." Or, in the words of another pork industry veteran: "Bacon suddenly became a condiment."

This coincided with a shift in diet trends that was more favorable to bacon. In 1992 Dr. Robert Atkins published the sequel to his 1972 diet book, called *Dr. Atkins' New Diet Revolution*. The core idea was a diet high in vegetables and protein and low in carbohydrates, but the key message that people took from it was that you could now have bacon and eggs for breakfast every day if you wanted. The Atkins Diet, and the residual high-protein trend it slowly spawned, finally killed the fear of fat that had held bacon back for so long. Suddenly bacon was transformed from the devil's meat into a blessed protein. A new generation of bacon burgers and sandwiches emerged from chains like Burger King, who went whole hog into the trend with a bacon cheeseburger, bacon sourdough burger—with four strips of bacon—and even a bacon sundae for dessert, among others. Denny's unveiled a whole seasonal menu packed with bacon items called the Baconalia, which remains one of their best-selling specials. Today, you'd be hard-pressed to find a fast food or casual restaurant chain that doesn't have a bacon burger or bacon sandwich on their menu.

Meanwhile, bacon was branching out into all sorts of new dishes at independent restaurants. A new generation of chefs were breaking the mold of the traditional fine dining hierarchy, with its focus on French technique, ornate dining rooms, and large kitchens. These chefs were young and adventurous, they gravitated toward full-fat comfort foods, and they absolutely worshipped the pig. Suddenly chefs everywhere were curing and smoking their own bacon, putting bacon into all sorts of crazy dishes, and even getting pork butchery guides tattooed onto their forearms, which sort of became the culinary world's equivalent of a tramp stamp. The restaurants these chefs cooked in were packed each night, and whether they were in New York, Denver, or Halifax, you found them filled with diners beating down the doors to try various bacon dishes. They roasted brussels sprouts with bacon, wrapped turkeys in bacon, infused bacon into cocktails, and candied bacon that they baked into brownies. Many just fried up thick-cut slabs of bacon like steaks. "Bacon, unlike a duck confit or charcuterie, doesn't require any skill to get it," said food writer and salty meat expert Josh Ozersky. "Any idiot can get a pound of bacon, cut it up into pieces, and toss it into a pan with chicken fricassee or smear bacon jam onto a pork chop. Because bacon has more flavor per square inch than any food you can make, it instantly made their food more tasty."

The more bacon these restaurants served, the more people wanted it. Offshoots of the bacon trend began emerging: some chefs dedicated their efforts to homemade charcuterie and other cured meats, and others wholeheartedly embraced the uncured pork belly, braising it Chinese style and then searing it so the fat acquired a caramelized crust that was irresistible. The consumer research firm Technomic reported that the number of bacon items on American menus rose steadily from 2006 through 2012, an increase of nearly 25 percent over that period. In 2013 it also noted that 87 percent of American diners were willing to pay at least 50 cents to add bacon to a burger or sandwich. Bacon was suddenly everywhere. As these chefs cooked more bacon, they demanded better-quality bacon, and they educated their customers about the differences between wet and dry cures, hickory and applewood smoke. Coveted boutique bacon brands such as Nueske's and Benton's not only saw an uptick in restaurant sales but they also became food world stars in their own right. Pig farmers and smokers from the backwoods of Virginia and Alabama were suddenly being profiled in *Bon Appétit* and *Gourmet* and invited to the best restaurants in the country, where they were lavished with praise.

As interest in eating bacon grew, bacon evolved from a food item to a cultural touchstone. A growing chorus of bacon evangelists, bacon obsessives, and baconheads began forming a community across the country. "I Love Bacon" was a bumper sticker-turned-rallying cry, as the bacon faithful came together online and in the greasy flesh to spread the gospel. One of the most prominent was Heather Lauer, a marketer who started the Bacon Unlimited blog in 2004. "I would never describe myself as being obsessed with it," said Lauer, who lives in Arizona. "When you're growing up you don't eat bacon with every meal . . . bacon's this special thing you only eat at holidays or on weekends. It is an affordable treat to look forward to." When she began Bacon Unlimited Lauer was one of half a dozen bloggers talking about bacon online. A year later their numbers were increasing significantly, and Lauer saw that it was actually becoming a movement of its own. She wrote the book *Bacon: A Love Story* in 2009 to chronicle this, in which she noted that the interest in bacon culture followed the rise in American bacon consumption, which grew 20 percent between 2000 and 2005.

There had always been bacon lovers. My younger brother Daniel became hooked on bacon during those summer camp canoe trips, and he used to fry up a few strips as an after-school snack. He put bacon on his pizza, on pancakes, and on burgers whenever he had a chance and would frequently utter Homer Simpson's drooling mantra "*mmmmm . . . bacon*" at its very mention. Now blogs like Lauer's and social media sites allowed a world of bacon fans to share their obsession. The Internet didn't make the bacon trend, but its effect was the equivalent of tossing a pan of bacon grease onto a fire. In 2008, when Kansas City barbecue aficionados Jason Day and Aaron Chronister, who ran the BBQ Addicts blog, posted photos of a new dish they had made called the Bacon Explosion—a football-sized orb of spiced sausage and crumbled bacon, wrapped in a lattice of bacon strips, entombed in foil, and then smoked— they unleashed the type of all-American culinary sensation that other nations point to in shock and jealous disbelief. The original Bacon Explosion recipe has since been viewed hundreds of thousands of times. One newspaper called it "the most popular recipe on the web." This gave rise to Bacon Explosion T-shirts, countless instructional YouTube videos, and a cookbook written by Day and Chronister featuring the Bacon Explosion on its cover. If you go to their website, bbqaddicts.com, you can purchase your own Bacon Explosion in three flavors (original, jalapeño, and cheese), and it will be shipped to your house in dry ice, ready to heat and eat.

Others indulged in flagrant, frat-boyish bacon porn. The You-Tube show Epic Meal Time, filmed by a crew of Jack Daniels–chugging carnivore Jewish punks in Montreal, made outlandish bacon-heavy culinary creations in a constant display of caloric one upsmanship. One episode featured a lasagna stuffed with bacon: fifteen Big Macs, fifteen A&W Teen Burgers, and fifteen Wendy's Baconators, plus a special Jack Daniel's meat sauce, onion rings, and one liter of Big Mac sauce, totaling 71,488 calories with 5,463 grams of fat. Nevertheless, Epic Meal Time's videos have been viewed tens of millions of times, and there is now an Epic Meal Time video game, a spinoff television series, a cookbook, and a large selection of merchandise you can buy on their website. If you prefer more restrained bacon entertainment, you can tune in to the Discovery Channel's, *United States of Bacon*, which is a bacon obsessive's road trip, very much in the style of the Food Network's bacon-centric ratings leader *Diners, Drive-Ins, and Dives*.

The bacon trend also inspired a cottage industry of bacon-themed products that didn't actually include bacon but *look* like bacon and sell on its appeal. Seattle novelty company Archie McPhee makes bacon bandages, bacon tinfoil, bacon stockings, bacon-scented spray, bacon Christmas tree ornaments, bacon tuxedos, bacon shirts, bacon socks, bacon-flavored toothpaste, and bacon dishes and cups. Some of these products, like the toothpaste and the spray, don't just look like bacon but smell or even taste like it without containing any actual pork. Then there was the rapid, astonishing rise of J&D's Foods, whose motto "Everything Should Taste Like Bacon" has been taken to its extreme. Its founders Justin Esch and Dave Lefkow worked together at a technology company in Miami. Esch, who was from Telluride, Colorado, had always loved bacon and was particularly in love with a shot of bourbon a local bar served with a bacon garnish. "It was a discussion about these shots that was the impetus to the idea that led to the creation of bacon salt in 2007," said Esch, who cemented his business partnership with Lefkow at 3 a.m., drunk, on the beach in Miami as they bought the domain name baconsalt.com on a phone. The two worked at nights in Lefkow's garage to develop a salt that would deliver the smoky flavor of bacon without actually being made of bacon—the product is actually kosher. They financed the venture by borrowing from the $5,000 *America's Funniest Home Videos* prize that had been awarded to Lefkow's three-year-old son (who has since been repaid).

J&D's Bacon Salt was launched in July 2007, with sales coming exclusively from online orders, which Esch and Lefkow packed and shipped themselves. "We sold three thousand jars of bacon salt in seventy-six hours, in twenty-two states and twelve countries," said Esch. "J&D's was profitable in hour forty-two of being in business. The thing that blew us away was that we were looking at orders, and we didn't know the first twenty customers. Bacon salt became such a hot trending topic that it made MSN top search its second day, and then on Google. It just blew up. The bacon fanatics and bacon world just came out."

What the two lacked for in money, they made up for with a PT Barnum approach to marketing. They pressed the case of J&D's Bacon Salt to bloggers, the media, and potential buyers with relentless phone calls, samples, and campaigns on social media, where they rapidly acquired fans. "We produced a massive amount of bacon-related content," Esch said. "We reached out to the blogs I Heart Bacon and Mr. Baconpants and Royal Bacon Society . . . we just realized this fire was burning, and people were in love with bacon, and we asked, 'How do we throw bacon grease on this?' We put funny, easily shareable things online to feed this." In October 2008 they staged a wrestling match in the basement of a Seattle nightclub (where they had relocated), featuring two combatants, a strip of bacon and a jar of mayonnaise, fighting in a pit filled with six thousand pounds of mayonnaise to promote their newest product, Baconnaise, a bacon-flavored mayonnaise. "If you pour six thousand pounds of mayo on the floor of a nightclub in a basement, you'd better have a plan to get it out," said Esch.

Baconnaise propelled J&D's and the bacon trend to the next level. When Jon Stewart sampled the product on *The Daily Show*, he spat it into the trash and then told the camera, "I think my tongue just shat in my mouth." Esch thought the joke would kill the company, but Stewart's on-air revulsion only drove up demand further. Next thing they knew J&D's products were on *Oprah*, newspapers were running feature stories on their business, and retailers like Walmart and Costco were placing huge orders for Baconnaise and other products. These include the marquee lines of Bacon Salt (now in nine flavors) and Baconnaise (in regular and light) as well as bacon-flavored popcorn, ranch dressing, croutons, gravy, and spice rubs. The company also expanded into a line of novelty products, including bacon-flavored lip balm, shaving cream, stickers, and envelopes, bacon-scented candy roses, and a coffin that looks like it's made from bacon. It costs $3,000, and they have actually sold three of them. Did I mention the lube? J&D's makes a bacon-flavored sexual lubricant. It was conceived as a gag gift, available four times a year, but Esch estimates they have sold over a hundred thousand tubes of bacon lube, which means that somewhere in the world tonight, there is a very real chance that a child is being conceived in bacon-flavored passion.

∽

Chicago's Baconfest is not the largest bacon festival in the country. That honor goes to the Blue Ribbon Baconfest in Des Moines, Iowa, which began in 2008 as a charitable event in a local bar featuring local bacon producers and some bacon foods, like bacon cheeseburgers, ice cream, and cupcakes. Two hundred people showed up and raised $1,000 for charity. By contrast, the 2013 Blue Ribbon Baconfest sold out all nine thousand tickets in under four minutes to people who came from thirty-nine different states and seven countries. It featured a bacon queen beauty pageant in a dress made from bacon strips, former professional wrestler Hacksaw Jim

Duggan, as well as an estimated half a pound of bacon being eaten by each person attending the show. Brooks Reynolds, one of the event organizers, estimated that Blue Ribbon Baconfest generated over $1.5 million for Des Moines, split between ticket sales, out-of-town visitors, and related economic activity that day. There is also Camp Bacon, an annual retreat put on by the Michigan deli and food emporium Zingerman's, which is the World Economic Forum of bacon gatherings, attended by big movers in elite bacon and focused on high quality and sustainability. Though Chicago's Baconfest is smaller in total attendance than its Iowa counterpart, in many ways it is more ambitious. It is a mix between the high culinary ambitions of the Fancy Food Show and the religious geekdom of a Star Trek convention. Its organizers (Michael Griggs, Andre Vonbaconvitch, and Seth Zurer) have made Baconfest a profitable business and have been expanding the brand with similar events in San Francisco and Washington, DC, in recent years. Walking around the festival during the lunch session I got a firsthand taste of how the cultural momentum of the bacon trend translated into economic opportunity.

At the Jones Dairy Farm table I spoke with Doug McDonald, the sales manager in charge of the company's foodservice accounts. "Bacon is our fastest growing category. The past five years we've seen double-digit growth in foodservice sales. What you see now is bacon going from retail and pancake houses to mainstream bar and grills serving bacon during happy hour," he said. "There's a restaurant in Arizona called Fifty/Fifty that we sell to. They take our thick-cut bacon, cook it, and put it on the bar in brandy glasses like peanuts." At the other end of the hall Bob Nueske, the second-generation owner of Wisconsin's Nueske's, one of the largest independent bacon smokehouses in the country, looked out at the wild, ravenous crowd with wonder. "I always have a fear that trends are like hula hoops," Nueske, who is broad and tall, with a mobster's wall of coiffed hair, told me as strips of the company's applewood smoked bacon slowly sizzled on an electric griddle. "This bacon thing is beyond a trend. Thirty years ago I couldn't imagine kids making bacon like they are now."

Dave Miller, the owner of Bang Bang! Pie Shop, a Chicago bakery, was handing out bacon cherry rugelach, a traditional Jewish cookie rendered as unkosher as possible. "I see bacon as outdated," admitted Miller, "but it's a money maker and we do it because the economics demand it. It creates a cult following." The bakery sold strips of candied bacon at a dollar a piece, and these acted as a sort of honey trap for bacon lovers, who came to Bang Bang! for the bacon but invariably bought a loaf of bread or some other item. Bacon's economic power was a shock even to those who built businesses around it. Sven Lindén was the founder of Black Rock Spirits, which made Bakon Vodka, a bacon-infused vodka that debuted in 2007 as a joke. It now does over $1 million in wholesale sales each year. "We knew there was a novelty component," Lindén told me as we stood by his booth, where they were handing out bacon bloody Marys, "but even in states where we've been around for five years they'll have a small bar do seven thousand bacon Bloody Marys a year." One of the few vendors not selling food but doing brisk business was Rebecca Wood, who owned the gift boutique Enjoy: An Urban Novelty Store, which had an entire bacon section filled with over a hundred novelty products. When she opened the store in 2005 her top-selling item quickly became bacon strip bandages, and today it remained in the top spot, followed by bacon socks, and I Love You More Than Bacon signs, which sold like gangbusters online.

Surrounded by bacon maniacs downing shots of bacon black bean stew, bacon cotton candy, and bacon root beer floats, it was impossible not to get caught up in the infectious exuberance of Baconfest. There were people like Jeaneed Kalakr and her grandson Parker, who wore matching, homemade T-shirts printed with a poem written for the occasion: "From one porker to the next / Don't give me no fat / I squeal for bacon / One good snort deserves another / I am a bacon lover . . . undercover." The miraculously petite sisters Christina and Danielle Wade were dressed in matching bacon earrings, socks, and T-shirts made for their 2011 Bacon Takedown Tour. "It's not a trend for me," the enthusiastic Danielle said. "It's a way of life." There were dudes wearing muscle shirts that said, "Bacon Gives Me a Lardon" and "Drink First. Pork Later";

babies in little pig outfits; a man wearing a homemade matching hat and shirt that displayed a peace sign made up of strips of bacon he'd ironed on; and my favorite, a T-shirt of a cat surfing a strip of bacon in outer space. "That's the coolest T-shirt here!" I told the owner and then immediately regretted it, as I saw someone with a T-shirt that had *two* bacon-surfing space cats. Yes, the bacon trend was about food, but it was also a money-making meme, like a live version of an online joke that just gets spun round and round and round until you wonder where it will end.

"Before the bacon bubble came into being it was very niche," said Aaron Samuels, who had bought VIP tickets with his wife, Charlotte, as an anniversary gift. The two of them were decked out for battle, with pink headbands, backpacks, and a studied knowledge of what was on offer. Samuels, who had a giant beard and was decidedly zaftig, wore a T-shirt that proclaimed "Man Boobs Are Sexy," while Charlotte's shirt featured an angel pig with wings and a halo floating above a plate of bacon, with the caption "It's what I would have wanted." "If the bacon bubble bursts, we'll still be fans of bacon," Samuels said. "Most people at Baconfest are the O.G.s of bacon"—meaning its original gangsters, bacon's most hard-core fans.

Nearby I overheard a man ask a group of strangers in full-on bacon regalia whether they were baconheads. "No," said one of them, hoisting a bacon bourbon cocktail, "we're Chicagoans. Other cities do marathons. We do Baconfest."

∽

The overall economic impact of the bacon trend is difficult to quantify, but it is undoubtedly substantial. The bacon trend created small businesses—restaurants, smokehouses, festivals, food trucks, surfing bacon cat T-shirt conglomerates—that each generated jobs and tax revenues where none had previously existed. Since 2011, when Wesley Klein opened his New York City bacon bakery, the Baconery, which sells bacon-laced brownies and cookies, the business had already expanded to a retail location, with plans afoot for four new Baconery stores and warehouses around the country to service a growing on-line business. Klein expected the Baconery to make over $400,000 in sales during 2013, quadruple what the business made the year before. A constant stream of requests for franchises around America and the world led Klein to believe the businesses growth was far from limited. "We can probably wrap the world in bacon," Klein said when I asked about his potential market, noting that there are many countries that love bacon that are so far untouched by the trend. J&D's is an even more dramatic example: in their first year in business they went from a garage startup with a tiny investment to a million-dollar company with international sales. Though Esch would not reveal exact figures when we spoke in 2013, he hinted that the company now generated over $10 million in annual revenues. "I mean, Dave just bought a new sailboat yesterday and I bought an Audi," Esch told me when I asked about their economic output. "The bacon business is good."

The bacon trend's financial impact was really felt in the pork business. Starting with the increase in bacon consumption the fast food chains and their use of precooked bacon had driven, the demand for pork bellies increased steadily from the late 1990s, and the value of the belly grew with it. "Now spare ribs and bellies are the highest-priced cuts in a pig carcass," Stephen Gerike told me in February 2013. "You're getting right now thirty-five cents per pound more to make bacon from bellies than pork loins to make chops"— almost the opposite of decades before. Pork belly prices rose as high as $1.89 per pound and regularly hover well over $1. They are now more valuable than the boneless, skinless chicken breasts that once drove belly prices so low. Although a lot of that increase was driven by a parallel rise in commodity prices, especially the corn that pigs eat, and an upswing in pork exports to Asia, much of it was credited to the trend known as bacon mania.

At the retail level there are now more people producing and selling bacon at every price and quality level and more lines within those companies. Where supermarkets once carried three to four brands of bacon, now they sell fifteen to twenty. "In Texas HEB [a large supermarket chain] buys twenty-four brands of bacon—all different varieties," said Joe Leathers. "I mean, that's a bunch of bacon." There is more bacon being sold to restaurants and more bacon sold to diners at those restaurants in different dishes, bringing more money into the pockets of smokehouses and distributors, restaurant owners, chefs, waiters, and busboys, whether they are small independent operators or publicly traded chains. "At retail," Leathers said, "you're looking at a thirty-five to forty percent profit margin for selling bacon. Foodservice is much higher: fifty to sixty percent margins, because they sell by the slice."

All of this shifted the bacon market cycle. Suddenly, the seasonal habit of freezing pork bellies throughout the winter, then smoking them for the summer tomato season was replaced by a constant, year-round demand for bacon. "There's a bacon shortage," said Sam Edwards III, who runs his family's traditional smokehouse S. Wallace Edwards & Sons in Virginia, which is highly regarded for the quality of its bacon. "We buy from six suppliers of bellies, and a lot of the time we just don't get what we order because there's so much demand for it. We were joking that what needed to happen is that people needed to breed pigs with three bellies on them."

As the price of a pork belly increased, it elevated the overall price of the hog, which put more money into the hands of pig farmers. Steve Meyer, the pork economist, estimated that the increase brought on by the bacon trend added roughly $20 to the value of each animal. "That's a bunch," he said. "That's over a ten percent increase in value of the animal. That's twelve percent more revenue for the farmer. It's twenty thousand dollars if you're raising a thousand pigs a year. It's been a tremendous contribution to the value of the animal, this new interest in bacon." Farmers responded by breeding their pigs to have longer, fattier bellies and integrating belly-heavy breeds like the Berkshire and Landrace pigs into their livestock. "Twenty years ago, if you looked at the animal then and now, the animal now is much longer today than it was then," said pork trader Steve Nichol. "Now you have a longer belly. Before you would get seventeen slices, but now I can get twenty-two to twenty-three slices out of a belly." Others have talked about meat packers cutting bellies in half and charging even more for their product.

The scale of the economic impact of the bacon trend was most visible in the pork belly futures market at the Chicago Mercantile Exchange, not too far from where Baconfest was held. With a constant stream of bellies now going from the kill floor directly to the smokehouse, the need for warehouses banking millions of frozen bellies faded away. Where the belly market once provided a cacophony of financial speculation, of great fortunes made and lost by men shouting frantic trades, it had since become a ghost town. As the bacon trend took hold, pork belly became a year-round ingredient, and no one needed to speculate on it anymore. In July 2011 half a century after the trade in pork belly futures began, the contract was delisted from the market, and the pork belly's life as a financial instrument ended. Only three months before, the National Pork Board finally dropped "The Other White Meat" as a slogan, opting instead for the more bacon-friendly "Pork: Be Inspired." When it came to pork, the twenty-first century belonged to bacon.

୬

After two and a half hours of Baconfest the salt, booze, and the sheer decadence of the day began taking its toll on the crowd. Those who ran between vendors at first now shuffled, and those who ate everything in their sight were now cherry picking, taking one bite and tossing the rest away. After eating my fifth bacon-flavored macaron, I honestly never wanted to eat anything made from bacon again in my life. (That feeling has since passed.) A sea of bodies slumped against the walls of the hallway outside the main event, and there were bacon fans passed out in each other's arms like they'd fallen valiantly in battle against their salty foe. Everything reeked of bacon smoke. Michael Griggs and the other organizers took to the microphone and called for everyone's attention. "Hello bacon nation!" Griggs yelled to a cheer and random cries of "Bacon!" They announced the winner of the bacon poetry contest, which was "Winter vs. Bacon" by Steve Nordin, a selection of which appears below:

Bacon on a cold night
Bacon on a chilled morning.
Bacon on bread, in the middle of the day.
I bite down and my mouth fills with the warm
Smokey flavor, like boots crunching down
Through crisp fall leaves.
Suddenly the hollowed out surrounding winter
Is alive.

The Baconfest organizers then presented an oversized $50,000 check to the Chicago Food Depository. Griggs thanked everyone in attendance and told them to go home because the venue had to be cleaned and reset with a whole new slate of restaurants for the dinner shift. People slowly filed out, some drunkenly helped along by security guards, and I followed Griggs to the back of the venue, where several hundred bags of garbage were piled to the ceilings and spread along corridors. A dozen volunteers were sifting through some of the bags, separating compostable forks and bowls from food waste and plastic in a vain effort to recycle. The scope of Baconfest's business became apparent in that moment. Three thousand people had paid more than half a million dollars to eat several tons of bacon. The restaurants and food companies had served up hundreds of thousands of dollars in products that had been bought from suppliers, and many of these restaurants and food companies would see increased business from Baconfest fans in the weeks and months to come. The event paid tens of thousands of dollars to the day's hired staff and generated sales at Chicago-area bars, restaurants, and hotels—and, likely, cardiologist offices—in the hours after the event. As Griggs tried to get the staff to stop sorting and focus on clearing the hallway, he turned and asked me what exactly I was writing about anyway.

"It's about the economics of the bacon trend," I told him.

"Right," he said, sweeping out his hand at the mountains of trash that represented every paying customer that had passed through the doors of Baconfest so far. "Like all this business that wouldn't be done if the trend didn't exist."

11

AFTERMATH

FONDUE RETIRES TO
FLORIDA

I had come to Tampa at the end of my journey around North America's food trend landscape for a single reason. It was not the city's famous Cubano sandwiches, a food that actually originated with Cuban immigrants here, or the all-American grills that dominated the landscape (including Hulk Hogan's Beach Club, conveniently located in my hotel). Over the past year I had observed items, people, and phenomena whose trends were at various stages of their evolution: the cupcake trend cresting, a chef whose influence was starting to spread, an apple that was just budding, food trucks on the cusp of great power. All of these trends were relatively recent, some were a few years old, others had begun just over a decade back, but none of them were what I would consider past their prime. I wanted to know what became of a food trend once it had passed to the other side.

All trends have a life cycle. The old ones must inevitably decline to clear space for the new ones. We had to stop worrying about fat so we could start worrying about carbs, had to fall out of love with whole wheat bread to truly embrace multigrain flaxseed chia-infused pasta. Bacon will always be a part of the American diet, but the future of bacon-flavored sexual lubricant is no more assured than the relationships born of its smoky aphrodisiac. In this way food is no different from other trends, like fashion. I had come to Tampa to see the last stop for one of the most iconic food trends of the past century. This trend had started out with an elite audience of tastemakers, had spread through a media frenzy, grown into a phenomenon that defined that era's culture, and then dropped from fashion. It had enjoyed a brief resurgence, then flamed out once again, and it was now as far from being a current food trend as mutton, Jell-O molds, or hardtack biscuits. I had tracked this trend's history through archived articles, old cookbooks, and interviews with its few surviving, elderly tastemakers. Now I found myself before a half-empty strip mall in the Tampa suburbs, like an anthropologist standing at the foot of a temple in the jungle, ready to encounter the last tribe of American fondue enthusiasts and what they were doing with a food trend that has long since passed.

Ahh fondue. If there exists a food trend that elicits stronger images and associations, I have yet to encounter it. Fondue—with its whiff of simplicity and exotic continentalism, overtures of romance and sex, and memories of rib-sticking comfort. Fondue brings to mind melted cheese and a basket of cubed bread, cauldrons of molten chocolate waiting for strawberries, the sizzle of hot oil frying a hunk of filet. Fondue is a conjurer of the past, a food trend that exists primarily in memory, often decades removed from the last time you ate it. You hear its name and picture ski lodges, a fog of stinky cheese, crackling fireplaces, shag carpets, and Burt Reynolds lying there, shirtless and with a long-stemmed fork in his hand. It is not only a cultural anachronism, but a symbol of all cultural anachronisms, of the fate of forgotten food trends, now no more relevant than tie-dyed T-shirts or lava lamps. Fondue is a punch line. Fondue is a pet rock.

I was born just as the last blue Sterno flame flickered out on the fondue trend. By the time I first encountered it on ski trips with my parents, it was already cocooned in nostalgia. Once a winter we would be vacationing in a resort like Aspen or Whistler and find ourselves in a restaurant with other families, sitting around a large round table as a giant pot of cheese that smelled like a musty basement bubbled in the center. The parents would eagerly dip their bread cubes in the cheese, laughing about the fondue set wedding gifts languishing in their garages, of first dates at fondue parties and scrubbing hardened cheese from velour sofa cushions. The kids around the table would try one bite of the pungent fondue, wrinkle their noses, and eat plain bread cubes until our parents relented with an order of chicken fingers. Our reaction to chocolate fondue was another story, however. We would dunk anything we could in there—bananas, strawberries, marshmallows, napkins, sugar packets, spoons—to get at that sweet nectar. When I got a bit older we started a tradition at our weekend house of hosting a Christmas Eve cocktail party for all the other Jewish families we were friends with. We served shrimp cocktails, frozen Swedish meatballs, deli sandwiches, and chocolate fondue. One of my father's clients always sent a huge slab of chocolate as a Christmas gift, and this went into the fondue pot along with a few triangles of the oversized holiday Toblerone bars we bought at the supermarket. We had a small fondue set with a little enamel pot set over a tea light, accompanied by long-handled thin forks. One year my mother bought microwave-ready chocolate fondue, and it was so bad (an oily, runny, god-awful mess) that our Christmas fondue tradition died then and there. We went back to Chinese food after that.

Cheese fondue originated in Switzerland during the late nineteenth century as a simple peasant dish of melted hard cheeses, like emmenthal and gruyere, eaten with hunks of stale bread. Its ingredients were cheap, filling, and could be packed easily into a rucksack. The preparation couldn't have been simpler: all you needed was a pot, a fire, and possibly a dash of wine or brandy to improve the taste. Fondue became a staple of yodeling Swiss cow herders during winter months, though it soon came down from the mountain pastures to inns and taverns. The epicenter of fondue culture is Neuchâtel, a picturesque lakeside town in the hills of the Jura region, bordering France. Here is where the classic recipe of fondue Neuchâteloise emerged, with a mix of shredded emmenthal and gruyere cheeses, garlic, pepper and nutmeg, cornstarch (to keep the texture consistent), dry white wine, and a dash of kirsch, a clear cherry brandy. During my last year of high school I had several friends who went to Neuchâtel on exchange for a semester. When they returned they all looked like puffed up Butterball versions of themselves. I asked my friend Mike why they had gained so much weight, and he answered with one word: fondue. They had been lured by the delicious siren of Neuchâtel, which cast its pungent spell from every bar, restaurant, and pub. That summer, back in Canada, Mike would go on covert fondue missions to Swiss restaurants around the city. I can still picture him sitting alone in the corner of one of these places, swirling bread around a fondue pot as oompah music played, happy as anything.

In Switzerland fondue eating developed its own subculture, which only increased the food's popularity. "It was mostly a dish served in the wintertime with young people," recalled Erwin Herger, who grew up in Lucerne, Switzerland, in the 1930s and 1940s. "If you lost your bread in the pot, a girl had to kiss the boy to her left, and if a boy lost his, he had to buy the next bottle of wine. It was timeless. Everyone knew about fondue Neuchâteloise." I was having lunch with Herger and his wife, Gerda, at a loud dockside fish restaurant in Melbourne, Florida, a seaside community on the Atlantic coast, where they had retired some years back. Herger, now eighty-four years old and somewhat hard of hearing, was one of the instrumental figures of the American fondue trend, thanks to the twenty years he spent at the helm of the Chalet Suisse's kitchen, the New York City restaurant that made fondue trendy. The Chalet Suisse had opened in the 1920s during prohibition on West 52nd Street in a narrow, low-ceilinged room with painted murals of the Alps on the back wall. The restaurant served traditional Swiss food, including cheese fondue, schnitzel, and other specialties. Recipes for fondue had appeared occasionally in American newspapers or cookbooks, often from well-traveled individuals who had been skiing in Switzerland, like Helen Evans Brown, who wrote in her 1950 *Chafing Dish Book* (a WASP cookery classic) that "recipes for cheese fondue . . . are numerous and varied, but none can excel the classic one of Switzerland."

In 1953 the Chalet Suisse's original owner sold the restaurant to Konrad Egli, a Swiss businessman who would become the patron saint of fondue. Affectionately known as "The Boss" by his employees, Egli was a fondue purist in some ways. He instructed guests not to consume any cold drinks with their cheese fondue except white wine because it was believed the cheese would harden in the stomach, and he staunchly refused to serve fondue to pregnant women. Herger, who grew up working for his parents at their restaurants and inns in Switzerland, had arrived in New York in 1952 and began working at the Chalet Suisse shortly thereafter. Egli did a lot to promote cheese fondue in New York. In 1954 he arranged for Herger to demonstrate fondue with Steve Allan on the *Tonight Show*. Unfortunately, the power cut out before the segment began, so the cheese didn't melt properly, and Herger was forced to fake it on live TV.

During the summer of 1956 Egli was vacationing in Zurich when he encountered a new type of fondue that didn't involve cheese. It was called fondue Bourguignon, after the French wine region, and it involved cooking raw cubes of meat in a pot of hot oil at the table, then dipping them in sauces. Supposedly this was how French workers ate in the vineyards, and though the legend wasn't necessarily true, the name had a nice ring to it. "Let's try that!" Egli told Herger upon his return, and they quickly placed the item on the menu. They used beef tenderloin and set out small bowls of sauces that included chili, tartar, and béarnaise sauce as well as chopped onions and a mix of capers and chopped egg. "It became an instant success," recalled Herger, who said the restaurant's business suddenly took off as the smell of smoking hot oil filled the small kitchen. "On a Saturday night seventy-five percent of the dishes going out of the kitchen were fondue Bourguignon," said Herger, who was soon serving celebrity customers such as Elizabeth Montgomery and Ginger Rogers. The press came calling as well, from *Gourmet* magazine, the *New York Times*, the *Herald Tribune*, and *Time Life Books*, who solicited Herger's fondue recipes for their global cookbook collection. Seeing the Chalet Suisse's success, other restaurants in New York began copying the dish, and the American fondue trend began to bubble.

In 1961 Egli came back from Switzerland again, this time with something called fondue Oriental, a variation on Chinese hot pot cooking, where thinly sliced meats were poached in broth. Herger created a plate with paper-thin slices of beef tenderloin, pork and veal loin, chicken breast, and even veal kidney. The broth was made from chicken stock, carrots, leeks, shitake mushrooms, and water chestnuts, and the dipping sauces included teriyaki and soy sauce. At the end of the meal the waiter would take the broth back to the kitchen, where noodles, sherry, shredded peapods, mushrooms, and onions were added to make a soup, which was served to guests with great ceremony. A similar seafood fondue, cooked in a fish broth, also appeared, with shrimps, sea scallops, Dover sole, and tuna. As interest in these new fondues spread, first through New York's dining public, then out to the small circle of gourmands, it finally reached the general American public through articles in the press. In 1962 the *New York Times Magazine* published an article on fondue, calling it "one of the most interesting developments in the field of food within recent years."

For his coup de grâce, Egli turned his attention to dessert in 1964, developing a chocolate fondue at the request of the Swiss chocolate company Toblerone. The brand's American publicist, Beverly Allen, was looking for a way to sell more chocolate bars in America, and she approached Egli and Herger to help them create a recipe for dessert fondue that featured Toblerone as its base. Though there are claims that others invented chocolate fondue decades earlier, the Chalet Suisse version really caught the public's attention and blew the fondue trend through the roof. "We mixed Toblerone with heavy cream, and served it with fruits, ladyfingers, and our own profiteroles" said Herger, who had been astonished by how quickly it took off. Here was a fondue anyone could like. It wasn't complicated (like proper cheese fondue could be) or dangerous (like the Bourguignon or Oriental fondues), and most of the ingredients were readily available. Chocolate fondue became so popular, in fact, people began coming to the Chalet Suisse just for dessert. Toblerone even produced their own fondue kits, with ceramic bowls atop metal stands that held a candle as well as a recipe booklet featuring an adorable drawing of two smiling Toblerone triangles, sharing a chocolate fondue made from their cannibalized brethren.

Slowly fondue began creeping into homes. Select kitchen stores began importing enamel fondue pots and forks from Europe, especially those from modernist European brands like Dansk or Le Creuset, which became staple wedding gifts. Other American companies devised heat 'n' eat cheese fondue kits, with premixed cheese fondue in cans or other processed monstrosities that made fondue more accessible, if less authentic and tasty. Boston's cookware store the Pot Shop was an early importer of Swiss fondue sets and a supplier to noted cooks like Julia Child. In 1962 the Pot Shop's eccentric owner, Vincent Zarrilli, self-published *The Fondue Rule Book*, a fondue entertaining manual that stands as the fondue party's equivalent of the Port Huron Statement. Zarrilli laid out the rules for an evening of fondue, making the key distinction between a fondue dinner party and a fondue party, which is held later in the evening. A fondue party should host six to ten guests, selected for a variety of personalities, and all adults should hire babysitters for the night. Guests should avoid conversation touching on "divorce, domestics, domicile, dependents and disease," and hosts should keep the wine glasses filled and chilled. Setting the proper mood for a fondue party was essential. "Your light bulbs should not be using all their kilowatts," Zarrilli wrote, "but should be dimmed to the point where the actual firelight of the alcohol burner augmented by two candles casts only a degree of light sufficient to make friends out of strangers." Men and women were to be seated alternatively. Fondue games could be played as the evening progressed. One involved transferring orange slices from chin to chin without the use of hands. On the subject of "Fondue Flirtations," Zarrilli added that "something would be decidedly wrong if no fond glances were exchanged as the evening wore on." As though to drive the point home, the manual predicted that fondue for two was a perfectly acceptable activity, although what you did after that was not included in the instructions.

It is no coincidence that the fondue trend rose in concert with the budding sexual revolution in North America. The hot-pot gatherings involved inherent physical and social contact, even in their most G-rated form, and so North Americans were given permission to connect with one another while dining in a way they hadn't before. Fondue could not work with inhibitions—there were no individual portions, no fondue for one—it was a meal of forced intimacy. "It invariably proves to be a party ice-breaker, capable of thawing the glacial surface of even the Person Nobody Knows," wrote Anita Prichard in her 1969 cookbook *Fondue Magic: Fun, Flame and Saucery Around the World*, widely regarded as the best fondue tome in a genre littered with crap. "You simply can't stay aloof from people who are dunking and dipping alongside of you." Keep in mind that fondue took off at a time when riots were breaking out on the streets of American cities, urban crime was becoming more prevalent and violent, and many Americans were relocating to the suburbs, where social life was forced indoors. It was an early example of Faith Popcorn's cocooning trend, and fondue was the fad that answered cocooning's needs. With a bit of cheese and enough candles, your rec room in Cleveland could instantly become a luxury ski chalet in Zermatt. With enough wine and kirsch, a fondue party was the perfect setting to really get to know the Franklins from down the block, if you know what I mean. You can almost hear the Sergio Mendes record skipping softly against the turntable's needle in the background, its tracks forgotten in the heady haze of now-cold cheese, extinguished blue Sterno, and libido, as a jangle of keys sit in a bowl by the door. The Chalet Suisse and Konrad Egli may have been the tastemakers who introduced fondue to America, but it was the pill and the lifestyle it helped unleash that turned it into an era-defining food trend.

With fondues now associated with home entertaining and dozens of inexpensive fondue sets flooding department store shelves and wedding gift tables, interest in eating authentic fondue at the Chalet Suisse waned. "Fondue for us peaked around the early 1970s," said Dietmar Schlüter, a cook at the Chalet Suisse who had been there since the early 1960s, and took over from Herger as chef in 1975. We were sitting in Swizz, one of the few remaining fondue restaurants in New York City, not far from where the Chalet Suisse had last been before it closed in the 1990s. He had recently written a cookbook of the restaurant's recipes, and as Schlüter swirled his bread cube in a red enamel pot filled with a classic fondue Neuchâteloise (which he declared had a sufficiently balanced flavor), he sighed at the way fondue's favor had slipped away. "We tried all sorts of other things," he recalled. "We made flambées in the dining room, but they weren't so practical, and dishes like beef filet à la mode." The swinging couples of the sixties became more health conscious as the seventies wore on, and different diet trends cast dispersions on fat, sugar, oil, and cheese. The Me Generation moved from shared experiences to individual ones. People wanted to cook quicker, easier meals, and the microwave oven replaced the slow burner. Home dining fell out of favor, first with discos and then with the rise in a more exciting and varied restaurant culture. Continental Europe, once exotic, was replaced by Mexico and the Southwest, Japan, India, and other farther-flung destinations that offered newer, more exciting flavors. Meanwhile, the AIDS epidemic sucked the wind out of the sexual revolution and even made the prospect of sharing a common eating vessel a genuinely terrifying experience. Fondue became a punch line, a joke about a time of bad mustaches and Vaseline-smeared portraits, when people sat around their houses on a Saturday night eating melted cheese.

"It used to be that all everyone wanted for a wedding shower gift was a fondue pot," lamented Gerda Herger as we sat having lunch with her husband. "Now nobody wants that. No one throws cocktail parties anymore. No one does a full-course dinner with appetizers." The fondue set moved from the table to under the counter, to the basement, out to the garage, and finally to the end of the driveway at a yard sale, where it sold for just a few dollars. Recently she and Erwin had broken out their fondue pots and made the Chalet Suisse's original chocolate fondue for friends in Florida. But the evening was a dismal failure: No one even touched the fondue because they were on diets. Presented with what could be the world's best chocolate fondue, cooked by the very chef who invented the recipe that started the trend, their friends just sat there like fools and picked at the fruit.

☙

In 1975, just as fondue's oily bubble was bursting, a small fondue restaurant opened in the suburbs of Orlando. Its owners, Roy Nelson and Bruce Knochel, were two friends who had no restaurant experience. They wanted to open a bar that served food, but neither of them could cook, so it had to be the simplest food possible, and fondue was an ideal fit. People always drank with fondue (which was good for business), and because the guests essentially cooked the food themselves, the kitchen operation would be minimal. The Melting Pot restaurant's original menu featured five items: the classic Chalet Suisse fondues (cheese, oil, broth, and chocolate) as well as a dish of mushrooms stuffed with a creamy onion dip, which guests could dip in batter and then fry tableside. The Melting Pot was located in the windowless basement of a strip mall and only had fourteen tables—all high, cozy booths that were dimly lit with chandeliers made from used wine bottles, which has since become a big restaurant-decorating trend.

One of the Melting Pot's first employees was a young waiter paying his way through college named Mark Johnston. A transplant from Long Island, Johnston had never tried fondue before he began working at the Melting Pot, but he quickly saw the potential of the restaurant, and within two years of working there he acquired the franchise rights and opened the second Melting Pot in Tallahassee with his older brother Mike. Their younger brother Bob, then just fourteen, came aboard to clear tables, and the Johnston brothers began building up the business, first in Tallahassee and then opening three more Melting Pots around central Florida. "The cheese is sticky, and it gets on you and it's hard to get off," Bob Johnston, now CEO of the Melting Pot's parent company, Front Burner Brands, said, explaining how the brothers became obsessed with fondue. "I started developing a passion for it, too."

The Johnstons acquired the Melting Pot outright in 1985, with an idea of growing the chain into something even larger. Even though fondue was already well out of fashion, the Johnstons believed its inherent qualities contained a formula for franchised growth that was uniquely advantageous. "Fondue was a fad, and fads do tend to run their course," said Bob Johnston. "It was a challenge at the start, because we really came in at the tail end of it. A lot of people didn't believe we'd be anything other than a fad, including lenders. People weren't wearing wide-lapel leisure suits and bell bottoms anymore, and fondue was part of that. However, we were doing something that people liked. It's not steak on a plate with a baked potato on the side. It's fun. Fondue is a fun experience, and the guests were drawn to that, and that propelled the concept for about a decade."

The Melting Pot chain built its initial business around celebrations and special events: date nights, prom dinners, graduations, birthdays, and so forth—"What's the common thread you weave through these types of experiences?" Johnston asked me. "A celebration of something special and a desire to celebrate that something special in a unique way." The way the Melting Pot dining experience was designed added to the excitement. Instead of fondues prepared in a kitchen, the Melting Pot outfitted each table with its own burner (initially electric coils, today induction cookers). Waiters brought out trays neatly arranged with custom-made aluminum pots and many small dishes of fresh ingredients, then assembled the fondues on the table. While the waiters stirred the cheese, they kept up a constant patter, engaging with the diners, who peered in awe at the cold ingredients quickly melting into something extraordinary. The Melting Pot's early employees were all young, highly motivated, and eager to build something. New franchises were sold to existing staff who believed strongly in the brand. Mark and Bob Johnston built each franchise by hand, even constructing the tables themselves.

That concept served the Melting Pot well for its first two decades as the chain expanded to nineteen outlets around Florida (it is headquartered in Tampa), with a few restaurants in other southern states. But by the mid-1990s growth and sales were stagnant. The Johnstons responded by refreshing the brand. They expanded the Melting Pot's wine program, updated the décor of all the restaurants, and added a lot more variety to the menu, which until then had not changed since opening day. "Seafood fondue, marinated meats like teriyaki sirloin, broth-based fondues, even vegetarian dinners, pastas, pot stickers, and raviolis that could be cooked in fondue, marinated duck, crusted seafood like tuna covered in black sesame seeds," said Johnston, rattling off a list of the additions. "A lot of it was tied into trends at that time."

The most impactful change was "The Perfect Night Out," a service credo that came to define the brand, more for the quality of a guest's experience than for the consistency of their fondue. "We began to look for ways to go above and beyond what the guest might expect in serving them," said Johnston. "If someone was there celebrating something, we'd take their picture, and it'd go inside a frame and maybe go on their fridge on a magnet so they could remember their experience." Waiters took notes on guests, and these were entered into a database so when those same guests made dinner reservations months later, their server would ask how their bodybuilding business was going or whether their daughter had completed her SAT course. "When we did that, we started to build on an almost fanatical fan base that exists to this day. No longer was it 'That was a cool place to go because it's fondue and unique.' It became 'Man, these people made us feel like we're the only people in the restaurant.'"

Over the past decade and a half the Melting Pot has expanded from 19 locations to well over 130 all over the United States and a handful more around the world. Once again, however, the Melting Pot was looking to reinvent itself. American dining habits had continued to change, and the chain's strength had become its weakness. The focus on service and a unique dining experience may draw guests who spend well when they enjoy a four-course meal—but only once or twice a year. "The reality is that people's dining habits have changed when they dine out," Johnston told me in his large, modern Tampa office. "Even my wife and I eat smaller samples at the bar instead of a full meal because we're so pressed for time." Since the recession of 2008 diners sought greater value from restaurants, and the Melting Pot had trouble delivering this easily. To keep fondue growing and alive—across the Melting Pot essentially carries alone—the restaurant needed to rethink the way fondue would look and taste in the twenty-first century.

The man they tapped to do that was Shane Schaibly, who was recruited in 2007 as the Melting Pot's executive chef. A tall, brawny thirty-one-year-old from Dunedin, Florida, a small city outside Tampa, Schaibly was the type of badass chef you'd expect to find slinging foie gras bone marrow bacon burgers in a hipster restaurant. His father had been an undercover narcotics cop, and he grew up in the kind of ballsy Florida culture where you hunted sharks and alligators on weekends as part of what Schaibly called "Redneck fun." Schaibly had worked in restaurants since he was fourteen, including small trendy bistros and the large hotel kitchens of Miami Beach's Ritz Carlton, though he had only eaten fondue at the Melting Pot—or anywhere, really—twice in his life before taking the job on his twenty-fifth birthday. Covered in tattoos from his ankles to his neck, the mischievous, smiling Schaibly met me that morning in Tampa at the Melting Pot's main location, the third to open, wearing an iPot T-shirt with a Melting Pot logo on it. Unlocking the door was like unsealing a vault of cheesy 1970s decor that had been made worse with some hideous 1990s touch-ups. The dimly lit restaurant was a warren of narrow passages and tucked-away rooms, ringed by an endless flow of dark wood wainscoting, like a long-shuttered Holiday Inn lobby bar. Glass bottles filled with colored water and lit from the bottom provided ambience, and the walls were painted either Barney purple, stained mustard, or "baby puke green," as Schaibly so eloquently put it. The location was slated for a renovation within the next year or two to bring it up to the more current décor most of the other Melting Pot locations enjoyed. "We're all trying to steer these 130 ships in a new direction," said Schaibly, flipping on the lights to the kitchen.

The Melting Pot's kitchen was unlike any I'd ever seen. There was no stove, no oven, no fryer—no source of heat whatsoever. "This is totally different from the rock-star chef life," said Schaibly, who was shocked when he first took the job. "It's nine to five, with no cooking equipment." It was basically a big prep kitchen where platters of fondue and salads were cut and assembled according to pictures of how they should look, piled onto trays, and brought tableside, where the waiters would cook them in front of diners. Aside from Schaibly, there were no other cooks or chefs working in the chain, which was a big attraction to those who were operating franchises. So long as everything was portioned and displayed correctly and the servers followed their training, it was almost impossible to screw up a Melting Pot fondue. For the most part Schaibly's job consisted of managing staff, ordering the food, and ensuring supply quality across the chain, a huge logistical task that took him to suppliers around the country, including Nueske's for bacon and sausages and Emmi-Roth Käse, a Wisconsin cheese maker that made traditional Swiss cheeses in copper kettles.

Three times a year—spring, summer, and fall—Schaibly got to flex his culinary muscles with seasonal menus known in the business as limited time offers (LTOs). "This is my outlet as a chef to do new cool stuff," he said with a huge grin. "The guest likes what they like. It makes it challenging for me to update things. There's a certain amount of a fondue cage that I live in. Believe me, I'm pushing on the edge of the cage. For me, bringing fresh ideas is bringing in certified Angus sirloin for the bourguignon fondue. You'd have thought that I was trying to close the place down and turn it into a burger joint when I did that." The LTOs were Schaibly's opportunity to melt current dining trends, seasonal ingredients, and his own creativity into the fondue pot. He kept an eye out at farmer's markets and in restaurants, read culinary blogs and magazines, and experimented with ideas at home. Schaibly was fondue's creative edge, its future tastemaker, and he greatly enjoyed the challenge of keeping fondue relevant. "Yes, I live in a fondue cage," he said, "but once you embrace what's going on, you can do whatever you want, man. That's what's cool about my job. I love it." Each LTO involved a unique cheese fondue, a seasonal salad, and a fresh spin on dessert fondue. (Oil and broth fondues remained the same.) LTOs were devised a full year ahead of their chain-wide debut so the company could test them in select markets, tweak the recipes if necessary, and secure a consistent supply of ingredients. In the past Schaibly had made a fondue inspired by gyros (spiced lamb with a tzatziki-style dip) and an all-bacon fondue menu, a trend near and dear to his heart. Currently the chain was serving a goat cheese fondue because

Schaibly preferred lighter cheeses in the spring and summer months (imagine eating a bowl of hot gruyere in Florida in August), though it took ages to achieve the right consistency. The goat cheese turned grainy when melted, so it only really worked when it was folded in at the end with other melted cheese. He had also recently tried mixing red wine and cheese for a fondue, and although it tasted good, the purple color would never fly with guests.

That day in Tampa Schaibly was putting the finishing touches on several LTOs. The Spring 2014 menu was designed around the salad, which would be a classic caprese with Roma tomatoes and a fresh Wisconsin mozzarella he had encountered on one of his trips there. The cheese fondue was going to feature a sharp butterkäse and fontina cheese blend, white wine, tomato pesto, and diced fresh tomatoes. The idea had come from a recent trip Schaibly and the Melting Pot's executives took to Switzerland, where they reacquainted themselves with fondue's roots, eating fondue for a week straight. In one epic session they ate twenty-five fondues in a single sitting, a feat Schaibly described as "gross" and Bob Johnston called "torture," but it gave them a wealth of new ideas, including the tomato fondue. There were two items that Schaibly was still trying to perfect, and this is why the executive team was coming in for lunch today. One was a dessert for the Spring 2014 LTO that was a white chocolate peaches-and-cream fondue, and the other was a Fall 2014 LTO contender that Schaibly was particularly excited about: a lobster bisque fondue that he had been testing at home.

Because the Melting Pot is only open for dinner, the executive team sat around one of the tables in the empty restaurant. There was Bob Margait (director of operations), Mike Lester (Melting Pot president), Scott Pierce (Front Burner's CFO), and Kristy Galke (R&D coordinator). All were veterans of the multi-unit casual American restaurant business, whether they had been with Outback steakhouses in their grand expansion or had worked their way up from a Melting Pot server position. These weren't gourmet foodies and culinary tastemakers chasing the latest trend with bold experimentation but rather calculating restaurant business executives attuned to the market realities of the mainstream customer they were serving, someone who was typically a middle-class woman between nineteen and thirty-five years old. The Melting Pot targeted your average American fondue eater, so to speak. They weren't looking for culinary fireworks as much as a subtle shift that could bring in new customers and keep the old ones coming back. A nudge of the needle. Schaibly and a waiter put two empty fondue pots on the table's induction burners (which heat metal but are cool to the touch) and began explaining the lobster bisque fondue as he assembled it. He poured in just over a cup of lobster bisque he had sourced from a local supplier, then began folding in the cheese for the classic Swiss fondue, all the while whisking with a fork.

"It's gonna be heavy," said Lester, "but it's gonna be delicious."

"We might need that lemon juice," said Galke, watching the concoction rapidly thicken.

"Yeah," said Schaibly, "it's super thick. That might have been wishful thinking to think it's only a bisque base." He squeezed in another lemon. "I'm hoping this acidity will cut it more." He sprinkled in chopped cooked lobster tail and shallots to the fondue and kept whisking. "Careful," he said, finishing up, "it's gonna be stringy."

The fondue had the taste of a lobster grilled cheese mixed with a bisque, a hint of seafood but not overly cheesy, with a nice tang. "I love it!" Pierce declared. "I'd eat it all day." Margait dove in next with his fork, speaking as he swirled the lobster fondue with a twirl to coat his bread. "We'd have to lock in the bisque and fancier lobster meat now, while the price is low," he said, popping it into his mouth. Schaibly promised he could secure a good price and would fix the viscosity, but there was concern around the table that if it didn't fly, they'd be left with oceans of lobster bisque on their hands. "Remember when he had to give away a hundred thousand pounds of chicken pomegranate sausage?" said Margait, recalling a previously unsuccessful attempt to capitalize on a food trend.

The lobster fondue was taken away, and Schaibly returned with the ingredients for the white chocolate peaches-and-cream fondue. At the previous tasting a few weeks back, the peaches-and-cream fondue had been a big hit, but everyone agreed it was too thin and not peachy enough. Schaibly worked with a supplier to create a concentrated natural peach puree that, along with fresh diced peaches, could hopefully amplify the flavor of the fondue.

"I like the flavor of peach fondue," said Lester, "but compared to others it doesn't compel me to order it over other chocolate fondues."

"What about using fresh peaches to dip with?" asked Margait.

"On the plate?" asked Schaibly. "The problem is that when a peach is good, it's too soft to hold onto with a fondue fork." Instead, they used the classic Melting Pot dessert dipper plate, which included cubes of crumb cake, marshmallows, and sturdier fruits like strawberries. The peaches-and-cream fondue was powerfully sweet, almost overwhelmingly so, and the peach only really worked well with certain dippers, like the sponge cake, but when it did, it was fantastic, like some great chocolate bar that had yet to be invented or a Starbucks frozen drink developed in Mattson's lab. Schaibly was pleased.

After lunch I spoke with Lester about the company's new international efforts, which had begun picking up steam over the past few years as domestic growth slowed because the Melting Pot already had such a large market presence. There was now a location in Edmonton, Alberta, which had become one of the busiest in the chain, as well as several in Mexico, which were exceeding all expectations. "When you really look at it most cultures have some sort of communal-pot cooking," Lester said, though cultural differences required some adjustments. Whereas the chain's biggest challenge in North America was the long time required to eat there, in Mexico that was the Melting Pot's biggest strength. "Americans want to refuel and get out," Lester said, "and in Mexico they love how they can eat and don't get pushed out." In American Melting Pots the lowest-selling fondue was the traditional Neuchâteloise, but in Mexico it outsold all other fondues ten to one. Mexican customers were split evenly between men and women (in the United States women dominated the business), and lunch was a bigger meal than dinner. The latest frontier for fondue was in the Middle East, where the Melting Pot had signed agreements to open seventeen restaurants in several Arab countries, largely in wealthy Gulf states like Saudi Arabia and Kuwait as well as Lebanon. There were requests from

Brazil, China, and Indonesia for franchises, as the world's grow-ing middle class looked to the Melting Pot to deliver its own spin on a food that had originated in Switzerland, crossed the ocean to America, and evolved into a trend that was now ready for a global resurrection.

❧

Fondue had seen a second life once before. During the 1990s and into the early 2000s fondue enjoyed a brief return to favor, as the children conceived during those wild midcentury fondue nights dis-covered its charms for themselves. The *New York Times* reported in 1990 that sales of new home fondue kits were double what their manufactures expected and were now littering the shelves of house-wares stores nationwide. Magali Pelletier, the product development manager with the Quebec kitchenware company Trudeau credits the boom to the recession of the 1980s and, once again, Faith Pop-corn's behavioral cocooning trend. Trudeau had distributed other fondue sets for years, but in the mid-1990s they manufactured their own in a rainbow of bright colors and made three-in-one fondue sets, with interchangeable compartments so you could use just one boiler to make cheese, oil, and chocolate fondues, all with little mess. Between 1996 and 2001 the company's fondue business grew tenfold, selling one million sets in Canada and the United States at chains like Target, Crate & Barrel, and Bed Bath and Beyond. Restaurants also got back into the fondue revival. A 2003 story in *Time* magazine ("It's Now Hip to Dip") chronicled the inventive gourmet fondues popping up at restaurants such as Luna Park in San Francisco, Vine in Los Angeles, and New York's cheese-focused Artisanal. This continues today with places like the Bourgeois Pig, a restaurant in New York that is staking a claim to hipster fondue, with savory blue cheese and honey entrées as well as a dark choco-late, bacon (of course), and beer fondue for dessert.

During this period, for the first time in years, new fondue cook-books began appearing on bookstore shelves. The most popular was *Fondue* by Lenny Rice and Brigid Callinan, a book that was entirely cheese focused and began after the two friends, who were working in the food business in San Francisco, threw a fondue party in 2002 to use up various odds and ends from a cheese course they'd taken. "People were taking different things off the dessert tray and using it in the cheese," said Callinan, who now teaches culinary arts in Idaho. "They were dipping Fig Newtons in cheese. It was super fun. Everyone said, 'You've got to do that again.'" *Fondue* was even published as a special custom edition for Williams and Sonoma stores, which paired it for sale with their newly popular fondue sets. This fondue revival died down by the mid-2000s, pushed back to nostalgic territory for one reason or another (e.g., trends toward small individual tapas plates), but it wasn't hard to see how the fondue trend could reinvent itself every decade or so, melting and reforming with the flavors, ingredients, and influences of other trends in order to stay relevant. You could sprinkle chia seeds in a cheese fondue to make it ostensibly healthier, use Red Prince apples or purple sweet potatoes for dipping, and do a tikka masala curry fondue, with chunks of paneer cheese and naan bread for dipping. Perhaps the future of fondue was found in businesses like the DipStick, a Denver food truck that had taken fondue to the streets in 2012.

Everyone involved with fondue, past and present, readily acknowledges that the food would likely never return to the popularity it enjoyed as a trend in the 1960s. Nonetheless, the inherent qualities of eating fondue ensured that it would always occupy a place in food culture. Schaibly and Bob Johnston told me several times how first-time guests at the Melting Pot regularly marveled at what happened when they dined there. Their children's faces, normally glued to screens at the dinner table, were completely entranced by the experience, and their phones remained in pockets throughout the meal. Conversation between strangers eased into friendships, and dates blossomed into romance as cubes of bread kissed melted cheese. "It's not what's going on in the pot as much as what's going on outside the pot," Johnston said, repeating a company saying. Fondue was as much a social trend as an edible one.

I experienced this firsthand when Schaibly and I returned to the Melting Pot for dinner that night. It was a Thursday, and the restaurant was now alive. Every table was full: couples on dates, large families with kids and grandparents, a dozen well-dressed young women on a girl's night out, and a private room holding a church fund-raiser. We took a seat in "Lover's Lane," a row of high-walled booths that were the focal point of every Melting Pot. Our friendly waiter, John Martin, came over and explained every aspect of the meal, from the order of courses to the way the fondues are prepared, while asking about ourselves, my visit to Tampa so far, and whether we had any special requests. Schaibly ordered the seasonal goat cheese fondue with a side of premium dipper plates that included Nueske's summer sausage and sliced Granny Smith apples. Martin came back out a while later with a double-chambered fondue pot that he placed onto the table's cooktop, and he began assembling the fondue from the tray of ingredients. Creamy garlic and herb cheese, butterkäse, and fontina went into the pot with chopped garlic and white wine, and we watched it slowly liquefy, releasing a steam that smelled like a drive-through farmland. Right before the last solid bit melted, Martin tipped in the crumbled goat cheese and began folding it into the fondue with a fork, slowly and carefully.

I picked up one of the long fondue forks, speared a cube of bread, and coated it with the cheese. Because I had burnt my mouth eating fondue too eagerly with Dietmar Schlüter several months back, I paused to give it a cooling puff. The cheese was smooth, almost like a cream sauce, with the strong flavor of garlic and herbs that you would expect from a pasta. This wasn't the powerful, gooey Swiss fondues I'd grown up eating; this was something more subtle, modern, and inventive. I dipped in a slice of summer sausage, and suddenly it was deeper and earthier, the herbaceous fondue now brightening up the smoky sausage, then with the apple, which made it seem tart and fresh. "Careful," Schaibly warned me as I went for my tenth bite in the first minute, "fondue is a marathon, not a sprint. If you don't slow down, you'll never get through the meal." Had I known what was coming next, I would have heeded his advice. Martin exchanged our cheese fondue for an empty pot filled halfway with oil. As the pot slowly came to life with a series of pops and pings, he set down a buffet of raw food: fat prawns and slices of deep red tuna, a platter of fresh vegetables, bowls of sauces and batters, and at least two pounds of meat, including Angus sirloin, Cajun-spiced chicken breast, and big cubes of beef filet. Schaibly showed me how to stuff a mushroom cap with creamy green-goddess dressing, dip it in thick tempura batter, and set it in the oil to brown.

As the oil danced around our skewers in a lawn sprinkler's hiss, we waited and talked about fondue's ultimate impact in our food culture. The Melting Pot was an exception to the fondue trend's general fortunes, growing as fondue had faded, but the legacy that fondue had left in its wake was all around us, melted right into the way we ate. Schaibly saw fondue in several lasting food trends, from chocolate-dipped fruits and cookies to our eager embrace of warm dips and melted sauces for all sorts of dishes. Sure, it wasn't fondue in the Swiss classic sense, but wasn't something like the molten chocolate cake just a variation on the chocolate fondue? Weren't all the melted cheese–filled entrees in our culture just cheese fondues on the inside?

For the better part of an hour Schaibly and I sat there skewering and frying, eating and joking. We talked about our families, about work, travel, and, in Schaibly's case, the finer points of shooting an angry alligator in the head with a high-powered pistol (Florida, baby!). I'd barely known the man for a day, but with each skewer the barrier of unfamiliarity between us fell away, and I felt like we had been good friends for years. (A year later, Schaibly moved on from the Melting Pot to another job. He finally broke free of his fondue cage, perhaps bringing the promise of melted cheese creations to a whole new audience.) It made me think back to something Erwin Herger had told me the day before when we sat with his wife, eating separate plates of fish on the other side of the state. "The strength of fondue is the idea that everyone participates in eating or cooking from the same pot," he said. "It somehow creates a unity at the table." Fondue's fundamental strength, the core of what made it a trend, was the central idea of a shared eating experience. It occupied the same place as a giant banana split, something you ate for the dynamic it created with people at the table as much as for the taste. Whether it was melted cheese, boiling oil, or chocolate, fondue was just the vehicle toward the ultimate goal of conversation and familiarity, and no matter what the fads of the day were, whether low-fat or low-carb, frozen or Greek yogurt, small plates or big entrées, the pleasure we got from sharing food with other people would never diminish. It was a trend that would always reemerge in various forms but that fundamentally could never go out of style. "That's what the name of fondue means: it's melting," said Herger, looking off across the water in the direction of his native Switzerland and, perhaps, the first kiss he stole from a girl who dropped her bread into the fondue many years ago. "It's melting people together."

Perhaps I was being a little bit cheesy, but wasn't that the whole point?

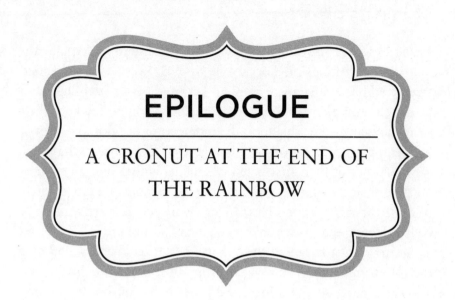

EPILOGUE

A CRONUT AT THE END OF
THE RAINBOW

On May 10, 2013, as I sat at home writing the cupcake chapter that opens this book, a new food trend was being born three hundred miles away. That was the day Dominique Ansel, a Parisian-born, New York–based pastry chef who had worked in the kitchens of star chef Daniel Boulud, debuted a new confection at his Dominique Ansel Bakery in the fashionable SOHO neighborhood of Manhattan. Ansel's creation began with a laminated dough, similar to the buttery, layered, proofed dough of a croissant. He shaped this into a ring, then fried it in grapeseed oil so that the dough puffed up crisp and golden on the outside, creating airy pockets between the flaky layers, which now peeled away in sheets. Ansel then piped in Tahitian vanilla cream so the thing practically bulged, rolled it in flavored sugar, and topped it all with a hot-pink rose-flavored glaze, which was sprinkled with rose sugar for added effect. Ansel named his new pastry the cronut, a croissant-donut hybrid. The cronut was extremely delicate, limited in number, and expensive ($5 each). You couldn't refrigerate a cronut, and it basically wilted like a flower after six hours, but its promise of novel decadence and deliciousness proved irresistible.

Because the popular food blog Grub Street had posted an article about the cronut the day before its official debut, its existence wasn't exactly a secret. But the public's response to the cronut was more than anything Ansel or anyone who has ever witnessed a food trend could have imagined. New Yorkers had been searching for an heir to the cupcake trend for years, and fancy donuts had been their rising contender, but this took the momentum of both and blew it up like a cream-filled hydrogen bomb. That first day Ansel and his staff sold out of their first batch of cronuts within half an hour of opening their doors, then scrambled to make more and immediately sold off the day's second batch. Dozens of people were frantically calling Dominique Ansel Bakery, trying to secure orders. FoxNews .com carried a story about the cronut's invention that day, and over the following week cronuts went from an unknown culinary creation to a feverish trend in record time. Food journalists looking to write reviews began heading to Ansel's bakery before opening, waiting in line in the early morning hours to score a batch. To try to control the madness, Ansel limited shoppers to a maximum of two cronuts per person. This only increased demand. Each day cronuts sold out quicker than the previous day. On May 15 someone gave one of Ansel's staff the middle finger when they were informed, upon reaching the end of the line, that the cronuts were already gone. Another person broke into actual tears of despair. On May 17 Ansel trademarked the word Cronut™.

It only got crazier from there. Within a week there were lineups for cronuts winding around the blocks near Dominique Ansel Bakery at all hours of the day, with the first eager customers showing up as early as five in the morning. Summer interns from businesses all over New York were dispatched to sweat it out in the line so their bosses could be presented cronuts at their desks. Enterprising Craigslist entrepreneurs began offering to wait in the cronut line on your behalf for a fee. A month after the cronut launched, a black market service called Premium Cronut Delivery opened for business, charging $100 to bring a single cronut anywhere in New York City (a 2,000 percent markup). If you wanted twenty cronuts, it cost $3,000 because larger orders required multiple rounds in line, the opposite of an economy of scale. Each day the cronut lineup formed a few minutes earlier, by August inching as early as three in the morning. The blog Gothamist even posted a photo of two young women rooting through the bakery's trash late at night, searching for rejected, overcooked, degenerate cronuts to eat or possibly even resell. Their desperation was tragic.

The shocking thing about the cronut trend was its sheer blitzkrieg speed. No one predicted its arrival, and no one had ever seen anything like this. It ushered in a new era of instant food trends. In the span of a month cronuts received the combined press coverage that the cupcake craze accumulated over a decade, with articles in every major national and international newspaper and website, TV news broadcasts all over the world, and a relentless onslaught of social media attention. *Vogue* magazine declared 2013 the summer of the cronut, the *Atlantic* called them "New York's favorite cruller on vanilla-flavored steroids," and cronut stories appeared on the Freakonomics blog as well as in the business magazine *Inc.*, questioning the long-term financial potential of the pastry's future. Cronut blogs, like funkincronuts.com, popped up to chronicle every minute development of the craze.

The cronut was unique because it was the first time a food had been born directly into a trend. Whereas cupcakes took one or two years to move out from Magnolia's kitchen into other New York bakeries, several more years to inspire cupcakeries in other American cities, and almost a decade to establish the cupcake trend internationally, the cronut emerged from Dominique Ansel's kitchen and leaped directly into the world of imitators, hybrids, and inspired pastry creations popping up as far afield as San Diego (the square cronut), London (the dosant), Singapore (crodos), and even Caracas, Venezuela (@MrCronut), to name but a few. All over the world pastry chefs were reverse engineering cronuts as the trend spilled from one country to the next. A bakery in Beijing reportedly got the idea from one in Australia, which had flown someone to New York to acquire a specimen in the same way that someone in Manila had done. In South Korea the country's Dunkin Donuts chain had already mass produced a "New York Pie Donut" by late July.

Few if any of these people had even tasted a cronut or even seen one up close, but the lessons of the cupcake trend were clear: get in early, catch the wave, and ride it for every dollar you can. I first encountered this early in July when Le Dolci, the bakery at the end of my block in Toronto specializing in cupcakes, macarons, and other sweets, began advertising cronuts on their chalkboard. They were smaller than Ansel's and more dense, but they were fried and flaky, and suddenly there were crowds of curious foodies taking photographs on my street with cronuts triumphantly displayed. Even after a year spent writing about food trends, this one amazed me.

As impressed as I was with the cronut trend, I only managed to observe it peripherally because my wife gave birth to our first child ten days after the cronut was born in Ansel's bakery. All summer long I saw the stories and Tweets and jokes about the cronut. People I knew were heading to New York for vacations and spending half their weekend in line for cronuts, which they chronicled as slideshows of photographs on social media. The cronut trend's sheer absurdity began to overtake reality. Karon Liu, a friend and fellow food writer at the Toronto newspaper *The Grid*, wrote an article about the potential of a crookie (croissant + cookie), almost as a piece of satire. To his surprise, the crookie instantly became a creation sold by bakeries in the city and then around the world, officially endorsed by the folks at Oreo, and covered in *Time*.

I was too stuck in a cycle of sleep deprivation, feeding schedules, colicky screams, and sheer parental joy to pay any real attention to all of this. I couldn't even manage to walk to the end of my block to buy a cronut before they sold out each day, despite regular promises to do so. In fact, my knee-jerk reaction to the cronut was a sign of how hard it was to shake the ambivalence I held toward food trends when I began this book. Each time a new cronut story came to my attention, each time someone excitedly asked whether I had already tried one, I groaned, as I once had for cupcakes, gluten-free diets, and restaurants that served bacon-flavored desserts. "It's just another fad," I said dismissively. "It'll be gone by Labor Day."

By mid-August my curiosity got the better of me, and I was finally ready to embrace the cronut. I marked a date in my calendar—the date my first draft of this book was due—when I planned on walking down the street to Le Dolci to pick one up, partly as a reward and partly as a fittingly delicious conclusion to my research. As my deadline approached, the excitement around Le Dolci's cronut reached fever pitch. The bakery had teamed up with a vendor called Epic Burgers and Waffles, which operated a booth at the Canadian National Exhibition (a giant end of summer carnival) that sold gut-busting creations like a waffle and fried chicken sandwich or a hamburger set between two halves of a Krispy Kreme donut. Together they unleashed the Cronut Burger, a seven thousand–calorie bomb that replaced donuts with a cronut, quickly becoming a media sensation and generating its own vast lines and celebrity status. The cronut was now in such hot demand that I was worried I wouldn't ever be able to get my hands on one.

On the day of my cronut appointment I woke up, checked Le Dolci's hours, and counted down the time until they were open. At eleven in the morning I strapped my daughter to my chest in her sling, put on my sunglasses, and strode confidently down the block. When I arrived at Le Dolci, however, the bakery was closed. I checked the time, peeked inside, and then turned to my phone, where I looked at my e-mails for the first time in a few hours, discovering only then why I would not be getting a cronut that day: a wave of violent food poisoning had affected over two hundred people who had eaten the Cronut Burger the previous night, sending several to the hospital. Both Le Dolci and Epic Burgers and Waffles were closed, pending an investigation by the city's health authority. Over the coming week it would be revealed that the culprit was neither the cronut nor the hamburgers but rather a maple-bacon jam Le Dolci had created as a topping for the monstrous sandwich that had been contaminated with the Staphylococcus aureus toxin. Le Dolci had fallen victim to the hubris of a food trend and had taken the cronut down with them. The bakery had opened the previous year, chasing the cupcake and macaron trends long after they had passed, and when the cronut came along, they were the first on the ground to offer it in Toronto. Drunk with the taste of a food trend's power, they sought to amplify their success and chased too many food trends at one time, combining the cronut, burger, and bacon trends into a hideous frankentrend that ultimately destroyed them—before Labor Day, no less.

That same summer a Japanese chef and blogger named Keizo Shimamoto invented a ramen burger at his pop-up noodle stand in Brooklyn. This dish, a hamburger set between two buns made from fried ramen noodles, was to some the high-water mark of food trend memes, the edible equivalent of a double rainbow video gone viral. Of course the lines began forming immediately, and of course the ramen burger attracted the scorn of many who had never even tasted it, but as one article pointed out, the ramen burger, in all its insanity, proved by its very existence what was great about our society. In Japan, where the food is delicious but governed by strict conventions and traditions, the ramen burger would be a blasphemy that would never see the light of day. The same could be said about cronuts, which would never fly in Paris, the city where Dominique Ansel was born. But here in North America we embraced food trends and allowed them to thrive. Kara Nielsen, the trendologist I spoke with in San Francisco, saw this as one of our greatest strengths. Food trends, she felt, were as powerful an example of the creative, democratic North American spirit than anything else out there in our culture. They represented the same force of entrepreneurship, fresh beginnings, and boundless destiny that drew immigrants to our shores with dreams in their eyes.

At their worst, food trends can be annoyingly shallow. They may start out as individual expressions of imagination, but ultimately they become victims of a herd mentality. One day everyone in your life is eating Greek yogurt, and you're not sure how it happened. In the case of trends like the cronut they literally attract stampeding herds of humans. It is easy to view the culture of trends as the vapid expression of a society obsessed with materialism, as insubstantial fads. We dine out for entertainment, watch hours of food being cooked and eaten on television, and plan road trips to taste the latest hot meal. Food has become fashion, chefs are hailed as rock stars, and photos of the latest dishes are our art. At the same time we live in a world where millions are starving or malnourished, and not just in distant poor countries but also within walking distance of our homes. In the United States alone more than 16 million children don't have reliable access to food. They've never heard of cronuts or chia seeds or the latest ceviche from Ricardo Zarate's kitchen, and they don't give a shit that you just posted a review of the top-twenty hottest food trucks in DC on your blog. These people wait in lines and dig through the trash for their next meal, not for some sense of culinary thrill-seeking.

It is hard to contemplate this reality when you're walking the halls of the Fancy Food Show, having so many culinary creations thrust at you that you can hardly swallow them fast enough. While writing this book I was often tempted to blame the ramen burger, the bacon explosion, or the chia-flavored Greek yogurt crookie for the sad absurdity of this problem, not to mention the much pettier but sometimes compelling problem: I was tired of hearing about new trends.

But somewhere in the midst of my year of decadent cupcakes, food truck festivals, and $2,000 worth of creamy, nutty black rice, it occurred to me how lucky I was—to be able to do this for a living, to live in a country that not only supported but encouraged these sometimes quixotic innovations, to have grown up in a time when food was so tasty and plentiful that we could sneer at steak and potatoes. It is a wonderful time to be eating.

Food trends bring us happiness. You can groan all you want about how cupcakes are "over" as a trend, but if I placed a cupcake in front of you, you would still peel back the folds of its paper cup with the same eager anticipation you had when you were a kid at a birthday party. You would chomp down on the sweet moist cake and the creamy icing with a single, ferocious bite and then lick the remnants from your sticky fingers until every last crumb is gone. For the same reason people will continue to eat Ricardo Zarate's food—not because it is cool and trendy but because it is fundamentally delicious and the experience of enjoying his uniquely composed causas and tiraditos brings diners a joy they cannot experience in other restaurants. Chefs like Roy Choi, David Chang, and Sang Yoon may have become known for a particular dish or a flavor profile that grew into a trend, but that was because that Korean taco, pork bun, or hamburger they created brought great happiness to the people eating it, and still does. The trends those chefs launched spread smiles to millions of diners everywhere, and this is why other chefs and other diners sought them out in their own cities and homes, where that happiness only grew.

Food trends are for everyone. They may originate as specialty items, available only in select cities for a high price and long wait, but eventually the nature of all food trends is democratic. The creation of a brilliant chef or a small food company will quickly be adapted, reinvented, and reborn in countless different ways at all different price points. Products and tastes that make their debut at the Fancy Food Show as rare, expensive indulgences will trickle down to the average supermarket buyer through the process of a trend's evolution, which is why goat's milk caramels may one day be as commonplace in our pantries as Hershey's chocolate. We now have a vastly greater selection of foods at our fingertips than we did a generation ago.

Food trends can also deepen and expand our culture beyond the plate. The success of Anson Mills grains has done more to further Glenn Roberts's goal of preserving the Carolina Rice Kitchen than any political campaign or charitable plea ever could. The quality and flavor of his grits and rice may propel their trendiness, but their ultimate cultural impact has resulted in a revived interest in southern history, traditional cooking, heritage ingredients, and farming practices that are spreading across the South and around the world. Trends also bring the kitchens of that world together. The years Sushil Malhotra, Sukhi Singh, and Hemant Bhagwani have spent trying to make Indian food popular in North America will soon pay off, as naan bread and chicken tikka masala become lunch staples in more homes, workplaces, and restaurants, and as fears about Indian food give way to an expanding curiosity and hunger, both for Indian cuisine and the greater culture it comes from. Our food isn't a static thing. It doesn't belong in a museum, hermetically sealed and unalterable. It shifts and changes to reflect our values, enriching us in innumerable ways as it does. Trends are what push it forward.

All of these trends created economic growth. The Botden family staked millions of dollars on the Red Prince apple because they knew that only a new, innovative apple could set them apart on the grocer's shelves. Their success will drive others to find and breed new apples, bringing greater diversity to what is available for us to eat while also increasing the fortunes of farmers and everyone who works with them, just as bacon's revival lifted the fortunes of the pork industry, buoyed restaurant profits, and helped farmers get more for their pigs. Chia created a global market for a seed that previously was sold only as a novelty item. The poor Argentinean farmers that Wayne Coates initially introduced to chia are now rich because of its growth as a health trend. Each cupcake shop, aspiring Indian restaurant, food truck, or small company winning a sofi award at the Fancy Food Show represents the hopes of several entrepreneurs, each of whom can possibly create hundreds or even thousands of jobs on the strength of their food trends. These are jobs in farms, offices, restaurants, and warehouses, jobs for highly educated individuals and for those who need steady entry-level work at a decent wage. Food trends represent capitalism at its finest: a good idea that the market rewards with dollars, creating jobs, tax revenues, and economies of scale as they expand.

With that economic might, too, comes the possibility of even more change. If enough people get behind a way of eating, policy will eventually follow. People had been crying about the lack of street food options for decades in North American cities and nothing happened. Only when gourmet food trucks became a trend did change actually occur and work its way into law. Within just a handful of years North American cities went from places where selling food on the street was illegal and the most you could hope for was a stale hot dog, to a roving smorgasbord of edible options that spurned innovation and new models of commerce that were legally available thanks to the political efforts of the food truck associations and the trend they rode in on.

Over the last few decades most of the food sold to us has become more processed, giving rise to particularly devastating health consequences such as obesity, heart disease, and diabetes. According to the Center for Disease Control and Prevention, around 17 percent of American children are now obese, and as many as a third are overweight. Those numbers have tripled in the past three decades and are now showing up in developing countries like China, India, and Brazil, where health problems related to overeating were entirely unknown twenty years ago. This shift, unfortunately, is also a food trend, and it is a hell of a lot more impactful than any hot pastry of the moment. Trends like these aren't easily diverted or slowed down; they are powerful and change the way we eat on a biological level. You cannot litigate them out of existence. They require a shift in the opposite direction with equal momentum and force to unseat them. The only thing that can do that is a countertrend.

Two years ago I found myself in the gymnasium of the Barrow Street Nursery School, a wealthy private school in New York's Greenwich Village, where Radha Agrawal was busy running around with a pack of shrieking three-year-olds. Agrawal, who was then thirty-three, was there to put on a puppet show with the Super Sprowtz, a posse of talking, singing vegetable superheroes that she had created years before. Formed after lightning strikes a New York City rooftop greenhouse, the Super Sprowtz use the power of their health benefits—Brian Broccoli is super-strong, Colby Carrot has super-sight, Suzy Sweetpea is super-speedy, Sammy Spinach is super-stretchy, and so forth—to fight their nemesis, Pompous Pollution and his unhealthy henchmen Greasy, Junk, and Processa, who hatch schemes tailor-made to rouse the ire of Whole Foods–shopping parents, like sending exploding grease carts into the Union Square farmer's market. Take the Justice League, infuse it with Dr. Oz's antioxidant gospel, wrap it in cuddly felt faces, and you've got Super Sprowtz.

Once the teachers seated all the school's children in front of a makeshift stage, Agrawal, who barely stood five feet, bounded out in front of them.

"So do you want to meet some of the Super Sprowtz today?" she asked the children.

"Yes!!!" the kids shouted.

"I can't hear you!"

"YESSSS!!!!!!" they shouted louder.

"I still can't hear you!"

Colby Carrot, the main hero of the Super Sprowtz, who wore a yellow eye mask, popped up from the stage. Screams erupted.

"Hi kids! I'm Colby Carrot! I heard all the yelling, and I came up here to see what that was all about! Let's cheer again if you like carrots!"

The kids went wild.

The Super Sprowtz began in 2006, when Agrawal created the cartoon vegetables for the kids menu at her twin sister Miki's organic pizza restaurant, Slice. Kids reacted by requesting those same vegetables on their pizzas, and Agrawal felt she was on to something. Over the next four years she wrote a backstory and hired artists to develop the Super Sprowtz characters, which she turned into a series of four self-published books. Eventually she quit her job in advertising to develop the Super Sprowtz into a kids educational nutrition and entertainment company with global ambitions. So far Super Sprowtz has produced plush toys and books, put on an interactive exhibit at the Children's Museum of Manhattan, shot a short television series that aired in the back of New York taxicabs, and performed hundreds of shows at schools, parks, zoos, and other venues, where the Super Sprowtz have appeared on the same bill as marquee kids' brands like Dora the Explorer and Olivia the Pig.

When I spoke with Agrawal in early 2013 the company was on the cusp of big things. It would soon secure a $2.5 million investment from one of the owners of the Century 21 department store chain, and talks were underway with merchandise licensers, book publishers, supermarket chains, and Amazon.com to take the Super Sprowtz characters and bring them all over the United States and the world. Improving childhood nutrition was a major cultural trend, and it was only growing. First Lady Michelle Obama had dedicated tremendous time and funds to raise awareness around it, and Agrawal had the support of her administration—even bringing Colby Carrot to the White House. "The first lady believes that the vibrancy and future of our country is truly at stake," said White House Chef Sam Kass when we spoke about Super Sprowtz. The dire scope of the problem translated into a potential market, complete with institutional support for people with potential solutions. "A lot of innovation is happening in this space," said Kass, "and Super Sprowtz is doing something that's very exciting."

Agrawal's hope was that the Super Sprowtz would eventually land a big TV deal. She pictured their show airing in every family's living room, with an Erica Eggplant puppet in every child's toy chest. Using the same aggressive marketing techniques that big food companies employ to get children to eat sugary cereals, Super Sprowtz would hook kids on vegetables, making carrots and spinach into a pint-sized food trend in the way the Vidalia onion farmers had done with Shrek. "It's not hard to get kids to eat vegetables if you start them young," Agrawal said. "But the only way to get that knowledge to a child is via strong and culturally relevant material." Agrawal was full of anecdotal tales of how this had already happened—of the little girl's father who wrote to her after the show, telling her about how his daughter suddenly couldn't get enough eggplant, or the investor who saw the company's future when his grandson began eating broccoli after a Super Sprowtz performance. If these individual successes could be replicated on a larger scale, to millions of children instead of thousands, imagine the potential trend it could unleash: kids tossing aside sugary cereals and soft drinks in favor of carrots and kale smoothies, eating healthier and better, and starting to reverse, however slowly, the decades' long trend in the other direction. A doctor at Columbia University was studying the potential effects of the Super Sprowtz on kids' food choices, and Agrawal had recently partnered with Cornell University to launch Super Sprowtz–branded salad bars in several New York schools.

Back at Barrow Street Elementary Suzie Sweetpea and Zach Zucchini swam to the Isle of Pollution and stole a key that controlled Pompous Pollution's deep fryer, saving the day once again. Agrawal ran out to the thunderous applause of a hundred tiny hands and grabbed the microphone again. "Okay, who wants to meet the Super Sprowtz?" she asked, and on cue dozens of squealing kids sprung from the floor to rush the stage. Their little hands tore at the felt puppets, desperately trying to touch Colby Carrot while Agrawal and her small staff frantically tried to keep the company's projector and laptop from falling victim to this pint-sized Altamont. Her goal of a broccoli in every lunch box was a lofty dream, of course. One child's nutrition expert referred to the Super Sprowtz as a "drop in the ocean" of addressing child obesity, but that was the thing about food trends: As much as the professional forecasters felt they could guess which ones were coming next, the big ones almost always hit the world by surprise. The Super Sprowtz had as good a chance as any at initiating a trend, and as I watched dozens of little children run into the arms of their parents, begging them, with tears in their eyes, for broccoli and zucchini, you could see a glimmer of hope for a new trend, small but still visible in the afternoon light.

ACKNOWLEDGMENTS

The Tastemakers was brought to life by dozens of wonderful, talented people who encouraged me and took chances with this project over the past few years and deserve no end of gratitude in these pages. Please call me anytime to collect a complimentary reward of a food trend item from within these pages, be it a fondue dinner or a tube of bacon lube.

First, I have to thank my stellar agent, Robert Guinsler at Sterling Lord Literistic. Robert has been a tireless and enthusiastic advocate of this project since the beginning and demonstrated the patience of a saint countless times, as this proposal (and others before it) was sent out into the rough waters of publishing with his wisdom and guidance.

The reward for all of Robert's stellar work was this book landing in the hands of Benjamin Adams, one of the smartest, sweetest editors I have ever had the pleasure of working with. Benjamin took a chance on a somewhat vague idea for a book about taste, carried it over to PublicAffairs, and transformed it into something even greater than I could have ever imagined. He put the Magnolia swirl on this humble red velvet base.

The other two publishing talents whom I forever remain indebted to are Doug Pepper and Jenny Bradshaw from McClelland

& Stewart in Toronto, who I have now worked with for close to a decade. Your vision has guided this book from a crumb of an idea to the final product, and I cannot express enough gratitude for everything you've done to make that happen.

At both PublicAffairs and McClelland & Stewart there are countless people who worked long and hard to bring this book to readers, from copy editors and designers to salespeople and publicists. Some, like Ashley Dunn, I have worked with closely for years. In other cases I am working with a whole new team: thanks to Clive Priddle, Susan Weinberg, Peter Osnos, Jaime Leifer, Alex Christopher, Melissa Raymond, Melissa Veronesi, Lisa Kaufman, Lindsay Fradkoff, and Matty Goldberg. A deep bow to each and every one of you.

The idea for *The Tastemakers* started out as a series of articles in *Bloomberg Businessweek* commissioned by the great editors Jonathan Kelly and Julian Sancton with the keen oversight of Brad Wieners. Thanks to all three of you for the opportunity to look at the food business in a way I could never have imagined. I'm also indebted to Laas Turnbull and Lianne George at the awesome Toronto newsmagazine *The Grid*, as they let me run wild with whatever idea I had, several of which found their way into these pages.

A particular thanks to those in the industry who went out of their way to explain the complicated world of food trends, including Kara Nielsen, Barb Stuckey, Suzy Badaracco, Darren Tristano, and Professor Josee Johnston. I also owe a great debt to friends and peerless food authorities Mitchell Davis of the James Beard Foundation, and Steve Dolinsky (a.k.a. The Hungry Hound) for advice, contacts, and suggestions along the way.

Over the course of my research I spoke to hundreds of people from around the world who spent countless hours detailing their work and thoughts and, in many cases, showing me around their little corners of the food business. A very special thanks to the Malhotra family and Hemant Bhagwani, the folks at Dole, the lovely people at the Specialty Food Association, Glenn Roberts, Shane Schaibly, the Baconfest folks, Che Ruddell-Tabisola and the

DCFTA, Radha Agrawal, Ricardo Zarate, Virginia Zimm, and the Botden family.

Wendy Litner, my research assistant, really made this book possible. A talented writer whose own books will one day top the best-seller lists, Wendy spent a year compiling arcane facts about fondue history, chasing down futile leads about chia seeds, and fearlessly tackled a gargantuan topic with surgical precision. Wendy, I cannot thank you enough for everything you've done.

Finally, I owe the biggest debt to Lauren, my darling wife, who coached me through the roller coaster of emotions any book will bring out in an author, especially when it coincides with buying and renovating our first house, immediately followed by pregnancy, a termite infestation, and the arrival of our daughter, which quickly led to three intense months of colic. Lauren, you were by my side the entire time, enduring sacrifices that were utterly humbling as you nurtured Noa, my shrieking muse, into the most beautiful creature in the world. I love both of you to no end.

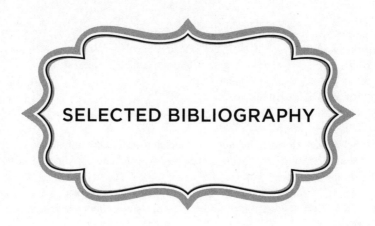

SELECTED BIBLIOGRAPHY

Interviews were either conducted in person, over the phone, or, in a few instances, by e-mail. Portions of Chapters 5, 6, and 8 originally appeared as articles in *Bloomberg Businessweek* and *The Grid Toronto*.

Chapter 1: The Cultural Trend
Cupcake sales statistics courtesy of *Modern Baking* and modernbaking.com, *Cake Statistics*, and *Baking Management*.
Cupcake history courtesy of thefoodtimeline.org.
Adam Sternbergh, "Sweet and Vicious," *New York Magazine*, September 2005.
Elizabeth Olson, "The Latest Entrepreneurial Fantasy Is Selling Cupcakes," *New York Times*, November 25, 2009.
Tim Carman, "An Alternative Take on the Profit Margins of Gourmet Cupcakes," *Washington City Paper*, December 2009.
Ellen Tien, "Baby Cakes Grow Up," *New York Times*, January 24, 1999.
Jacob Goldstein, "Are We in a Cupcake Bubble?" NPR.org, July 16, 2010.
Sumathi Reddy, "New York City's Cupcake Economy," blogs.wsj.com, July 16, 2010.
Burt Helm, "The Great Cupcake Wars," *Inc.*, May 1, 2011.
Joel Stein, "Food: Cupcake Nation," *Time*, August 20, 2006.
Brigid Schulte, "Once Just a Sweet Birthday Treat, the Cupcake Becomes a Cause," *Washington Post*, December 11, 2006.
Evelyn Juan, "Helping Afghanistan One Cupcake at a Time," *Christianity Today*, September 12, 2005.
Daniel Gross, "The Cupcake Bubble," *Slate*, September 2, 2009.

Andrea Aldeman, "The Psychology of Cupcakes," *Washington Post*, February 7, 2012.

Emily Maltby and Sarah E. Needleman, "Forget Gold, the Gourmet-Cupcake Market Is Crashing," *Wall Street Journal*, April 17, 2013.

Allison Robicelli, "Cupcake Wars," Medium.com, April 25, 2013.

Chapter 2: Agriculture

Kay Rentschler, "A Grits Revival with the Flavor of the Old South," *New York Times*, March 24, 2004.

Oliver Schwaner-Albright, "True Grits," *New York Times*, September 17, 2006.

Julia Moskin, "Southern Farmers Vanquish the Clichés," *New York Times*, December 27, 2011.

Eva Moore, "Columbia: Secret Grits Capital of the World," *Free Times*, April 21, 2011, www.free-times.com/archives/columbia-secret-grits-capital -of-the-world.

Jeff Gelski, "Modern Markets for Ancient Grains," *Food Business News*, February 9, 2011.

Sarah McSimmons, "A Tour of Anson Mills," sarahmcsimmons.com, July 6, 2011, http://sarahmcsimmons.com/2011/07/06/a-tour-of-anson-mills/.

"Anson Mills," Know Your Farms, http://knowyourfarms.com/j/index.php ?option=com_content&view=article&id=83:anson-mills&catid=12: producer-profile&Itemid=14.

Eva Moore, "Shrimp and Grits," *Free Times*, May 29, 2008, www.free-times .com/archives/shrimp-and-grits.

"Glenn Roberts" (interview), *Common Place: American Food in the Age of Experiment*, www.common-place.org/vol-11/no-03/roberts/.

"History," Arroz Preto Ruzene, www.arrozpreto.com.br/historico_en.asp.

Virginia Phillips, "'Heritage Grains' Return as Tasty Alternatives, and the Trend Is Sprouting Here," *Pittsburgh Post Gazette*, August 2011.

Chapter 3: Chefs

James Oliver Cury, "Epicurious Predicts Top 10 Food Trends for 2009," Epicurious.com, December 1, 2008.

Gregory Dicum, "Food of the Andes by the Golden Gate," *New York Times*, August 20, 2009.

Andrew Curry, "The Next Superchef," *Upstart Business Journal*, November 7, 2008.

Mitchell Davis, "A Taste for New York: Restaurant Reviews, Food Discourse, and the Field of Gastronomy in America" (PhD dissertation, New York University, 2009).

Jonathan Gold, "Mo-Chica: The Best Peruvian Ceviche Might Be in a Warehouse South of Downtown," *LA Weekly*, May 27, 2009.

David Kamp, *The United States of Arugula: How We Became a Gourmet Nation* (New York: Clarkson Potter, 2006).

Chapter 4: Health

Woody Allen quote from "Hypochondria, an Inside Look," *New York Times*, January 13, 2013, http://www.nytimes.com/2013/01/13/opinion/sunday/hypochondria-an-inside-look.html.

Gluten quote from *This Is the End*, Columbia Pictures, 2013.

Ricardo Ayerza and Wayne Coates, "New Industrial Crops: Northwestern Argentina Regional Project," in *Progress in New Crops*, ed. Jules Janick (Alexandria, VA: ASHS Press, 1996).

Dr. Coates's website: azchia.com.

Margaret Conover's website: chiativity.org.

Christopher McDougall, *Born to Run: A Hidden Tribe, Superathletes, and the Greatest Race the World Has Ever Seen* (New York: Alfred A. Knopf, 2009).

Wayne Coates, *Chia: The Complete Guide to the Ultimate Superfood* (New York: Sterling, 2012).

Lindsey Duncan, "Chia: Ancient Super-Seed Secret." Doctoroz.com, November 14, 2011.

Mehmet Oz, "Recharge Your Body," *Dr Oz Show*, October 12, 2011.

———, "Change Your Life with Chia," Doctoroz.com, October 9, 2013.

———, "The New Superfood," oprah.com, http://www.oprah.com/health/The-New-Superfood.

Mary MacVean, "Chia Seeds Are Popular Again—This Time for Nutrition," *Los Angeles Times*, June 2, 2012.

"Chia Demand Outstripping Supply to Lead to Big Crop Increase in Drop Area Next Year: BI Chief," Nutra Ingredients USA, July 20, 2012, http://www.nutraingredients-usa.com/Suppliers2/Chia-demand-outstripping-supply-to-lead-to-big-crop-increase-in-crop-area-next-year-BI-chief.

David C. Nieman, Erin J. Cayea, Melanie D. Austin, Dru A. Henson, Steven R. McAnulty, Fuxia Jin, "Chia Seed Does Not Promote Weight Loss or Alter Disease Risk Factors in Overweight Adults," *Nutrition Research* 29, no. 6 (June 2009): 414–418.

Catherine Ulbricht, Wendy Chao, Katie Nummy, Erica Rusie, Shaina Tanguay-Colucci, Carmen M. Iannuzzi, Jeena B. Plammoottil, Minney Varghese, Wendy Weissner, "Chia (Salvia hispanica): A Systematic Review by the Natural Standard Research Collaboration," *Reviews on Recent Clinical Trials* 4, no. 3 (September 2009): 168–174.

Leah Price, "Acai: Superfood or Harmful Fad?" *Gourmet*, April 2009.

Lynda Resnick with Francis Wilkinson, *Rubies in the Orchard: How to Uncover the Hidden Gems in Your Business* (New York: Doubleday, 2009).

Louise Foxcroft, *Calories and Corsets: A History of Dieting over 2000 Years* (London: Profile Books, 2011).

A. J. Jacobs, *Drop Dead Healthy: One Man's Humble Quest for Bodily Perfection* (New York: Simon and Schuster, 2012).

Marion Nestle, *Food Politics: How the Food Industry Influences Nutrition and Health* (Berkeley: University of California Press, 2002).

Legal information related to POM lawsuit: "In the Matter of POM Wonderful LLC and Roll International Corp., companies, and Stewart A. Resnick, Lynda Rae Resnick, and Matthew Tupper, individually and as officers of the companies," FTC File No. 082–3122, Docket No. 9344.

Chapter 5: Sales
Facts on the specialty food industry come from the Specialty Food Association.

Chapter 6: Data
Elizabeth Weise, "Coconuts, Beer? Six Food Trends for 2013," *USA Today*, January 22, 2013, www.usatoday.com/story/money/business/2013/01/22/food-trends-2013/1855189/.

"What We're Reading," NYTimes.com Diner's Journal Blog, January 22, 2013, http://dinersjournal.blogs.nytimes.com/2013/01/22/what-were-reading-612/?_r=0.

The Food Mirror Game can be found and entered at thefoodmirror.com.

McCormick Flavor Forecast can be found at flavorforecast.com.

Barb Stuckey, *Taste: Surprising Stories and Science About Why Food Tastes Good* (New York: Simon and Schuster, 2012).

Josh Schonwald, *The Taste of Tomorrow: Dispatches from the Future of Food* (New York: Harper, 2012).

Chapter 7: Marketing
Sarah Elton, "When A Is for Apple and H Is for Hype," *Globe and Mail* March 9, 2010.

Jordan Timm, "Farming: How Do You Like Them Apples," *Canadian Business*, April 7, 2011.

Jennifer Bain, "Meet Ontario's Newest Apple," *Toronto Star*, February 16, 2010.

G. Bruce Knecht, *Hooked: Pirates, Poaching, and the Perfect Fish* (Emmaus, PA: Rodale, 2006).

Florence Fabricant, "Chilean Sea Bass: More Than an Identity Problem," *New York Times*, May 29, 2002.

"Restaurants Remove Toothfish from Menus," *USA Today*, February 19, 2002.

Miriam Jordan and Lauren A. E. Schuker, "The Onion's Best Friend Is an Ogre," *Wall Street Journal*, June 28, 2010.

Chapter 8: Ethnic Foods
Immigration statistics: the Migration Policy Institute, the 2008 American Community Survey, and the US Citizenship and Immigration Service's Office of Immigration Statistics (OIS).

Industry statistics: NPD Group, Mintel, Nation's Restaurant News, and Private Label Manufacturing Association.

Helen Bullitt Lowry, "The Old World in New York," *New York Times*, April 3, 1921.

Krishnendu Ray, "Exotic Restaurants and Expatriate Home Cooking: Indian Food in Manhattan," in *The Globalization of Food*, eds. David Inglis and Debra Gimlin (Oxford: Berg, 2009).

———, "Traveling Tastes: Authority, Authenticity, and Publics for Indian Cooking in Manhattan," www.soas.ac.uk/migrationdiaspora/seminars events/food_migration_abstracts/file49147.pdf.

———, "Dreams of Pakistani Grill and Vada Pao in Manhattan: Reinscribing the Immigrant Body in Metropolitan Discussions of Taste," *Food, Culture, and Society* 14, no. 2 (June 2011): 243–273.

———, "A Taste for Ethnic Difference: American Gustatory Imagination in a Globalizing World," in *Globalization, Food and Social Identities in the Asia Pacific Region*, ed. James Farrer (Tokyo: Sophia University Institute of Comparative Culture, 2010).

Peter van der Veer, ed., *Nation and Migration: The Politics of Space in the South Asian Diaspora* (Philadelphia: University of Pennsylvania Press, 1995).

Lizzie Collingham, *Curry: A Tale of Cooks and Conquerors* (Oxford: Oxford University Press, 2007).

Thomas Rogers, "Can Indian Food Conquer America?" *Salon*, January 10, 2011.

Laresh Jayasanker, "Indian Restaurants in San Francisco and America: A Case Study in Translating Diversity, 1965–2005," *Food and History* 5, no. 2 (May 2009): 219–244.

Jane Nickerson, "Spicy Cookbook Sheds Light on Indian Dishes" *New York Times*, October 11, 1956.

Craig Claiborne, "Indian Actress Is a Star in the Kitchen, Too," *New York Times*, July 7, 1966.

Chapter 9: Food Politics

Adam Davidson, "The Food-Truck Business Stinks," *New York Times Magazine*, May 7, 2013.

Baylen J. Linnekin, Jeffrey Dermer, and Matthew Geller, "The New Food Truck Advocacy: Social Media, Mobile Food Vending Associations, Truck Lots, and Litigation in California and Beyond," Keepfoodlegal.org, 2011, http://www.keepfoodlegal.org/PDFs/linnekindermergeller.pdf.

Baylen Linnekin, "Chicago's Disgusting New Food Truck Regulations," Reason.com, July 28, 2012.

David Weber, *The Food Truck Handbook: Start, Grow, and Succeed in the Mobile Food Business* (Hoboken, NJ: Wiley, 2012).

Additional city food truck facts and figures: the Institute for Justice and *Mobile Food News*.

Quotes from the DC City Council hearing on vending regulations: video archives of the testimony, PR 20–125, May 10, 2013.

Jessica Sidman, "Mobilizing: How D.C.'s Food Trucks Learned to Love Lobbying," *Washington City Paper*, November 14, 2012.

Eric P. Newcomer, "D.C. Food Trucks, Restaurants Look Forward to New Regulations," *Washington Examiner*, February 25, 2013.

Tim Carman, "Public Is Hungry for Better Vending Regulations for Food Trucks," *Washington Post*, April 10, 2013.

Chapter 10: Money

Monica Davey, "Trade in Pork Bellies Comes to an End, but the Lore Lives," *New York Times*, July 30, 2011.

"Iconic Chicago Pork-Belly Trading Pit, Remembered in 'Trading Spaces,' to Close" *Fox News*, August 29, 2007.

Andrew Clark, "Rising Pork Bellies Prices Hit All Time High," *The Guardian*, August 2010.

"Pork Belly Price Rise Persists," *National Hog Farmer*, August 6, 2010.

Steve Meyer, "Hog Prices Just an Anomaly?" *National Hog Farmer*, May 2, 2008.

R. W. Mandigo, "A New Look at Belly and Bacon Values," *National Hog Farmer*, April 15, 2002.

Mark Rahner, "It's Mayo, It's Bacon, It's Baconnaise—and Sales Are Sizzling," *Seattle Times*, April 28, 2009.

Bacon consumer sales statistics: Technomic's February 2013 *Food Flash: Bacon Bits*.

Heather Lauer, *Bacon: A Love Story: A Salty Survey of Everybody's Favorite Meat* (New York: HarperCollins, 2009).

Chapter 11: Aftermath

Anita Prichard, *Fondue Magic: Fun, Flame and Saucery Around the World* (New York: Hearthside Press, 1969).

Sylvia Lovegreen, *Fashionable Food: Seven Decades of Food Fads* (Chicago: University of Chicago Press, 1995).

Vincent Varrilli, *The Fondue Rule Book*, self-published, date unknown.

Helen Evans Brown, *Chafing Dish Book* (Los Angeles, The Ward Ritchie Press, 1950).

Dietmar P. Schlüter, *Chalet Suisse: Fondues*, Veal, self-published, date unknown.

Mimi Sheraton, "Delicious, Solid, Countrified Swiss: Chalet Suisse," *New York Times*, December 19, 1980.

Catherine Phipps, "A Fondness for Fondue," The Guardian blog, March 24, 2010.

Dena Kleiman, "Fondue, Refreshed, Re-emerges," *New York Times*, March 7, 1990.

Lisa McLaughlin, "Restaurant Trends: Fondue: Now It's Hip to Dip," *Time*, February 10, 2003.

Melissa Clark, "A Little Nostalgia, a Long Fork and Lots of Cheese," *New York Times*, January 23, 2008.

Diane Duane and Peter Morwood, "Switzerland: Chocolate Fondue: Its True History and the Basic Recipe," europeancuisines.com.

Vintage Toblerone promotional materials: Mondelez.

Epilogue

Hugh Merwin, "Introducing the Cronut, a Doughnut-Croissant Hybrid That May Very Well Change Your Life," grubstreet.com, May 9, 2013.

Hilary Dixler, "Q&A: Dominique Ansel on Cronut Mania and Imposters," eater.com, May 30, 2013.

Bianca Prum, "The World's First Interactive Cronut- (and Cronut Impostor-) Finding Map," thrillist.com, August 11, 2013.

Jeanette Settembre, "Cronut Mania Hits South Korea via Dunkin Donuts," *New York Daily News*, July 30, 2013.

Jen Carlson, "Here Are Two Young Women Digging for Cronuts in the Trash," Gothamist.com, August 13, 2013, http://gothamist.com/2013/08/13/spotted _two_young_women_digging_for.php.

"Contaminated Cronut Burger Cause of 150 Illnesses at CNE," CBC News, August 23, 2013.

Melinda Maldonado, "Cronut Burger: Poor Refrigeration of Jam Likely Cause of CNE Food Poisoning," *Toronto Star*, September 5, 2013.

Karon Liu, "Double Bake," *The Grid*, June 20, 2013, www.thegridto.com /life/food-drink/double-bake/.

INDEX

Christopher Farber

David **Sax** is a freelance writer specializing in business and food. His writing appears regularly in the *New York Times, Bloomberg Businessweek, Saveur, The Grid Toronto,* and other publications. He is the author of *Save the Deli: In Search of Perfect Pastrami, Crusty Rye, and the Heart of Jewish Delicatessen* and has won a James Beard Award for writing and literature. He lives in Toronto, Canada.

...shing house founded in 1997. It is a tribute ...values, and flair of three persons who have ...rs to countless reporters, writers, editors, and ...f all kinds, including me.

...NE, proprietor of *I. F. Stone's Weekly*, combined a com-...ent to the First Amendment with entrepreneurial zeal and ...orting skill and became one of the great independent journal-...sts in American history. At the age of eighty, Izzy published *The Trial of Socrates*, which was a national bestseller. He wrote the book after he taught himself ancient Greek.

BENJAMIN C. BRADLEE was for nearly thirty years the charismatic editorial leader of *The Washington Post*. It was Ben who gave the *Post* the range and courage to pursue such historic issues as Watergate. He supported his reporters with a tenacity that made them fearless and it is no accident that so many became authors of influential, best-selling books.

ROBERT L. BERNSTEIN, the chief executive of Random House for more than a quarter century, guided one of the nation's premier publishing houses. Bob was personally responsible for many books of political dissent and argument that challenged tyranny around the globe. He is also the founder and longtime chair of Human Rights Watch, one of the most respected human rights organizations in the world.

. . .

For fifty years, the banner of Public Affairs Press was carried by its owner Morris B. Schnapper, who published Gandhi, Nasser, Toynbee, Truman, and about 1,500 other authors. In 1983, Schnapper was described by *The Washington Post* as "a redoubtable gadfly." His legacy will endure in the books to come.

Peter Osnos, *Founder and Editor-at-Large*